Microfinance, Poverty Alleviation and Financial Inclusion of the Poor

MICROFINANCE, POVERTY ALLEVIATION AND FINANCIAL INCLUSION OF THE POOR:

Reflections from Andhra Pradesh and Telangana

Naveen Kolloju

KALPAZ

First Published, 2017

Published by

Kalpaz Publications
C-30, Satyawati Nagar,
Delhi – 110052
E-mail: kalpaz@hotmail.com
Ph.: 9212142040

Printed at: G. Print Process, Delhi

Cataloging in Publication Data—DK
Courtesy: D.K. Agencies (P) Ltd. <docinfo@dkagencies.com>

Kolloju, Naveen, author.
Microfinance, poverty alleviation and financial inclusion of the poor: reflections from Andhra Pradesh and Telangana / by Naveen Kolloju.
pages cm
ISBN 9789386397034

1. Microfinance—India—Diwancheruvu. 2. Microfinance—India—Taduku. 3. Microfinance—India—Chinabonala. 4. Poverty—Prevention—Government policy—India—Diwancheruvu.
5. Poverty—Prevention—Government policy—India—Taduku.
6. Poverty—Prevention—Government policy—India—Chinabonala.
7. Financial services industry—Social aspects—India—Diwancheruvu.
8. Financial services industry—Social aspects—India—Taduku.
9. Financial services industry—Social aspects—India—Chinabonala.
I. Title.

HG187.I42A53 2017 DDC 332.10954 23

Contents

Foreword

Even after seventy years of independence, a large segment of Indian population hitherto remained untouched with the institutional banking system. The problem of over-indebtedness and continuous exclusion from the formal banking has led generation of financial instability and pauperism among the lower income groups. In the larger developmental discourse, it has been argued that bringing the hitherto unbanked poor in general and rural women in particular into the ambit of institutional finance is expected to bring significant changes in the economy, especially the rural economy. It is evident from the recent financial inclusion policy that the government has been initiating various schemes and programs in order to achieve financial inclusion. Given this context, an attempt to bring this manuscript into a book is timely and relevant. In order to have a thorough understanding on financial exclusion/ inclusion and how to achieve complete financial inclusion, it is pertinent to trace the roots of the concept of microcredit/microfinance and have a theoretical understanding of financial inclusion. This book largely succeeded in providing a rich theoretical framework along with key empirical insights in relation to microfinance, poverty alleviation and financial inclusion.

Bringing this book is increasingly important as it highlighted the issue of human rights in relation to the functioning/performance of MFIs in India. In the absence of an adequate formal banking system, MFIs have proliferated like mushrooms in rural India. It has been advocated that MFIs have come to bridge the increasing gap between the demand and supply by providing microfinance at the doorstep to the needy sections without cumbersome procedures and time loss. However, this phenomenon has had several social repercussions in the southern states of Andhra Pradesh and Telangana. For instance, the exorbitant interest rates, coercive recovery methods adopted by few private MFIs have resulted in suicides by some of the hapless borrowers in both the states. Many such unanticipated developments have put the microfinance sector at a crossroads, which is in contrast to the belief that MFIs have huge potential in alleviating poverty through accelerating livelihood opportunities. Having said this, the author strongly believes that there is an immediate need to critically examine the contributions of microfinance and the role of the state in response to the microfinance crisis in Andhra Pradesh and Telangana.

This book greatly helps the academicians, researchers, bankers, development practitioners and students to unravel the inter dynamics and the potential correlation among microfinance, poverty alleviation and financial inclusion. This book made a laudable attempt to fill the knowledge gap in relation to the potential synergies among the said three subjects. The author believes that the efforts to achieve complete financial inclusion without alleviation poverty is a futile exercise and financial inclusion would be successful only if financial literacy is vigorously promoted along with poverty alleviation schemes and programs. This book succeeded in examining the possible synergy between the two by thoroughly examining and analyzing the key microfinance models and initiatives. Apart from rich theoretical insights on microfinance and financial inclusion, the two field survey chapters on two southern states of India -Andhra Pradesh and Telangana - made the book different from the other several books on the same subjects. The empirical study on the potential contributions of three important microfinance models such as SHG-Bank Linkage Program (SBLP) model, Business Correspondent (BC) Model and Microfinance Institutions (MFI) model offered some interesting observations, which are quite relevant in the present policy context. This attempt, in fact addressed one of the fundamental questions as why the poor are unabatedly depending upon MFIs, despite the successful functioning of SBLP and the newly initiated BC models in fulfilling the same objective.

One of the strong areas of the book is its in-depth field survey analysis. Amidst of the recent microfinance crisis in the states of Andhra Pradesh and Telangana, where its repercussions are still visible, a detailed empirical analysis on the impact of microfinance is much appreciated. Last but not least, the key observations with regard to the three microfinance models certainly will be an added knowledge in the subjects of microfinance and financial inclusion and offer valuable suggestions at the policy level too. I strongly hope this book is worth reading. Wishing the author all the best.

I. Ramabrahmam

Professor, Department of Political Science,
University of Hyderabad.
2017.

Preface

With the ascendancy of the concept of microcredit in development literature, access to credit is widely debated. It is believed that lending small loans to the rural unbanked population would create small-scale self-employment opportunities to improve their income levels and uplift them from the clutches of poverty. An argument has been put forward that besides various welfare and developmental policies, it is imperative for poor to become financially aware and economically independent. Accordingly, an alternative strategy to poverty alleviation has been advanced to not only uplift the poor, particularly women, but also to enhance their resilience. It did not take much time for the policy-makers to understand that offering tiny loans and promotion of self-employment opportunities alone may not be a substitute for the holistic development of rural people. In the larger developmental discourse, it has been argued that the need of the hour is to bring the hitherto unbanked poor and women into the ambit of institutional finance by providing basic financial services. Thus, the achievement of poverty alleviation and financial inclusion has received greater attention. In this context, the study made an attempt assess the impact of SHG-Bank Linkage Programme (SBLP) model and Business Correspondent (BC) model on poverty alleviation and financial inclusion of the poor. Besides, it also examined the functional aspects of Microfinance Institution (MFI) model in providing microfinance to the rural poor and to understand credit holders' experiences with relation to financial transactions.

A field study was conducted for this purpose in three villages of Andhra Pradesh; one of them is now in the state of Telangana. The three villages are: Diwancheruvu village of East Godavari district, Taduku village of Chittoor district in Andhra Pradesh; and Chinabonala village of Karimnagar district in Telangana state. From each of these three villages, 50 respondents were selected from the SBLP model by using simple random sampling. Another 150 respondents were selected from the BC model by using stratified random sampling method. Put together, a total sample of 300 respondents was selected for this study.

The study found that availing microcredit through SBLP model with subsidised interest rates has a significant impact on the creation of various livelihood opportunities vis-á-vis alleviating poverty of the rural women. Utilising their loans in various productive activities like buying agricultural equipment, livestock rearing and creation of various self-employment activities has made considerable progress in improving their income levels. The contribution of their income for family expenditure like purchasing food items and electronic goods, children's education, healthcare purpose, house construction and repaid old debts has significant impact in reducing their vulnerability to poverty. Despite these benefits, the SBLP model has several limitations as well. With regard to MFIs, the study identified three main factors responsible for the microfinance crisis in the erstwhile Andhra Pradesh: (i) exorbitant interest rates (ii) weekly repayment collection practices, and (iii) coercive and highhanded behaviour of MFI staff in recovering the loans. As far as the BC model is concerned, the study concluded that this model can be seen as an alternative to the formal banking structure and the traditional banking process and has the potential to bridge the gap between the service providers (the banks) and the service seekers (customers). However, the lack of adequate infrastructure and training programmes; lack of awareness of this model among the rural people and banker's lackadaisical approach towards this model are seriously limiting the success of this model.

The study concludes that the goal of poverty alleviation and promoting financial inclusion in rural areas, especially women, through different microfinance and banking models is a laudable attempt. In particular, encouraging women to start self-employment activities, making them to be economically independent and further promoting them to be a part of banking system through SBLP and BC models could be seen as a forward linkage from poverty alleviation to financial inclusion. However, merely providing subsidised credit for self-employment through SBLP model and providing individual bank account alone may not successfully contribute for poverty alleviation and financial inclusion. The study suggests that the government with the help of banks should promote various skill-based training programmes and come forward to create market linkages and required infrastructure to promote the indigenous goods produced by rural communities. Financial inclusion is an ongoing and a progressive process in the banking system. Its success depends up on access to adequate, affordable and timely credit along with the availability of basic financial services and its optimum usage by the people. In other words, achieving financial inclusion is a concerted effort of government, bankers and the end users. Therefore, the beneficiaries, especially women and low-income groups must be empowered to utilise all the available financial services and reap the perceptible benefits. This is an essential condition for their economic upliftment and the larger goal of financial inclusion.

Acknowledgements

This book would never have been possible without the help and support from several people.

First and foremost, I would like to thank my supervisor, Professor Niraja Gopal Jayal for her guidance, help, support and patience through the entire journey. She has been much more than one would have expected from a study and degree supervisor. I am also deeply indebted to my teachers Professor Ramabrahmam and Professor Chinna Rao.

I would like to express my greatest debt of gratitude to my late father, Panduranga Chary for his encouragement and support over the years and who had struggled throughout his life for my well-being and always dreamt of my bright future. My next highest debt is to my Amma, Bharathamma for her unconditional love and constant encouragement throughout my life.

I gratefully acknowledge the help and support provided by all means by Jeevan Anna, Sudhakar Vaddi Anna and Mohan Anna. They were with me in all my difficulties and shared my joys and sorrows and encouraged me to complete the book. Their moral support and invaluable suggestions greatly helped me at every stage in the preparation of this book. A Special mention to my best friends Ramakrishna Anna, Prakash, Brahmaiah and Sahana who have been great inspiration to me; I express my heartfelt gratitude for their constant encouragement, unconditional help and support by all means at every stage of my life.

This book is also the result of healthy support and efforts of many people who are part of my field study in the three districts of Andhra Pradesh and Telangana. I am indebted to those who willingly helped me during my interview process and in collecting valuable information for my book.

With all this feeling of indebtedness and appreciation in mind, I shall keep moving forward, hoping that it could be at least a partial repayment to all those to whom I am so grateful.

—Naveen Kolloju

Acronyms

ADB	:	Asian Development Bank
APGVB	:	Andhra Pradesh GrameenVikas Bank
APMACS	:	Andhra Pradesh Mutually Aided Cooperative Societies
BC	:	Business Correspondent
CGAP	:	Consultative Group to Assist the Poorest
DWCRA	:	Development of Women and Children in Rural Areas
FICCI	:	Federation of Indian Chamber of Commerce and Industry
FIF	:	Financial Inclusion Fund
IFI	:	Index for Financial Inclusion
IKP	:	Indira Kranthi Padham
KCC	:	Kisan Credit Cards
KYC	:	Know Your Customer
MFI	:	Micro-Finance Institutions
NBFC	:	Non Banking Finance Company
NFA	:	No Frills Account
ROSCA	:	Rotating Savings and Credit Association
RRB	:	Regional Rural Bank
SAP	:	Structural Adjustment Programme
SBLP	:	SHG Bank Linkage Programme

SERP	:	Society for the Elimination of Rural Poverty
SGSY	:	Swarnajayanti Gram Swarojgar Yojana
SHARE	:	Society for Helping Awakening Rural Poor through Education
SHG	:	Self Help Group
UIDAI	:	Unique Identification Authority of India

Chapter - I

Introduction

In a country where the vast majority of the people continue to live in rural areas, rural development must necessarily be a crucial element in building an inclusive society. Given the high percentage of rural population (69 per cent[1]), a number of developmental policies have been initiated with an overall emphasis to alleviate poverty (Jodhka, 2014). It is believed that improving the living standards of rural people by providing access to rural resources is crucial for rural development (Majumdar and Gupta, 2013). In fact, Sen's (2000) capability approach emphasises the need for enhancing capabilities of the poor and disadvantaged by providing access to various services and opportunities in order to help them to improve their socio-economic conditions. In this regard, provision of access to institutional credit has gained wider attention to ensure financial sustainability of the rural poor. The literature suggests that access to adequate and affordable institutional credit is one of the most crucial factors that influence rural development as it enables the rural poor households to uplift themselves from the clutches of poverty (Pitt and Khandker, 1998; Das, 2005; and Campbell, 2010).

An additional benefit of access to subsidised bank credit is that it encourages the rural poor to invest financial resources in various income-generating activities and maximise the returns, which in turn reduces their vulnerability to financial risks in their daily lives. Further, it enlarges the rural economy through increased participation from the marginalised sections. In other words, it promotes participation of the rural poor in market economy and also social and political spheres. The other important benefit of ensuring access to subsidised institutional credit in rural areas is that it augments agricultural production, enhances women's economic empowerment and improves the efficiency of rural credit delivery system (Arora and Leach, 2005; Bapuji and Masthanvali, 2008; Puhazhendhi *et al.,* 2000; and United Nations, 2006). In particular, this approach has brought women's empowerment to the forefront through their enhanced entrepreneurial spirit. In other words, provision of lending tiny loans to poor women represents a ray of hope for those who have been compelled to depend upon pawnshops and conventional moneylenders (Arora and Leach, 2005; and Biju, *et al.,* 2013).

However, with regard to the development of on-farm sector, it is argued that despite significant contribution to the Gross Domestic Product (GDP), the agricultural sector has been undergoing a major crisis since the 1990s in India. In terms of economic aggregates, India's development and expansion of markets have largely been confined to metropolitan centres, away from its rural areas and agrarian economies. This is reflected in a gradual decline of agriculture's share in the national economy (Jodhka, 2014). Some of the causative factors for the decline of agricultural productivity include, lack of adequate access to institutional/farm credit, lack of innovative approach for agricultural development, steep increase in the prices of fertiliser and fuel, decline in investment, poor returns, high indebtedness, escalating cultivation cost, imperfect market condition and so on (Deshpande and Arora, 2010; Golait, 2007; and Nair, 2011). In addition to these factors, majority of the operational landholdings are small and marginal, cultivating of which require adequate and timely loans. However, this proposition is not viable for the banks, as the formalities involved in the lending process do not allow the banks to provide loans to small and marginal farmers. Due to the institutional limitations, the poor and tiny landholders who largely depend on on-farm activities are generally being excluded from the benefits of rural institutional credit. As a result, rural poor are compelled to depend upon semi-formal institutions (Microfinance Institutions) or other informal sources (moneylenders) that in turn aggravate the problem of rural indebtedness, which shrink the existing livelihood opportunities (Jodhka, 2014; Nair, 2011; and Vatta, 2003).

It is therefore, imperative to recognise that the provision of extending timely, adequate and affordable loans to the poor in rural areas through the formal banking system would not only lead to their socio-economic enrichment but also include them in rural economy. The arguments highlight the fact that lack of access to adequate institutional credit makes the farmers and the poor to dependent on their own limited savings, which in turn restricts their choice of investment. As a result, it compels them to depend on informal financial sources, which in the longer run, traps them into a cycle of perpetual debt and poverty.

Financial Inclusion

Financial inclusion is a global phenomenon that has gained wider currency in the development literature in contemporary times. Given the magnitude of poverty in the Third World economies, wherein a large segment of the population does not have access to basic financial services, the idea of financial inclusion has become conspicuous in these economies. A recent United Nations (UN) study observes that financial inclusion of the poor is a global challenge to the achievement of the Millennium Development Goals (MDGs) (2006). This report draws attention to a plethora of problems that are being faced by the poor in accessing financial services, and reveals that a large number of people are unable to save money as formal banking services are not within their 'reach'. Structural barriers, as the report states, prevent the poor from accessing banking facilities, thereby resulting in financial exclusion. The study further argues that a significant proportion of the poor in developing countries do not have savings bank accounts, let alone insurance policies (*ibid*).

In India, despite a well-developed banking system, a large number of groups remain excluded from the basic opportunities and services provided by the financial sector for a variety of supply and demand side reasons (Report of the Steering Committee on Microfinance and Poverty Alleviation, Government of India, 2007:12). The report observes that the credit needs of the financially excluded population are often met by the informal and non-institutional sources rather than the formal institutions. The excluded sections are drawn from the small and marginal farmers, women, unorganised sector workers including artisans, the self-employed and pensioners (Dev, 2006). A recent study points out that only 55 per cent of the population in India have bank accounts. India has the highest number of households (145 million) excluded from banking system (Biju, 2013). The 59th round survey of National Sample Survey Organisation (NSSO, 2008) finds that 89 million (73 per cent) farming households in the country do not have access to credit either from institutional or non-institutional sources. Among the excluded, the financial exclusion of the dalit households is especially deplorable. The All India Debt and Investment Survey (AIDIS, 2002-03) claims that dalit households in rural India obtained more than half of their total debt from informal sources. The share of formal sources in the total debt of these households was only 44.8 per cent, lower than the corresponding share of 59 per cent for non-dalit households. Among informal sources, conventional moneylenders were the predominant sources of debt.[2]

The Report of the Committee on Financial Inclusion, Government of India (2008:5) adds a geographic dimension to understand the extent of financial exclusion. The report attributes the factors such as inaccessibility, distance and lack of proper infrastructure to financial exclusion in rural India. It suggests the need for expansion of geographical coverage and ensuring outreach of various financial services to the needy population without any demand and supply constraints. According to this report, financial exclusion is high in India with geographical variations and as well as social groups. The report laments that the existing policies, programmes and vast banking infrastructure have not brought about desired changes in pooling necessary financial services. This has been a major barrier to the rural poor in opening up other avenues of livelihood opportunities to uplift their financial status. One of the fundamental reasons is inadequacy of assets and lack of collateral of the poor; this discourages the commercial banks in providing financial services.

Given this backdrop, in recent times, the phenomenon of 'microfinance' has emerged as an innovative and bottom-up approach to offer tiny loans directly to the rural poor, predominantly for women (Firedman, 2005). It has become a fulcrum for alleviating poverty in developing economies, and harbingers as one of the most promising and cost-effective tools in fighting against global poverty (Morduch, 2006). In the realm of financial services, it is acting as a credit facilitator and investment creator, which addresses the vulnerability of the poor and financially excluded (Basu and Srivastava, 2005). In India, since 1990s, it has expanded its outreach and acting as one of the major alternative strategies in providing several financial services to the low-income people, including credit, savings, insurance and remittance. Microfinance serves the rural people through the mainstream financial players such as commercial banks, MFIs and innovative delivery models such as SHG-Bank Linkage Programme (SBLP).

SHG-Bank Linkage Programme (SBLP) Model in India

In the post-independence period, numerous measures were taken to provide credit facilities to the rural poor. The rural credit structure in India has been evolved gradually over a long period of time, from 1947 to the 1980s. This began with the starting up of State Cooperative Banks (1955), the Reserve Bank of India (RBI) in banking policies (since1955) and the creation of Regional Rural Banks (RRBs) in 1976 (Misra, 2006 and Shah *et al.,* 2007). The 1980s witnessed a paradigm shift in the Indian rural credit structure. The formal Banking sector took the initiative to develop a 'supplementary credit delivery mechanism' through the establishment of the National Bank for Agricultural and Rural Development (NABARD). During 1980s, there was active involvement of RBI and NABARD in providing microcredit to the rural poor. These initiatives have gained a momentum with the launching of SBLP model by NABARD in 1992 (Mohan, 2008).

The formation of Self-Help Groups (SHGs) and provision of credit and other microfinance services to group members is an important feature of SBLP model. Of late, this model emerged as a major microfinance programme in the country (Thakur, 2010; and Vaish and Agarwal, 2010). In the course of time, every SHG was required to be linked to banking system to meet the financial requirements of the group members. Gradually, the practice of group lending approach received popular appreciation and evolved as an important microfinance model in the country (SERP Report, 2013). A recent report of NABARD reveals that as on 31st March, 2013 there were 7.3 million savings-linked SHGs covering 970 million poor households under the microfinance programme. The report further states that though this phenomenon was impressive in Andhra Pradesh and Karnataka, the movement later widely spread to various parts of India such as Tamil Nadu, Kerala, Maharashtra, Gujarat, Uttar Pradesh, Bihar and so on

(The Status of Microfinance in India, 2012-13). Besides the SBLP model, The RBI adopted a 'technology-based agent bank model' through Business Correspondent (BC) model in 2006. This model envisages providing an alternative banking structure to branch-based banking services.

Business Correspondent (BC) Model and Financial Inclusion

The BC model is acknowledged as an alternative banking structure to the branch-based banking services, which enables public sector banks to use the services of NGOs, SHGs and MFIs as intermediaries in providing financial and banking services (RBI, 2006). The model primarily intended to reach out to a geographically diverse population, particularly in rural areas and those who are financially excluded from the institutional banking. It ensures doorstep delivery of financial services to these sections. According to the RBI guidelines, the Business Correspondents (BCs) are permitted to act as agents to carry out financial transactions on behalf of bank, therefore, this banking is called as branchless banking. This model is being aided by technology oriented tools such as point of service (POS) handheld devices, mobile phones and biometric scanners (Karmakar, 2009).

With regard to the functioning of the BC model, the Report of the Committee of Financial Inclusion, Government of India (2008) observes that adopting appropriate technology enables the BCs to go directly to the customers instead of the other way round. Banks can use the services of BCs for opening a bank account, under the compliance with KYC norms.[3] As per the RBI guidelines, BCs cannot charge any fee from the customers for services. Recently, the RBI has expanded the scope of BC model responding to government policy of opening 'no frills accounts'[4] and some of the electronic benefits have been transferred to these accounts to process government payments such as the Mahatma Gandhi National Rural Employment Guarantee Scheme (MGNREGS), pensions and other social payments with the help of POS devices (CGAP, 2012). In this regard, BC model has the potential to deliver services even to rural regions, which is one of the core strategies of accelerating financial inclusion.

Recently, the Government of India has come up with a socio-economic initiative in the realm of Indian banking sector, named as the Pradhan Mantri Jan-Dhan Yojana (PMJDY) on 28 August, 2014.

It is primarily intended to financially empower the people by encouraging them to open bank accounts and providing basic banking services. The main objective of the scheme is "ensuring access to various financial services like availability of basic savings bank account, access to need based credit, remittances facility, insurance and pension to the excluded sections such as low income groups and disadvantaged sections" (A Report on Pradhan Mantri Jan-Dhan Yojana: A National Mission on Financial Inclusion, Government of India, 2014: 1). The Scheme emphasises that every household in our country must have a bank account and he/she is in a position to avail credit and other banking facilities and get benefit out of it. The report believes that having a bank account and availing banking services enables them to come out of the grip of moneylenders and financially helps them from emergencies. Thus, the report suggests that the BC model has to play a major in not only encouraging the poor and unbanked sections to open a bank account but also ensure them to utilise those accounts with appropriate financial services.

Therefore, under the broad rubric of financial inclusion, provision for delivering institutional credit and other financial services, particularly through the SBLP and BC models gained critical importance. Some of the earlier studies on this subject claimed that these two models stood at the forefront of addressing the financial needs of the rural poor in Andhra Pradesh. However, the recent microfinance crisis in Andhra Pradesh[5] (AP) has questioned those claims. To explore this mismatch further, the following section attempts to focus on SHG movement in Andhra Pradesh and traces the emergence of MFIs. While doing so, it also critically examines the recent microfinance crisis in the state.

SHG Movement and Microfinance Intervention in Andhra Pradesh

In scripting the success of SHG movement, the case of AP became noteworthy. In fact, the Government of Andhra Pradesh (GoAP) introduced the concept of SHGs in the early 1980s itself. Along with other developmental programmes, the state has been encouraging the growth of SHGs as a strategy to address poverty, in particular a reduction in feminisation of poverty in rural areas. It is believed that SHG as a rural credit intervention and as a group approach primarily intends to economically empower rural women by promoting various small-scale income-generating activities and enables their participation at the community developmental activities (Bapuji *et al.*, 2008).

The state of Andhra Pradesh has been at the forefront of microfinance interventions through the SBLP model in India since the late 1990s. The public sector banks in the state have given priority to the SBLP model and encouraged rural women to be part of financial inclusion (Status of Microfinance in India, 2012-13). In fact, the penetration of credit intervention through SHGs is greater than any other state in India. According to the Annual Report of the Society for Elimination of Rural Poverty, GoAP (2013-14), the implementation of SBLP model has been taken up on a larger scale since 2005, covering all 1098 mandals in the 22 rural districts. As of 31st January 2014, there are a total of 10,59,777 SHGs with 1,16,08,418 members. These members have been formed and organised into 44,433 village organisations (VOs), which in turn were categorised under 1098 Mandal Samakhyas (MSs). Upto 31 January 2014, the total loan amount disbursed under the SHG-Bank Linkage was Rs 10,724.81 Crore and Rs 2,98,791 per group.

Parallel to the SHG movement, other microfinance models also emerged in AP. The state has the highest penetration of MFIs in India which started operating since 1997. It is home to some of India's biggest MFIs such as SKS, Spandhana, Basix and Share etc (Johnson and Sushmita, 2010). MFIs aim at providing small loans to both group borrowers and individual borrowers who have no access to group lending (Ross and Savanti, 2005). Though the MFIs were primarily concerned with rural women, these institutions have also expanded their outreach to the rural farmers and other disadvantaged sections. Since 2000, the fastest growing MFIs have resulted in a rapid proliferation of credit across AP with the number of borrowers more than doubling each year. By the year 2005, AP emerged as one of the thriving centres for MFIs in India (CGAP, 2001). According to Sa-Dhan, a network body of India's MFIs revealed that upto 31st March, 2010, AP has the maximum outreach of 62.5 lakh borrowers with the borrowed amount being Rs 16,466 Crores.

It has been argued that despite the existing rural banking system and the functioings of SHGs in Andhra Pradesh, the financial needs of the rural poor have not been met by a large margin and that the prevailing system of finance and credit has proved to be ineffective (Rajalaxmi, 2007 and Roy, 2008). A recent study reveals that the incidence of indebtedness, particularly among small and marginal farmers in AP was the highest in India. The 'rural distress' in the state has been more than evident in reported incidents of farmer's suicides. It is argued that the vacuum created by the state as a major credit facilitator has been adroitly filled up by the private sector (Nair, 2011). Earlier, the state used to be the major player in providing credit and subsidies to the rural poor. However, the advent of the neo-liberal economic order has relegated the state to the back seat and paved the way for the emergence of private sector as a dominant actor in the provision of goods and services. It shifted the focus of 'development' from being state-centric to market force-driven, with no qualms about pursuing profit. For instance, MFIs have recognised the need for providing credit to the rural poor by bridging the gap between the unbanked rural poor and banks (Consultative Group to Assist the Poor (CGAP), 2010). A recent study on the rural economy in AP argues that the shift in agriculture towards commercial cropping coupled with limited and inadequate access to institutional credit pushed the farmers into debt[6] (Sukumar, 2010). This indebtedness engenders diffidence in the rural communities to invest freely in on-farm or off-farm activities. All these factors have become major hurdles in ensuring adequate livelihood security in the rural areas, resulting in the deprivation of the economic capabilities of the poorer sections (Nair, 2011).

Microfinance Crisis in Andhra Pradesh: Issues and State's Intervention

The success of any policy or programme squarely depends on the legal and regulatory frameworks and the government's intervention in various phases (Basu, 2005). In the context of microfinance models, the SBLP has been regulated by the government. However, with regard to MFIs, these institutions have not been adequately controlled by the government and this has caused a tremendous setback in achieving the goals and objectives of the programme. The number of these institutions has grown at a frantic pace and this resulted in a major crisis in the microfinance sector in March 2006 and again in October 2010. As a result, the district authorities in AP closed down about 50 branches of two major MFIs in Krishna district (Nair, 2014 and Shylendra, 2008). There were about 40 very small lending institutions in AP, which merely lend and collect money. These institutions were not familiar with the concept of MFIs and that made the rural poor to take credits from multiple sources. The MFIs follow a weekly repayment schedule to recover debts from the borrowers and thus put a lot of pressure on them. Sometimes the borrowers are forced to depend upon other lending sources (other MFIs or moneylenders) to repay the initial MFI loan in order to retain their access. It is alleged that the strict and often coercive debt recovery methods adopted by the MFIs, and their exorbitant interest rates have caused some of the hapless borrowers to end their lives (Kumar 2006 and Nair, 2014).

Recently a fact-finding report prepared by the Gender Unit of the Society for the Elimination of Rural Poverty showed that 54 people committed suicides due to the charging of high interest rates and coercive recovery methods practiced by the MFIs (SERP, 2010). There are three major allegations against the MFIs that came up during the crisis: It was alleged that MFIs are collecting exorbitant interest rates, and lack transparency regarding their interest rate practices, which helps them to transfer various costs on to the borrowers; MFIs are portrayed to have resorted to unethical ways of recovering loans by confiscating title deeds, using intimidation and abusive language; and MFIs are aggressively poaching from government and bank led SHGs to capture their borrowers (Shylendra, 2008). Due to such practices, it is argued that MFIs are causing a huge burden on the poor, rather helping them to come out of the poverty trap, which further pushed them into a vicious cycle of debt, poverty and even deaths. The weekly repayment schedule normally followed by these MFIs put a lot of pressure on the members to maintain regular repayment (Nair, 2014).

Statement of the Problem

In the absence of an adequate formal banking system, Micro-Finance Institutions (MFIs) have proliferated like mushrooms in rural India. It has been advocated that MFIs have come to bridge the increasing gap between the demand and supply by providing microfinance at the doorstep to the needy sections without cumbersome procedures and time loss. However, this phenomenon has had several social repercussions in Andhra Pradesh. For instance, the exorbitant interest rates, coercive recovery methods adopted by some of the private MFIs have resulted in suicides by some of the hapless borrowers in the state. The methods employed by these MFIs to expand their presence and emerge as viable models in Indian microfinance have not been the subject of critical scrutiny, partially due to their popularity and due to the absence of a regulator. Many such unanticipated developments have put the microfinance sector at a crossroads, which is in contrast to the belief that MFIs have huge potential in alleviating poverty through accelerating livelihood opportunities (Campbell, 2010; and John and Montgomery, 2005). Given this backdrop, the issues pertaining to access to microfinance through MFIs and their role in poverty alleviation and financial inclusion must be scrutinised. Further, there is a need to examine the role of state in response to the microfinance crisis in Andhra Pradesh.

Besides, there has been dearth of studies to assess microfinance on poverty alleviation and promoting financial inclusion through different models. As discussed earlier, primarily there are three models of credit lending to the rural poor in India: the SHG-Bank Linkage Programme model, the MFI model and the Business Correspondent (BC) model. Though all these models aim at lending credit to the rural poor, they differ from each other in their functioning. There have been variations with regard to loan sanction, duration, methods of repayment and interest rates. Resultantly, the impact of these models on the rural poor would be different in nature. Moreover, the literature claimed that the MFI model is the second best option for the poor, both in terms of interest rates and financial services after the SBLP model. However, there has been insufficient examination of the fundamental questions as to why people are unabatedly depending upon MFIs, despite the SBLP and the newly initiated BC models in fulfilling the same objective. In fact, the recent microfinance crisis in AP has raised many important questions regarding the role and credibility of the rural banking system, particularly the SBLP model. These issues call for examining the role of state in mitigating the crisis and reflect on trust of government intervention and the regulatory mechanism.

The literature argues that financial inclusion is one of the means to provide various financial services (through no-frills bank account) to low-income and under-privileged sections at an affordable cost

(Karmakar, 2009; Khan, 2012; and Thorat, 2006). In this regard, the Business Correspondent (BC) model is one such initiative from RBI that allows banks to partner with third party agents to provide basic financial services such as credit and savings to households that do not have banks in their neighbourhood. Achieving financial inclusion, however, is still a distinct dream for many households in rural India (Rangarajan Committee Report on Financial Inclusion, Government of India, 2008). With this background, the present study is an attempt to assess in detail whether merely having a bank account, or accessing various financial services, improve the economic position and social enrichment of the rural poor through SBLP or BC models? The survey of literature indicates that ensuring financial inclusion without poverty alleviation is a futile exercise, and financial inclusion would be successful only if financial literacy is promoted along with the government led developmental schemes. Therefore, achieving poverty alleviation and ensuring financial inclusion are very much interrelated. The earlier studies have not examined the possible synergy between the two; and the present study attempts to fill this gap.

Hypothesis

H1: SHG-Bank Linkage Programme (SBLP) and Business Correspondent (BC) model have a positive impact on alleviating poverty and promoting the process of financial inclusion of the poor.

H2: The easy accessibility of microcredit may lead to over dependency on the MFIs that lead to serious repercussions for the rural poor.

Objectives of the Study

The central objective of the study is to assess the impact of SHG-Bank Linkage Programme (SBLP) model, Microfinance Institutions (MFI) Model and Business Correspondent (BC) model on poverty alleviation and financial inclusion of the poor.

The specific objectives of the study are:

(i) To assess the impact of SBLP model on the respondents with reference to self-employment, income generation, housing, education, health and access to financial services in the selected three villages of Andhra Pradesh and Telangana.

(ii) To examine the functional aspects of MFI model in providing microfinance to the rural poor and to elicit credit holders' experiences with relation to financial transactions.

(iii) To assess the impact of Business Correspondent (BC) model on respondents' access to various financial services.

(iv) To ascertain the views of the credit holders on the factors that determined their participation levels in all the three models.

(v) To critically examine the reasons for recent microfinance crisis in undivided Andhra Pradesh, and state government's response to mitigate this crisis.

Research Methodology

Scope of the Study

The study is confined to an examination of the impact of microfinance models and initiatives on poverty alleviation and financial inclusion among the poor and deprived sections. SBLP and BC models are central to the research. In order to elicit required information on the functional aspects of MFI model, the study depended upon the respondents of SBLP model. While examining its impact, the study collected data pertaining to respondent's occupation, year of joining SHGs, purpose of availing loan from SBLP model, improved income levels before and after joining SHGs, contribution to family expenditure, and social and economic transformation that the respondents have witnessed after joining SHGs. Similarly, to examine the impact of BC model on respondents' access to various financial services, the study collected data on source of information in knowing about the BC model, reasons pertaining to open a savings bank account, availability of business correspondent, operation frequency of bank account by the respondents and so on. Considering the time and resource availability, the study is limited to three districts of undivided Andhra Pradesh. Though the study is limited to only three districts, it represents all the three regions of the undivided state. The districts selected for the study include East Godavari district from Coastal Andhra region, Chittoor from Rayalaseema region and Karimnagar district from Telangana region. However, on 2nd June 2014, the combined Andhra Pradesh state was divided into states: Andhra Pradesh and Telangana. The first two districts, namely East Godavari and Chittoor fall under

Andhra Pradesh state and the Karimnagar district fall under newly formed Telangana state.

Sampling Procedures and Sample Size

Each district in the sample was represented by a village located within the district selected. Chinabonala village of Siricilla Mandal in Karimnagar district, Deevanchervu village in Rajanagaram Mandal in East Godavari district and Taduku village in Puttur Mandal in Chittoor district have been selected after having due consultations with the concerned Mandal Revenue Officers. According to them, these villages are witnessed high presence of SHGs and availed bank loan more than three times. From each of these three villages, 50 respondents, that is, a total of 150 respondents were selected from SBLP model by using simple random or probability sampling. Probability sampling facilitates equal chance to each item in the target population to get included in the final sample. In other words, each one of the possible samples has the same probability of being selected (Kothari, 2010). Since, all members of the SBLP model are women, the researcher adopted simple random sampling. The researcher has visited SHG Village Samakhya Office and approached Assistant Project Manager (APM) in order to select the sample size. On an average, each village is consisting of 30-40 SHGs. Among them the researcher has visited 10 SHGs randomly and approached all the members of the each group and finally selected five respondents from each group according to their willingness to respond to the questionnaire. It is therefore, the final sample size is 50 from each village. The research has followed uniformity in the size of the sample.

As far as the BC model is concerned, another 150 respondents were selected from the above mentioned villages (50 respondents from each village) by using stratified random sampling method. This sampling method was used to divide the total sampling frame into sub-sections based on certain variables such as gender, caste, religion, education, respondent's occupation, income levels and so on. Through this method, the total sample frame (population) is stratified into a number of non-overlapping sub-groups and then sample items are selected from each sub-group (Rajendra, 2008). Since, the clients of the BC model are both men and women, the researcher stratified the total sample frame into two sub-groups by using gender as a variable.

The total respondents of the study comprised of SHG members, SHG leaders, BC clients and MFI borrowers. The following table represents the total sample frame from all the three villages.

Table 1.1. Sample Size Distribution

Study Area	*Number of SHG members*	*Number of clients of BC model*	*Total Respondents*
Chinabonala (Karimnagar)	50	50	100
Deevanchervu (East Godavari)	50	50	100
Taduku (Chittoor)	50	50	100
Total	**150**	**150**	**300**

Data Collection

The study relied upon both the primary and secondary sources for data collection. For the primary data, a field study was carried out and the respondents were drawn from SHGs under SBLP model and clients of the BC model. To know the policy aspects, the researcher has consulted Bank Managers, Business Correspondents and other government officials. The field study was carried out in two phases. In the first phase, a pilot study was conducted to test the questionnaire in the month of October 2013 in the selected three villages. During the pilot study, it was found that some of the SHG women were also clients of MFIs. This helped the researcher to elicit information on the functional aspects of the MFIs. In the second stage, primary field study was conducted during November-December 2013. The study employed different methods to collect the data. Interviews were conducted to both the SHG members and BC clients to know their experiences as clients. The primary data was collected on different socio-economic factors like region, religion, caste, gender, age, education levels, family size, landholdings, occupation of the respondents and income levels. Besides, the study also collected information relating to year of joining in SHGs, their economic status and micro financial services before and after borrowing money from the rural banks and under BC model. During this visit, the researcher also accessed documents related to the study in the respective government and private offices. In the process of data collection, the researcher used different tools such as interviews with the SHG members, BC clients, business correspondents and bank managers by using structured questionnaires and Focus Group Discussions (FGDs) to elicit necessary information pertaining to the objectives of the study. The researcher also followed direct observation method in the process of collecting the data at the field site.

For the secondary data, the study depended on Annual Reports of the World Bank, RBI, NABARD, Government of India documents, SERP reports of the Government of Andhra Pradesh and Telangana as well as scholarly books and articles published in this area. The researcher also accessed various websites, in order to make the data up-to-date.

Data Analysis

After the data collection, the responses in the filled questionnaires were codified in order to simplify the data entry process. The study used Excel sheet in order to compute the data. The data has been tabulated and analysed by using Statistical Package for Social Science (SPSS version 20). Descriptive statistical tools such as frequency distribution and cross-tabulation have been used to describe the socio-economic profiles of the respondents. These tools have also used to assess different variables such as year of joining in SHGs, purpose of availing loans, caste profile and purpose of availing loan, improved income levels before and after joining SHGs, contribution to family expenditure, awareness and usage of no-frills accounts, awareness on Know Your Customer (KYC) norms, financial services available under BC model, role of business correspondent in promoting financial inclusion etc.

Organisation of the Book

The remaining chapters of the study are organised as follows:

Chapter II, titled, *Literature Review* is divided into three major sections. The first section aims at reviewing the extant literature on poverty. While doing so, it attempts to conceptualise the multidimensional nature of poverty. It analyses the phenomenon at the global level in general and India in particular and offers an operational definition to poverty. Further, it also analyses three important perspectives to understand poverty and its gendered nature. It documents poverty estimates in India by various committees constituted by the Planning Commission and briefly highlights some of the important poverty reduction strategies. The second section makes an effort to trace the conceptual underpinnings of microfinance and the emergence of the microfinance movement in India. It reviews the theoretical and empirical literature, which deals with microfinance, SHGs and poverty alleviation. Further, the section introduces a recent phenomenon in the Indian banking sector, that is, financial inclusion. It identifies key challenges and offers different strategies and recommendations to address the problem. The third section is central to this chapter as it provides the theoretical framework of the study, Amartya Sen's theory of 'Development as Freedom' (1999) and Nussbaum's construction of 'Capability Approach' (2000).

Chapter III, titled, *Microfinance: A Theoretical Framework,* deals with various issues pertaining to microfinance that are especially relevant to understanding its impact in promoting self-employment opportunities and alleviating poverty. Having said this, it traces the emergence of microcredit in the backdrop of neo-liberal agenda. It delineates how donor agencies promoted the microcredit approach as a strategy of poverty reduction. The chapter offers a detailed explanation on definitions of microfinance and the difference between the concepts of microcredit and microfinance. It discusses the features of microfinance and scope of microfinance services to the rural poor. Importantly, it summarises different perspectives on microfinance, that is, women's empowerment and poverty reduction; financial inclusion and Millennium Development Goals (MDGs). It summarises microfinance experience at the global level in general and India in particular. It also attempts to offer critical arguments pertaining to microfinance vis-à-vis women's empowerment, poverty reduction and financial inclusion. The chapter sums up with concluding remarks.

Chapter IV, titled, *Financial Inclusion in India: A Conceptual Analysis*, briefly discusses the concept of financial exclusion and gives an overview of financial exclusion in India. While doing so, it highlights the supply and demand side causes of financial exclusion. An important section of the chapter provides a conceptual analysis of financial inclusion, which captures various perspectives in understanding the concept and its importance, and attempts to illustrate the financial inclusion life cycle. By way of background, the chapter traces the evolution of the banking system in India. It discusses Sarma's (2008) 'Index of Financial Inclusion' (IFI) and reports the statewide financial inclusion in India measured by the author. It reviews some of the recent policy initiatives being implemented by Government of India (GoI), Reserve Bank of India (RBI), and National Bank for Agricultural and Rural Development (NABARD) to promote financial inclusion in India. It also attempts to look at the relationship between SBLP and Financial Inclusion. The final section summarises the chapter.

Chapter V, titled, *SHG-Bank Linkage Programme (SBLP) Model on Poverty Alleviation: Findings from Andhra Pradesh and Telangana,* attempts to examine the impact of India's largest public sector microfinance model, that is, the SBLP on poverty alleviation of rural women in Andhra Pradesh. This chapter examines the central hypothesis of the study, that is, 'access to subsidized credit and other financial services through SBLP has significant impact in terms of reducing poverty levels of poor women'. To test the same, this study reports the findings of field research in three villages from the state of Andhra Pradesh. To assess its impact, some important variables such as the respondent's period of association with the group, purpose for availing loans, the correlation between respondent's caste and purpose of availing loan, improved income levels of the respondents before and after joining SHGs, and also their financial contribution to family expenditure were taken into consideration. The study also deals with an important aspect, that is, SBLP vis-á-vis rural entrepreneurship development. It identifies some of the important challenges to the functioning of SBLP model from both officials as well as SHG members. The study draws observations regarding the functioning of MFI model and identifies constraints in its implementation through the feedback of the respondents. The inferences of the study are explained in detail in the chapter.

Chapter VI, titled, *Microfinance Models and Initiatives on Financial Inclusion of the Poor: Findings from Andhra Pradesh and Telangana*, is also based on empirical data. It attempts to examine the impact of two microfinance models such as (i) Self Help Group-Bank Linkage Programme (SBLP) Model and (ii) Business Correspondent (BC) Model on promoting financial inclusion of the poor in the selected three field surveyed areas. In this regard, the chapter is divided into two main sections. As part of section I, the chapter, on the one hand, examines the contributions of SBLP model in promoting financial inclusion among the SHG women and on the other hand, identifies the challenges faced in its execution. Section II examines the impact of the BC model in ensuring financial inclusion. The chapter further offers a comprehensive understanding on the formation and functioning of BC model vis-à-vis inclusion of the hitherto financially excluded sections into the banking fold. It also brings out the constraints involved in both SBLP and BC model in achieving the said objectives.

Chapter VII *Conclusion* synthesises various arguments put forth in the preceding theoretical chapters and summarises the main findings of the empirical chapters. In doing so, the chapter highlights and analyses the potential of SHG-Bank Linkage Programme (SBLP) and Business Correspondent (BC) models in terms of the two main claims: poverty alleviation and financial inclusion of the poor. Further, it offers a few suggestions for the successful functioning of SBLP and BC models with a special emphasis on Microfinance Institutions (MFIs). The chapter draws three inferences: First, the provision of delivering subsidised credit through SBLP has a positive impact on creation of various livelihood opportunities for the rural poor. However, it is argued that merely providing subsidized credit and individual bank accounts may not address the multidimensional nature of poverty. Second, financial inclusion is an ongoing and a progressive process. Its success depends upon access to adequate, affordable and timely credit along with the availability of basic financial services and its optimum usage by the people. Third, as far as the BC model is concerned, it is primarily an agent driven model and its success depends upon the efficiency and motivation of the business correspondents in connecting with the customers and creating awareness among them.

References

1. According to the Census of India, 2011, out of total population of 1210.2 million population in India, the size of rural population is 833.1 million (68.84 per cent of the total population). The total number of villages in India has increased from 6,38,588 (2001 Census) to 6,40,867 (2011 Census); an increase of 2,2279 (Hazra, 2012).
2. Cited in Pallavi (2007): Access to Bank Credit: Implication for Dalit Rural Households, Economic and Political Weekly, p.3219.
3. With a view to simplify the applying procedures for the customers, the Reserve Bank India introduced Know Your Customer (KYC) norms in August 2005. According to the RBI norms, banks can accept any evidence to their satisfaction for establishing the identity and address proof of the

customer. In other words, these KYC norms simplified the procedures to open an account for those whose financial transactions are of modest amounts. See Ramji (2007:16).

4. The 'no-frills account' (NFA) is an important financial product that allows financially excluded individuals to access banking services with low or nil minimum balances; and also either with low or no charges. NFA encourages the poor people to save more by providing the credit in the form of overdraft facility. See Khan (2012).
5. The present study, including primary survey, is carried out prior to the division of the state into Andhra Pradesh and Telangana. The issues raised in the study are still relevant to both the states and therefore, the researcher used the name of the state as 'Andhra Pradesh' that also includes Telangana.
6. In India, 49 per cent of the rural farming poor has been highly indebted, out of which 64 per cent of them have taken loan from informal sources. In Andhra Pradesh alone, 82 per cent of the households are stated to be indebted, of which 74 per cent of the households taken loan from informal sources (59th round survey of NSSO data, 2005). The data underscores that most of the rural households are hitherto financially excluded by the formal financial institutions and further, emphasising the need of including the same in the formal financial fold.

Chapter II

Literature Review

The chapter is divided into three major sections. First section primarily aims at reviewing the literature on poverty. While doing so, it attempts to conceptualize the multidimensional nature of poverty. It analyses the phenomenon at the global level in general and India in particular and offers an operational definition of poverty. Further, it also analyses three important perspectives to understand poverty and its gendered quality. It documents the poverty estimates in India offered by various committees constituted by the Planning Commission and briefly highlights some of the important poverty reduction strategies. Second section makes an effort to trace the conceptual underpinnings of microfinance and the emergence of the microfinance movement in India. It reviews the theoretical and empirical literature, which deals with Microfinance and Self Help Groups (SHGs) in relation to poverty alleviation. Further, the section introduces a recent phenomenon in the Indian banking sector, that is, financial inclusion. It identifies key challenges and offers different strategies and recommendations to address the problem. Third section is central to this chapter as it provides theoretical framework of the study: Amartya Sen's theory of 'Development as Freedom' (1999) and Nussbaum's construction of 'Capability Approach' (2000).

Introduction

The problem of poverty has a central concern of academicians and policy planners. It has assumed critical importance with the debate on the new goal for global poverty reduction, that is, "to reach zero extreme poverty by 2030" (The Chronic Poverty Report, 2014-2015). It is argued that even after implementing various anti-poverty measures and welfare policies by the governments and International agencies, many of the Asia, Africa and Latin American countries continue to witness the stubborn persistence of poverty. According to Global Multidimensional Poverty Index (MPI) (2014), in June 2014, a total of 1.6 billion people were living in multidimensional poverty with more than 30 per cent of the people living in one hundred and eight countries. Of these 1.6 billion people, 52 per cent live in South Asia, and 29 per cent in Sub-Saharan Africa. With a view on estimating rural and urban poverty, it is documented that, of the said 1.6 billion poor people, 85 per cent live in rural areas (Alkire *et al.,* 2014).

With reference to India, poverty alleviation has consistently been one of the important challenges since its independence and recognised as an avowed objective in policy-making. Accordingly, the Indian government has been initiating and implementing various developmental strategies and welfare policies from time to time to meet the proposed objective. Despite the government's initiatives and commitment through these strategies and policies, the grassroots reality makes it clear that the country still has a long way to go in alleviating poverty (Alkire *et al.,* 2014 and Goshal, 2012). As far as the rural areas are concerned, scholars are of the view that poverty in India is largely rural in character. While arguing about which section of people come under poor category in rural regions of India, casual agricultural labourers were identified as the largest group, and small and marginal farmers were the second largest group among the poor (Gaiha, 1989). In terms of caste stratification, the people belonging to Scheduled Castes (SCs) and Scheduled Tribes (STs) are far more likely to be poor than those of other social groups, because of their low status (Dev, 2007; and Haughton and Khandker, 2009).

In addition to the above categories, a significant proportion of rural women remain caught in the poverty trap. They have been suffering more from poverty due to landlessness, unemployment, inaccessibility of resources, primary health, education, transportation, market and so on. Due to landlessness, they often work as daily-wage labourers in agriculture and various other activities. In their off time (or if there is no work to do) they would remain without any earnings. The unpredictability and inconsistency of earnings, therefore, compelled them to remain bound in the shackles of poverty and dependent on their male relative (Sukumar, 2010; Visaria, 2008 and World Bank Report, 2003). Corroborating the above, scholars have attributed the problem of poverty to low national income, unequal distribution of resources and inequitable distribution of development gains (Dandekar and Rath, 1976). Some have argued the case for seeing poverty as deprivation of multiple capabilities ranging from socio-economic, political and cultural spheres (Sen, 2000 and Sengupta, 2007) and also seeing the problem through a gender lens (Alkire *et al.*, 2014; Nussbaum, 2000; and Upalankar, 2005). Given this context, the following section, as a part of literature review, attempts to conceptualise multidimensional aspects of poverty in the Indian context and offers an operational definition for it. Further, it also analyses three perspectives on poverty and the gendered nature of it.

SECTION - I

The Multidimensional Nature of Poverty

Conceptually, the notion of poverty is a multifaceted phenomenon in its content and definition. While conceptualizing poverty, academicians and international organisations have used different criteria to understand and define the term poverty. It is therefore, difficult to give a concise meaning to it. The following section, however, attempts to bring out an inclusive definition, which accommodates various dimensions of poverty. With reference to India, the section also examines the factors affecting poverty in rural areas, and highlights the relationship between microfinance and poverty alleviation.

At the global level, during the late 1960s-early 70s, poverty has been observed into three aspects: subsistence, inequality and externality. First, subsistence is primarily concerned with the minimum provision of access to food, maintaining health and working capacity. In other words, it is understood as having minimum capabilities to survive and lead one's life. Second aspect, that is, inequality deals with differences of income levels between various groups within the society. It also accommodates the consumption power or purchasing capacity of a person. The third aspect of poverty is attributed to externality, which is correlated with the social consequences of poverty for the rest of the society rather than with the mere material needs of the poor (Rein, 1970). In mid-1970s, the European Council (1975) defined poverty as the lack of some important indicators of human well-being, which are the consequence of low-income levels. The Council believes that poverty is primarily related to income levels of the people. To put in succinctly, inadequate income levels preclude them from having a standard of living. In this disadvantaged stage, they may experience poor housing, inadequate health and may be excluded and marginalised from partaking in various activities of the society. While correlating the problem of poverty with individuals' participation in socio-economic and political spheres in any given society, Singh (1989) argues that poverty is a 'social determinate' as it depends substantially on the structure of caste, class and family as well as social attitudes and values. Only a part of it is economic inefficiency which can be measured economically. This argument brings a sociological perspective to understand the nature of poverty, particularly in Indian context.

The World Bank report (2000-2001:5) put forward a comprehensive definition of the term poverty by including some of the basic amenities of the human survival. The report defines poverty as a situation of "pronounced deprivation in well-being". Further, it adds, being poor means "to be hungry, to lack shelter and clothing, to be sick and not cared for, to be illiterate and not schooled". With reference to poor people's legitimate claims from the state and participation in the society, the report states, "they are often treated badly by institutions of the state and society and excluded from voice and power in those institutions". Similarly, the United Nations report[1] (2006) argues that the phenomenon of poverty has various manifestations. It observes that the notion of poverty includes:

> lack of income and productive resources sufficient to ensure sustainable livelihoods; hunger and malnutrition; ill health; limited or lack of access to education and other basic services; increased morbidity and mortality from illness; homelessness and inadequate housing; unsafe environments; and social discrimination and exclusion. It is also characterised by lack of participation in decision-making and in civil, social and cultural life. (Annex II, para 19, 2006)

The above two definitions offer a comprehensive idea of how to understand the phenomenon of poverty and its severe social consequences. Importantly, the definitions make it clear that poverty is multidimensional in nature and it is not just limited or restricted to one aspect. The definitions include some of the key human development indicators such as health, education, housing and safe environment. Importantly, correlating poverty with sustained livelihoods needs to be highlighted as it has gained wider currency across the globe in recent times.[2] The definitions also expose the plight of the poor people in claiming their legitimate share in the state and their passive participation in the society due to their socio-economic disadvantages and continued discrimination from the mainstream.

Toye (2007:505) offers a generalised, yet simplified definition of poverty by stating that "poverty is a kind of generalised lacking, or state of being without some essential goods and services. Poor people are those deprived of things that they need to live a normal life". Haughton and Khandker (2009:3) add financial and agricultural issues to analyse poverty. They define poverty as "inequality and vulnerability". According to them, inequality focuses on the distribution of income or consumption across the whole population. Vulnerability is defined as the risk of falling into poverty in the future, even if the person is not necessarily poor at the present situation. It is often associated with the effects of 'shocks' such as drought, decline of farm prices, or a financial crisis. They are of the view that vulnerability is a key dimension of well-being as it affects individual's behaviour in terms of investment, production patterns and cropping strategies, and in terms of the perceptions of their own situations. As mentioned, this definition offers a new dimension to poverty by relating it to investment, particularly in the farm sector. They add the term vulnerability to poverty by arguing that drought and crisis in farm production may also push poor people into the poverty trap in the future.

The Global Multidimensional Poverty Index (MPI, 2014) lists ten indicators to measure multidimensional poverty under three important dimensions: (i) Health (ii) Education and (iii) Living standard (Alkire *et al.*, 2014).

Table 2.1: The Dimensions, indicators and deprivation

Dimension	*Indicators*	*Deprived if...*
Health	Nutrition	Any adult or child for whom there is nutritional information is malnourished.
	Child Mortality	Any Child has died in the household.
Education	Years of Schooling	No household member has completed five years of schooling.
	Child School Attendance	Any school-aged child is not attending school up to the age at which they would complete class 8th.
Living Standard	Electricity	The household has no electricity.
	Improved Sanitation	The household's sanitation facility is not improved, or it is improved but shared with other households.
	Safe Drinking Water	The household does not have access to safe drinking water or safe drinking water is more than a 30 minute walk from home, roundtrip.
	Flooring	The household has a dirt, sand or dung floor.
	Assets	The household does not own more than one radio, TV, telephone, bike, motorbike or refrigerator and does not own a car or truck.
	Cooking Fuel	The household cooks with dung, wood or charcoal.

Source: Alkire *et al.*, 2014: 2.

The above table clearly demonstrates the three dimensions of poverty under ten indicators listed above. According to the Global Multidimensional Poverty Index (MPI), poverty is defined as being deprived of three important dimensions under ten indicators. It is understood that improvement in health, education and decent standard of living are critical for a person to come out of poverty. It is said that if any individual is deprived of these ten indicators, they are victims of multidimensional poverty. However, the above diagram and table need to be critically analysed. Though the authors identified the three important dimensions of poverty, they did not discuss an important indicator to measure poverty, that is, employment opportunities and income levels. Without proper employment opportunities and sustained income levels, the poor and disadvantaged people are unable to access these indicators on their own. If they do not have income-earned activities on their own, they have to rely on either state sponsored policies or work as daily-wage labourers.

In the Indian context, Dandekar and Rath (1976) succinctly define poverty as the problem of low national income, slow pace of development and inequitable distribution of the small gains of development. The authors observe poverty only from the economic perspective which means low national income and its unequal distribution. However, they do not include socio-economic perspective to the term poverty. Unlike the above scholars, Kurien (1987) opines that poverty is primarily a socio-economic phenomenon whereby the resources and services available to a society are used to satisfy the wants of the few while many do not have even their basic needs met. The author offers a definition of poverty by highlighting the unequal distribution of resources and services among all sections of people in the society. According to Sen (2000), poverty is not simply a state of low income or consumption but lack of freedom of a person to choose and live the life he has reasons to value. Further, he interprets poverty as deprivation of multiple capabilities. He understands poverty in terms of undernourishment or malnourishment, and inadequate human capability, which is dependent on access to education, public health, housing and so on. Deprivation in the above factors restricts the ability of the people to participate in social and political spheres as well. The author's definition gives prime importance to the well-being of an individual and his/her values.

Sengupta (2007) identifies poverty as a composite of extreme forms of income poverty, human development poverty and social exclusion, eradication of which may be regarded as human rights entitlements in each society. It is therefore, the denial of a number of recognised rights such as right to food, health, education, and adequate standard of living. The absence of these rights would be equivalent to the denial of basic capabilities. The previous studies observed poverty from the developmental or economic perspective. However, Sengupta's definition brings a human rights perspective to understand the nature of poverty. Here, some of the basic human rights have become important indictors to measure poverty. In fact, this kind of recognition generated an urge among the policymakers for complementing poverty alleviation strategy with a special emphasis on the enhancement of basic human rights such as right to food, shelter, education, health and so on.

Sukumar (2010:149) is of the view that poverty involves "one's inability to satisfy basic needs, lack of control over resources, lack of education and skills, poor health and malnutrition, lack of shelter, poor access to water and sanitation, vulnerability to violence and crime, and lack of political freedom and voice". In addition to other common causes of poverty, the rural sector is also especially affected by agricultural stagnation. The author expanded the definition of poverty by adding vulnerability to violence and crime, and lack of political freedom and voice as causes of people falling under poverty. World Bank Report (2011:17) identified access to six basic amenities, in addition to consumption of food, to understand poverty, particularly with reference to India. The six basic facilities of which the poorest segments are deprived lack of access to education, health, infrastructure, clean environment and benefits for women and children.

The recent Rangarajan Committee Report (2014:72) defines poverty as "the inability of a household to meet its current consumption expenses with its incomes". The report makes it clear that households whose incomes are insufficient to meet expenses and who cannot either raise incomes or curtail expenses, usually borrow to bridge the shortfall of their income. For such low levels of incomes, borrowing is expected to be the last resort for a household. However, it is said that borrowings increase the probability of falling into a debt trap. This argument attempts to show the correlation between low-income levels and the need of borrowing to overcome the basic deprivations. This definition fall under the category of Sen's idea of "poverty as capability deprivation,"[3] wherein the households, due to low-income levels and people who are under the below poverty line, may be deprived of multiple capabilities.

From the above definitions both at the global and national level, we observe three dominant views advanced by various scholars. In fact, the arguments largely fit into three perspectives to understand poverty: (i) income perspective, (ii) basic needs perspective and (iii) capability perspective (Parr and Kumar, 2003:15). According to the authors, the 'income perspective' explains that a person is poor if his/her income level is below the defined poverty line. Similarly, the first stream of thought makes it clear that 'poverty as lack of income or low consumption levels'. Scholars defined 'below poverty line' by saying that the poor people are those whose income (consumption) is less than a specified amount be it $ 1 per day or $ 1.25 per day. In other words, poverty is understood as low income levels of those who are below poverty line.

To put it succinctly, this stream of thought assesses poverty predominantly in its monetary aspect (Bhalla, 2002, Ravallion *et al.*, 1999, and The World Bank, 2003). In fact, in India, during the early years of independence, poverty was measured through income and consumption levels. Dandekar and Rath's (1976) idea of poverty fits into this domain. Though this line of thought receives greater significance to define and measure poverty, it is a very narrow way of understanding the phenomenon. It can also argue that reducing poverty to a single dimension, that is, merely income levels, denies socio-political and cultural aspects, which are pertinent for any individual for a decent standard of living. Corroborating the above argument, Kakwani and Subbarao (1990) assert that defining poverty exclusively in terms of income or expenditure has resulted in the neglect of other aspects, notably education and health, which expand and ensure the long-run capabilities of the population.

According to Parr and Kumar (2003), the second perspective on poverty is the 'basic needs perspective'. For them, the basic needs perspective means poverty as deprivation of material requirements for a minimal acceptable fulfillment of human needs, including food. It also recognises the need for employment and participation. Similarly, the second stream thought argues that poverty is comprehensive in nature. It primarily encapsulates the denial of some of the basic human needs include; lack of access education, primary health, malnutrition, inadequate housing, sanitation and so on. Importantly, the recent literature on this subject highlights the concept of poverty in terms of social exclusion and vulnerability, which is gradually receiving wider currency (Haughton and Khandker, 2009; Sukumar, 2010; United Nations Report, 2006 and World Bank Report, 2011).

The third perspective on poverty is the 'capability approach', which highlights the absence of some of the basic capabilities to function. In other words, poverty indicates the lack of opportunity to achieve some functionings such as being well nourished, being adequately clothed and sheltered, and being able to participate in the community and society (Parr and Kumar, 2003). In this context, Sen's projection of poverty rightly fits into this domain. According to Sen, poverty is one of the "deprivations of the basic capabilities rather than merely as low levels of incomes" (2000:87). He believes that the inability to function or participate in any society is a sign of poverty and emphasises that it is the individual's level of functioings[4] that matters, rather than the quantity of money he or she owns (*ibid*). To put it succinctly, the capability perspective on poverty primarily emphasises individuals' capabilities to discharge their functionings and claim their entitlements in the given society, rather than merely their income.

By analysing the definitions in a chronological order, it can be understood that the scope of poverty has been widening over time. In other words, the concept of poverty has been enriched by including socio-economic, political and cultural indicators from different dimensions. Further, it is understood that poverty is an extremely complex phenomenon, which manifests itself in a wide range of interlinked socio-economic and political deprivations. These include low income levels, poor health, lack of assets, social insecurity, social exclusion, vulnerability and political powerlessness. As far as the income levels are concerned, if a household's total earnings are insufficient to meet the basic necessaries for his/her survival, then the person is considered to be living under the conditions of poverty. When it comes to social exclusion, caste, illiteracy and powerlessness renders the poor unable to receive the government's benefits, which are actually meant for them. In other words, due to their poverty, they are excluded even from the state sponsored welfare and developmental programmes within the society.

However, most of the arguments related to poverty focused on lack of income, education, health, housing and so on. Very few scholars argue that lack of access to adequate credit also influences employment opportunities and that in turn augments income levels. It encourages the small and marginal farmers and landless labourers to invest in sustained income generating activities. For instance, investments in farm production, livestock rearing or dairy farming certainly improve the income levels of the poor. Given the above definitions and understanding of poverty, the present study adopts the second and third perspectives advanced by various scholars, particularly by Sen (2000). The author considers poverty as 'capability deprivation', wherein people are deprived of basic services or opportunities such as lack of access to education, primary health services, housing, lack of access to institutional credit, lack of livelihood opportunities and so on compelling them to stay in the clutches of poverty. Among the factors, one of the identified constraints faced by the poor who engage in on-farm and off-farm activities are lack of access to formal credit, which restrains them from taking advantage of economic opportunities and to increase their income levels, hence move out of poverty.

Poverty: Gender Perspective

In recent times, the gender dimension of poverty assessment has also gained significant momentum. This perspective primarily deals with the poverty of women. In fact, it has deviated the central focus on general poverty to poverty of women in particular. It has also become central to debates in most of the developing countries on how to address gender inequality and bring qualitative change in the lives of women. Nussbaum in her book, *Women and Human Development: The Capability Approach* (2000) elucidates that women are less well nourished than men, less healthy, more vulnerable to physical violence, sexual abuse, lead a far from dignified life and are being treated as *'second class citizens'*. She also draws attention to how women are being treated as burdensome and even dispensable in traditional families. Following Sen's approach, Nussbaum underscores the importance of human development through the enhancement of capabilities. She argues that human functional capabilities like quality life, health, emotions, reason, body integrity, imagination, thought etc., are essential for human development. In similar vein, Upalankar (2005) observes that women are among the poorest of the poor suffering from malnourishment. The voices of poor women would not carry any weight in a family structure, particularly in rural India. Among many other causes, this situation largely attributed to lack of economic independence. They have been long neglected in their role as beneficiaries of the process of development. These social and economic inequalities relegate women to a lower status and make them less important, less capable, less central, and less valuable than men. Such discrimination and exclusion has multiple implications for the overall growth of a healthy society.

Exclusion in different capacities acts as a cause and consequence for women to take active participation in mainstream. Ironically, in developing countries women play a significant role in both agriculture and household activities (Wong and Veroinique, 2014). However, the benefits of agricultural production are reaped by men. For instance, it is estimated that 43 per cent of women are engaged in farming in developing countries, ranging from 20 per cent in Latin America to 50 per cent in Eastern Asia and Sub-Saharan Africa. Yet women have little or no access to agricultural related assets, inputs and services (Food and Agriculture Organisation, 2011). It is needless to state that men monopolise the asset base, leaving women to extreme poverty and vulnerability. Despite the contribution of women, their capabilities have been severely underestimated. The trends project that a total of 60 per cent of the 1.6 billion people living in extreme poverty are women (Alkire *et al.,* 2014). The Millennium Development Goals (MDGs) Report (2014) reveals that, 781 million adults and 126 million youth worldwide lack basic literacy skills, and more than 60 per cent of them are women.

In India, poverty among rural women is mounting compared to poverty among rural men. Over the past 20 years, the number of women in absolute poverty rose by 50 per cent as against 30 per cent for rural men. As far as the work participation is concerned, though the country has a large percentage of women workers, there is a serious underestimation of their contribution in the nation's economy. It is estimated that women in India form 89.5 per cent of the informal and unrecognised sector, and in particular, their work participation rate is higher in rural areas (Razi, 2012). As far as the female work force in agricultural sector is concerned, it is estimated that 66 per cent of them are engaged in farming. However, they are invariably paid lower wages than men for the same work. Besides, it is emphasised that women shoulder the entire burden of looking after livestock, bringing up children and doing other household chores. Though there is a significant increase in women depending on farming as a means of livelihood, they have no access to institutional credit as the land titles are in the names of men. It is observed that only 11 per cent of women have access to land holdings, that too, mostly as small and marginal farmers (Amrit, 2012).

Apart from their working conditions, sufficient literacy is a necessary condition for attaining qualitative change in the lives of women (Hazara, 2010). In particular, educating women in rural areas promotes quality of life with regard to life expectancy, infant mortality, learning and nutritional levels (Maulick, 2011). Even though the literacy rate in India has increased in comparative terms, the gender gap remains very high. According to Census 2011, of the 74.04 per cent of literacy rate, the figures for male and female are 82.14 and 65.46 per cent respectively. The figures denote that there has been a tremendous increase in the literacy rates, however, the gap between the genders continue to take its central stage. In particular, Rajasthan state reports a nearly 28 percentage point gap and other North Indian states like Bihar, Uttar Pradesh, Madhya Pradesh, Chhattisgarh and Jharkhand report a more than 20 percentage point literacy gap (Visaria, 2011). Overall in India, the literacy gap between men and women is reported as much as 16.7 per cent. Thus, the figures both at the global and national level indicate the existing inequalities faced by women in socio-economic fronts. Further, it highlights the immediate need for recognising the problem of feminisation of poverty and to address the same.

There are a variety of techniques and methods developed across the globe to alleviate feminisation of poverty and bring gender equality. Nayyar (2005) opines that reduction of gender inequality in access to resources and opportunities leads to an increase in the rate of economic growth which in turn reduces the poverty levels. This happens because gender equality enables women to take up income-earning opportunities, and participate in the growth process. The author correlates reduction of gender inequality with economic opportunities. To put it succinctly, he emphasises creating various income-generation activities for women so that they can become financially stable on their own. Morrison *et al.,* (2007) are of the view that economic empowerment is one of the most important ingredients in the process of women's empowerment. They also add that women's access to markets and their decision-making power within households not only leads to the reduction of poverty but also increases their productivity at the individual and household level. Having recognised the need of providing small loans to rural women, other scholars also promote the same strategy by giving emphasis to the promotion of Self-Help Groups (SHGs) in rural areas (Ramalakxmi, 2003; Malhotra *et al.,* 2005; Sylendra, 2008; Nair, 2011). The proceeding sections of this chapter review the literature on the role and impact of SHGs in this direction.

Poverty Estimates in India

Estimation of the poverty line has been a much debated issue in India since the 1960s and expert groups have been set up from time to time to review the methodology for estimation. In this regard, the Planning Commission constituted various committees in order to estimate the poverty ratio, that is, the percentage of people living below the poverty line in India. One of the first of its kind in estimating poverty was the Working Group set up in 1962 to identify a desirable minimum level of living for the population (Gangopadhyay and Singh, 2013). The Working Group recommended a poverty line in the same year, set a minimum level of expenditure of Rs 20 per day for rural areas and Rs 25 per day for urban areas at 1960-61 prices, below which households would not be able to meet the basic requirements for living. This minimum per capita expenditure was determined by taking into account the requirements of balanced food and, in the case of urban areas, some provision of housing expenditure. However, the expenditures on health and education were not considered as they were expected to be provided by the state (Dandekar, 1996). Fifteen years after the Working Group, the Planning Commission constituted a Task Force in 1977 under the chairmanship of Dr Y.K. Alagh to estimate the poverty levels based on consumption levels, which submitted its report in 1979. The Task Force report estimated the average calorie requirements both in rural and urban areas, pegging the calorie norm as 2400 kcal per capita per day in rural areas and 2100 kcal per capita per day in urban areas (Mehta and Bhide, 2009; Rangarajan Committee Report, 2014). Twelve years after the constitution of the Task Force, the Planning Commission constituted an Expert Group in 1989 under the Chairmanship of D.T. Lakdawala. The Expert Group submitted its report in 1993 and the Planning Commission accepted its recommendations in 1997. By adopting the Lakdawala Expert Group methodology, the Planning Commission estimated the poverty ratio and the number of poor for different years at the national level. The percentage of people living below the poverty line in 1993-94 has been estimated as 37.3 per cent in rural areas and 32.3 per cent in urban areas and 36.0 per cent for the country as a whole (Rangarajan Committee Report, 2014).

Suresh Tendulkar Committee Report (2009)

Sixteen years after the constitution of the Lakdawala Expert Group, the Planning Commission constituted another Expert Group under the chairmanship of Suresh Tendulkar in 2005. It submitted its report in November 2009 and the Planning Commission accepted its recommendations in January 2011. Following the Tendulkar Committee methodology, the Planning Commission appointed another review committee to estimate the extent of poverty in the country in 2012. Table 2.2 shows the poverty levels at the national level for the last twenty years.

Table 2.2: National Poverty Estimates (per cent below poverty line) (1993-2012)

	Poverty Ratio (per cent)			*Number of Poor (million)*		
Year	*Rural*	*Urban*	*Total*	*Rural*	*Urban*	*Total*
1993-94	50.1	31.8	45.3	328.6	74.5	403.7
2004-05	41.8	25.7	37.2	326.3	80.8	407.1
2009-10	33.8	20.9	29.8	278.2	76.5	354.7
2011-12	25.7	13.7	21.9	216.5	52.8	269.3

Source: Press Note on Poverty Estimates, 2011-12, Planning Commission (2013), Government of India; Review of Expert Group to Review the Methodology for Estimation of Poverty (2009) Planning Commission, Government of India. PRS (p. 3).

Table 2.2 demonstrates that the percentage of people below the poverty line in 1993-94 was 45.3 per cent and it was 50.1 per cent in rural areas and 31.8 per cent in urban areas. In 2004-05, the poverty ratios were 37.2 per cent at the all India level and for the rural and urban areas 41.8 per cent and 25.7 per cent respectively. In 2009-10, it has been estimated that 29.8 per cent at the all India level and it was 33.8 per cent in rural areas and 20.9 per cent in urban areas. With regard to 2011-12, as per the estimations of Planning Commission (2013), the poverty ratio for the country was 21.9 per cent[5] and it was 25.7 per cent in rural areas and 13.7 per cent in urban areas. According to the above estimates, poverty ratio declined at an average rate of 0.74 percentage per year between 1993-94 and 2004-05, and at 2.18 percentage per year between 2004-05 and 2011-12. The all India poverty ratio has declined by 15 per cent from 37.2 per cent in 2004-05 to 21.9 per cent in 2011-12. Regardless of various committees, it is observed that the extent of poverty ratio is higher in the rural sector compared to the urban sector. Nevertheless, significant decline in poverty ratio has been observed in both rural and urban areas during this period as the rural poverty head count ratio declined by 16 percentage from 41.8 per cent to 25.7 per cent and urban poverty declining by 12 percentage from 25.7 per cent to 13.7 per cent.

However, the poverty measurements estimated by Suresh Tendulkar Committee report came under serious criticism. The main criticism of the report was that its poverty line was primarily based on the level of urban poverty. It is also argued that the report had delinked consumption poverty from calorie norms and focused on price differentials over space and time. As a result, the total poverty ratio at the national level was too low, as it was figured at 21.9 per cent (Manohar, 2014:7). It was therefore, seven years after the Tendulkar Committee, that the Planning Commission constituted an Expert Group under the chairmanship of Rangarajan in 2012, which submitted its recommendations in 2014. The Rangarajan Committee (2014:8) reviewed the poverty estimates reported by Tendulkar Committee. It has come up with different estimates, wherein it has attempted to extend its concern beyond food to some basic non-food essentials, which are not similar to the Tendulkar Committee report.

Rangarajan Committee Report on Measurement of Poverty (2014)

The Rangarajan Committee Report on 'Measurement of Poverty' (2014:5) estimates that about 30.9 per cent of the rural population and 26.4 per cent of the urban population are below the poverty line in 2011-12. The poverty ratio at the all India level for 2011-12 prices comes to 29.5 per cent, as against to 21.9 per cent of the methodology followed by Suresh Tendulkar Committee. In other words, 260.5 million individuals in rural areas and 102.5 million in urban areas a grand total of 363 million were under the poverty line in India in 2012. This means that three out of every ten Indians are poor. The Committee has based its methodology for estimating poverty on observed data of household income and expenses. Accordingly, it has suggested that persons spending less than Rs 47 a day or Rs 1,407 per month in urban areas and upto Rs 32 per day or Rs 972 per month in rural areas should be considered poor. For a family of five members, the monthly consumption expenditure is estimated at Rs 7,035 in urban areas and

Rs 4860 in rural areas. The report has showed a significant difference from Tendulkar Committee report that had suggested that the poverty line should be kept at Rs 33 per day in urban and Rs 27 per day in rural areas. The Committee is of the view that the better way of looking at poverty would be through the monthly consumption expenditure per household rather than the 'per person' or 'per day' method. Besides, it adds, apart from the monthly consumption expenditure, a household's well-being must be measured in the context of government spending on public services. The report also emphasises that the estimates proposed by this Committee would be a useful input for the government in initiating any welfare and developmental programmes for poverty reduction as well as for subsidy schemes. The following section attempts to briefly highlight some of the important poverty reduction strategies in India since its independence.

Strategies of Poverty Reduction in India

The literature on poverty tells us about the complex systems and procedures that create poverty and its prevalence among one-sixth of the global population. There is a need to understand the causes of poverty and identify important strategies to alleviate it. One important question relevant to the strategies adopted is about access to adequate and sustainable credit to poor women and its impact in reducing poverty levels. The context and consequences of the microcredit system require proper attention to understand whether the position of rural women improved or worsened. In particular, this question has gained much relevance against the backdrop of the microfinance crisis in Andhra Pradesh as discussed in the earlier chapter. In fact, the microfinance crisis in Andhra Pradesh has not been adequately addressed in the current literature.

The Government of India has been formulating various developmental and welfare measures to reduce poverty levels since independence. Academicians have also contributed by proposing various strategies for this. For instance, during the mid-1970s, in the process of finding various strategies to alleviate poverty and to accelerate nation's growth, Chakraborthy (1974) proposed the idea of 'poverty-reducing growth process' and recommended for adopting a nationwide poverty reduction strategy. This strategy emphasises the acceleration of national growth in manner that increases income levels of the people living below the poverty line. The Government of India has primarily relied on two approaches to reduce poverty levels since its independence. First, it was anticipated that the effects of aggregate rural growth would spread to all sections in society such that poverty reduction would be achieved side by side with increases in economic growth. Second, it was based on poverty reduction through the implementation of various anti-poverty and welfare programmes. The reliance placed on each of the two objectives has varied over time. Further, the report argues, the slow reduction in poverty through the 1950s and 1960s in particular, reinforced skepticism regarding the strength of any trickledown effect (The World Bank Report, 1997). The state led planning ignored the existing unevenness and inequality within the households of rural areas. Thus, the focus of development shifted to this dimension.

Using state-level data for 1957-91, Datt and Ravallion (1996) identified the unevenness of the rise in rural living standards in various states of India since the 1950s. They proposed two important strategies of rural poverty alleviation. The first strategy is development of on-farm and off-farm sectors vis-à-vis economic growth. In some states such as Punjab and Haryana, they argue, robust growth in rural areas appears to have been the main factor in poverty reduction. Corroborating the above argument, Jayaraman and Lanjouw (1999) highlight three important forces of economic change: agricultural intensification, changing land relations and occupational diversification, and the role of various institutions as conduits of change. They believe that land and labour are the two key determinants of the rural economy. In the mid-1960s, the northern States of Punjab and Haryana saw a most significant growth in output. Improvement in the agriculture sector, multiple cropping and a shift to high-value crops appear to have made a significant contribution to the rural economy. Second, the study also observed a decline in traditional caste occupations and increase in the creation of off-farm income-generating activities. The study concluded that the green revolution and the expansion of the non-farm economy had raised agricultural wages in rural India by increasing the demand for labour.

The second strategy by Datt and Ravallion (1996) pertains to development of human resource development in rural areas. They assert that this approach can also reduce poverty even if there is little output growth in the domestic economy. By referring to Kerala as an example, the authors state that the ability to export skilled labour to other countries and consequently benefiting and improving the living standards back home through remittances could be a useful practice. On the other hand, the study found uneven progress in rural living standards in some other states. It argued that unfortunately some states like Bihar and Madhya Pradesh were unsuccessful on both counts as they were reported to have achieved little economic growth, and underdevelopment of human and physical resources. Of late, scholars such as Sen (2000) and Nussubaum (2000) have underscored the significance of human resources in the poverty alleviation. In a study by Sen (2000) highlighted that the improvement in human development indicators such as health and education in Kerala significantly contributed in improving living standards of the people. One can identify a paradigm shift in understanding of development from income perspective to non-income perspective. This development reinforced the need for investing more in human resource development. By adopting Sen's idea of 'poverty as capability deprivation', Bhide and Mehta (2007:201) identified some of the key causes of poverty, which are linked to the capability of a household to utilise economic opportunities for income and employment. They argue that lack of adequate economic opportunities may limit a household's access to different occupations. Poor infrastructure facilities, such as roads or communications may limit a poor household's access to information or markets. Lack of assets would restrict a household's access to credit or services. Lack of education limits a household's access to opportunities for jobs. All these factors may also influence a poor household's ability to break out of poverty.

Banking system in rural areas is not sufficient to deliver adequate and sustained credit to various sections of the society. As a result, they are unable to invest the capital in any small-scale income generating activities that in turn aggravates unemployment and poverty (Rajkumar and Chennakrishna, 2009). De Sliva and Denby (1989) offered a critical discussion of banking to the poor, particularly credit to women in Third World countries. They argue that the strategies adopted in these countries emphasised the need to increase agricultural production and to bring the rural poor out of poverty. Shortage of working capital is regarded as one of the major obstacles to generate self-employment opportunities. In particular, access to affordable credit to the poor women in these economies is dismal. The reasons are many: blatant discrimination; the failure of planners to recognise the role of women in development; the assumption that women do not need or cannot effectively use credit; and the failure of credit programmes to take into account the particular conditions under which women live and work. They emphasise that access to institutional finance is an important development strategy. However, its effectiveness depends on its usage. It also depends largely on the particular conditions under which it is employed. They add that the active participation of poor not only enables them to be recipients of loans and also integral partners in the process of development.

Referring to rural disadvantaged women, Vatta (2003) argues that even today most of the rural women are income-less, economically dependent on male members. According to him, inadequate access to primary health, education and decent living compel them to stay in the clutches of poverty. The author attempts to establish a link between human development to poverty alleviation. Anupam and Shobit's (2008) study characterises microfinance as a poverty alleviation strategy in so far as individual development of the poor, particularly women is concerned. It encourages small entrepreneurial activities in economically weak societies and regions. For instance in Bangladesh, microcredit through the Grameen Bank managed to yield benefits where poor-led market participation is enhanced, thus helping many poor and excluded to cross the poverty line. Since poverty alleviation is the prime objective, the Government of India and policy planners have been seeking the most suitable ways to deal with this situation. Along with other anti-poverty programmes, Government of India in its 2006-07 Union Budget formally recognised the contribution of microfinance in the alleviation of poverty for the first time.

Most of the developing countries have recognised as well as adopted microfinance as a mechanism to address the problem of rural poverty and empower the rural poor. Some of the literature on microfinance attempts to find out the potential links between microfinance intervention and livelihood promotion of rural women. The literature shows that microfinance significantly plays a productive role in the lives of rural women. The above arguments also underscore the efficacy of SHGs in lending credit. Given this backdrop, the following section attempts to review the literature on the emergence of microfinance and microfinance intervention in India. Further, it examines the impact on alleviating poverty of the rural poor, particularly women.

SECTION II

The Genesis of Microfinance

The genesis of microfinance can be traced to experiments in Latin America and South Asia (Armendariz and Morduch, 2004). Bangladesh is particularly notable in this context, as the Grameen Bank was initiated here by Professor Yunus. He started in 1976 with providing microfinance facilities to 42 rural women to start income-generating activities on an experimental basis. He found that given a chance women were able to increase their income and improve the socio-economic status of their families (Ahmad, 2008). Identifying the importance of subsidised credit, he established Grameen Bank in 1983, and started lending tiny loans to the rural poor in a full-fledged manner (Rahman, 1999). Since the mid-1980s, microfinance has become a favoured intervention for poverty alleviation in other countries too (Leach and Sitaram, 2002).

The definition and objective of microfinance was discussed at the 1997 Micro-Credit Summit in Washington DC. The Summit defined microfinance as "microcredit programmes provide credit for self-employment and other financial and business services to very poor persons". The draft declaration of the summit also proclaims that "the time has come to acknowledge microcredit as a powerful tool in the struggle to end poverty and economic dependence" (Micro-Credit Summit, 1997, Declaration and Plan of Action, p. 45). The same year, Kofi Annan, the former United Nations (UN) Secretary General, declared that microcredit is a critical anti-poverty tool, a wise investment method in human capital. Considering the advantages of microcredit, George (2008:62) defines microfinance as "a provision of thrift, credit and other financial services (loans) and products of very small amount to the poor in rural, semi-urban and urban areas for enabling them to raise their income levels, improve living standards and empower them in different spheres". Another scholar on microcredit, Oommen (2008) believes that microfinance means providing financial services to the poor and vulnerable who are being excluded by the mainstream banking and finance market.

Globally, the World Bank has adopted the concept of microcredit as a targeted approach to poverty reduction since the 1980s. In the early 1990s, microcredit was endorsed as an approach to reduce poverty in most of the third world countries. These countries initiated different plans to invest in various microfinance models. It significantly increased women's access to facilities for tiny loans and savings, thereby contributing to poverty reduction and financial sustainability (Weber, 2004 and IFAD, 2009). In Indonesia, the provision of delivering microfinance services to poor sections have profound implications for their social and economic development, as it effected a shift from government and donor subsidized credit system to self-sufficient MFIs providing voluntary savings and credit services to the poor and deprived (Robinson, 2001). The Bank Kredit Desa System (BKDS) in rural Indonesia provides small-scale credit to the poorest households, with an accent on petty traders. However, here is a huge demand for microfinance services by the poor who have hitherto being dependent on informal institutions. The demand can be met at reasonable cost to borrowers only in the formal sector and only by public sector banks (Roy, 2008).

While highlighting the supply-side constrains faced by the poor in accessing institutional credit, Abdullah and Fontaine (2008) argue that poor people are often neglected by the commercial banks in most of the developing countries by imposing strict rules and regulations. Resultantly, demand for the product and services offered by commercial banks is low among the poor as the products and services are not designed to meet their requirements. They need credit on a minimum rate of interest and in relaxed terms. In such circumstances microfinance is envisaged to enable borrowers to attain higher household incomes, increase savings rates, acquire smooth consumption pattern over their lifetime and finally diversify their sources of income generation. A study by Mosley (2001) documents that the success of microfinance in alleviating poverty in Bolivia, Bangladesh and Indonesia as it reached a sizeable number of poor people in these countries. In particular, Khandker (2005) showcases the microfinance intervention through MFIs in rural Bangladesh resulted in 40 per cent reduction in moderate poverty. The study further reiterates that microfinance enables low-income people to expand their economic mobility, and helps them move from 'survival mode to planning mode'. In this context, it is seen that access to finance is essential to enable people to participate in the modern market-based economy. In fact, it is analogous to access to improved housing, safe drinking water, basic healthcare services, primary education and so on. Since the 1980s, microfinance was successfully operated and popularised by the Grameen Bank, propounded as a bottom-up approach mobilising the marginalised communities, particularly poor women (Basher and Rashid, 2012).

In India, the Report of the Committee on Financial Inclusion, Government of India (2008:5) reiterates that financial access to the poor and vulnerable sections is a prerequisite for 'poverty reduction and social cohesion'. This could be understood as the state's obligation to benefit the poorest of the poor and facilitate them to become an integral part of efforts in promoting 'inclusive growth'. The Eleventh Five Year Plan (2007-12) also acknowledged the significance of microfinance as it can contribute immensely to the financial inclusion of the poor without which it will be difficult for them to come out of the vicious cycle of poverty (Report of the Steering Committee on Micro-Finance and Poverty Alleviation, 2007). Thus, the Government of India, along with the RBI, recognised role of banking sector in achieving financial inclusion. This approach aims at ensuring easy access to and usage of formal financial services for all people at an affordable cost. These measures are expected to promote financial deepening by expanding the outreach of banking facilities to wider sections of the population (Takeshi and Hamori, 2012; Majumdar and Gupta, 2013).

In recent times, attention has been paid to critically examine the role of MFIs in poverty alleviation in the wake of microfinance crisis in Southern India, particularly in Andhra Pradesh. The crisis has raised fundamental issues concerning MFI borrower's welfare and questioned the very purpose of the emergence of MFIs. For instance, a recent study by Hulme and Mairot (2014) argues that microfinance in South Asia, particularly in Bangladesh and India has lost its moral compass. The study finds that in recent times, MFIs have focused excessively on financial performance and neglected their social mission, that is, poverty alleviation and women's empowerment. More importantly, the impact of loans on beneficiary welfare has become a secondary issue as the loan officers or staff of the MFIs were pressurised to achieve individual financial targets set by the institutions. In that process, they routinely mistreat clients, especially poor women. It suggests that the MFIs should be held accountable for monitoring levels of indebtedness to protect their clients.

In this context, research on microfinance has received much significance in recent times. Parallel to microfinance intuitions, in recent times, SHGs have also been the focus of development discourse in the third world countries, as they seem to offer a platform for economic empowerment of women. In fact, the reason for studying the idea and practice of SHGs as a strategy is because these groups enable women's easy access to credit facilities and the possibility of creating self-employment opportunities that in turn, enable them to become economically independent and reduce their poverty in the longer run (Galab and Rao, 2003; Malhotra, 2005; Morrison *et al.,* 2007; Roy, 2008; Misra, 2010; and Vaidyanathan, 2014). The following sub-section attempts to theorize the concept of SHGs in general and India in particular, and bring out its potentialities.

Self-Help Groups and Poverty Alleviation: Theoretical and Empirical Analysis

The idea Self Help Group came into vogue in development literature since the 1970s. This approach became a unique form of effort, believed to enhance effective coping skills, improved self-esteem, personal growth and collective mobilisation for social change (Hasenfeld and Gidron, 1993). One of the earlier studies defined SHG as "a human service-oriented voluntary association (apart from voluntary organisations) made up of persons who share a common problem and who band together to resolve the problem through their mutual efforts". It presented the idea of *experiential knowledge,* which serves as a primary source of truth in SHGs (Borkman, 1976:446). It is also said that "these groups emphasise face-to-face interactions and informal and interchangeable roles" (Hasenfeld and Gidron, 1993:217).

Tripaty defines the SHG as

> a homogeneous group of rural poor, voluntarily formed to save whatever amount they can easily save out of their earnings and

> mutually agree to contribute to a common fund of the group to be lent to the members for meeting their production and credit needs. (2005: 45)

Similarly, Suguna observes the SHG as

> a small economically homogeneous group of rural poor which is voluntarily ready to contribute to a common fund to be lent to its members as per group decision, which works for group's solidarity, self-help, awareness, social and economic empowerment in the way of democratic functioning. (2006: 15)

Kumar highlights the basic structure and importance of SHGs by stating that

> SHG consists of a group of people of, ten to fifteen members on the condition that each of them would be assuming responsibility for the development of all. It represents an institution that is the result of a participatory endeavour of people trying to secure three types of power – social, economic and political that would empower them and improve their lives. (2009: 68)

The above definitions provide a clear understanding of the structure and functioning of the SHGs; and have the voluntary savings enable the targeted group to become self employed and also gain self-esteem through establishing their own enterprises. However, Suguna (2006) offers a broader definition as she argues that the SHGs also work for unity of the group members and promote their social and economic empowerment. As far as the last definition is concerned, SHG is a visible portrayal, which includes the dimensions of participation, responsibility and development of each group member. The author also draws our attention to social inclusion as a whole, with the usage of three types of power, that is, social, economic and political. Simply put, membership in the SHGs enables women to gain control over their well-being through nutrition, health, education (i.e. social power), control of household income and decision-making through income-generation activity (i.e. economic power); and the SHG as a group approach, enables women to participate in grama sabha meetings, and facilitates their awareness of the voting pattern and how to claim their entitlements through their elected representatives (i.e. political control). The author opines that these are all feasible through membership and effective participation in the SHGs. As a result, it enhances their capabilities to overcome their hurdles and further enriches their lives.

Shylendra (1996) in his study assessed the impact of Regional Rural Banks (RRBs) in delivering credit to the poor people. He examined the role of RRBs in achieving institutional reforms in rural credit in terms of loan diversification in Andhra Pradesh. The study concluded that RRBs are partially successful in reaching to the poorest as they benefited the rich. Thus, the vacuum created by the RRBs in delivery of tiny loans to the poor, particularly women, paved the way for the current innovative group-based lending system through the initiation of SHGs. These groups aimed at supplementing the formal credit agencies in reaching the rural women more effectively with mutual collateral facility. While Corroborating the above argument, Rao (2002) argues that the existing formal financial institutions such as banks have failed to lend finances to the landless, marginalised and disadvantaged sections in which women are particularly distanced. In these circumstances, SHGs encourage savings and promote income-generating activities through tiny loans.

Satish (2001) raises some important issues relating to the formation and function of SHGs. According to him, adequate care should be taken to ensure homogeneity of the socio-economic status of the members. He emphasises that the process of SHG formation of an organisation has to be systematic, whether it is a bank or Non-Governmental Organisation (NGO). He also emphasises the need for formation of SHGs throughout rural India, instead of being concentrated in only a few pockets of the country Manimekalai and Rajeshwari (2001) highlight the relationship among the banks, microcredit and women's empowerment. They believe that the lending facility of microcredit by the banks to SHG women significantly helps the group members to achieve economic and social empowerment. It also enables them to develop a sense of leadership, organisational skills, mutual help and management of various business ventures through the help of microcredit.

Malhotra (2004) discusses the opportunities and challenges that microfinance provides to women. According to him, the microfinance programmes increase women's income levels and this in turn leads to greater levels of economic emancipation. Microfinance programmes also enable women's access to networks, markets, access to information and possibilities for the enhancement of other social and political responsibilities. A study conducted by Galab and Rao (2003) in the state of Andhra Pradesh (AP) observes that organising women around thrift and credit services is one of the most effective methods for their economic empowerment. The study also add that the Development of Women and Children in Rural Areas (DWCRA) programme was started in 1982-83 in AP to provide opportunities for self-employment on a sustained basis for rural poor women, which enabled them to start new businesses and expand old ones.

Malhotra (2005) in his study elucidates the promotion of SHGs in India through the formal banking system, initiated by NABARD in 1992. The sole objective of the initiative was to ensure access to institutional credit for the rural poor in general and women in particular. The author takes AP as a model of the SHG movement in India. The state government also decided to provide credit from the banks to SHGs at a highly subsidized rate, besides exempting the SHGs from stamp duty on loan documents. A field observation by Ramalaxmi (2003) in AP reveals that this state alone has about half of all the SHGs organised in India. The author also emphasises the impact of SHGs by pointing out that every village in the state has at least one SHG and 75 per cent of the villages have 15 to 20 groups in each. The Government of Andhra Pradesh (GoAP) felt the need for building institutions to strengthen the implementation of SHG at the village and mandal (block) level. Besides, the author highlights the role of an innovative scheme promoted by the GoAP popularly known as the *Deepam* (light) scheme, which has been under implementation since 2002. Through the *Deepam* scheme, 20 per cent of the SHG members have access to safe cooking fuels (LPG).

The Report of the Committee on Financial Inclusion, Government of India, (2008) showed that microfinance through the SHG-Bank Linkage Programme (SBLP) has empowered women in terms of enhancing their contribution to household income and increasing the value of their assets, which in turn gives them better control over decision-making that affects their lives. Further, savings and credit schemes provide opportunities for women to generate income in their home areas and develop their communities instead of migrating to urban areas (Roy, 2008). A recent study conducted by Reeta *et al.,* (2010) in six States of India (Andhra Pradesh, Karnataka, Maharashtra, Orissa, Uttar Pradesh and Assam) assessed the impact of SBLP model on rural poor. The study found a significant improvement in the net household income (6.1 per cent), annual growth rate (5.1 to 5.4 per cent), household annual expenditure on education (5.6 per cent) and health (5.5 per cent) and increase in the ownership of productive assets. A similar study by Misra (2010) assessed the impact of SBLP model of the rural poor on 93 client households from five SHGs from three different locations in Western and Central part of India. It confirmed the beneficial effects of the SBLP model. The study observes that all beneficiaries were saving regularly at monthly/bimonthly intervals and thereby building up the group savings. The reliance on moneylenders for credit decreased for two-third of beneficiaries. However, only six per cent of beneficiaries had taken up any economic activity, as most of the bank credit as well as loans used overwhelmingly for consumption purposes. One of the important reasons is that the group members are often unwilling to borrow to take up economic activity due to credit risk and absence of skills.

The following section introduces the recent phenomenon in the Indian banking sector: financial inclusion. As a part of literature review, some of the major works on this subject have been reviewed and key challenges to ensure financial inclusion in India identified. Different strategies to address the problem financial exclusion have been discussed. Dev (2006:4310) defines financial inclusion as "delivery of banking services at an affordable cost to the vast sections of disadvantaged and low-income groups". The author argues that due to lack of formal credit, many households are being exploited by moneylenders, especially in states like Andhra Pradesh, Punjab and Tamil Nadu. Financing for housing is another area where many poor people are excluded. The study, therefore, highlights the need to bring these households under the ambit of the formal banking system and provide adequate credit at an affordable cost. The study also suggests that financial inclusion requires a holistic approach addressing both supply and demand side aspects. The supply side problems include: narrowing of the branch network; fall in credit deposit ratios in rural areas; decline in agricultural credit; steep decline in credit-deposit ratio in eastern and north-eastern regions and so on. On the demand side, the problems include: low productivity and risk, and vulnerability of small and marginal farmers; low skill and poor market linkages for rural non-farm and urban workers; vulnerability to risk for rural landless; and inadequate awareness and low financial literacy. The study asserts that SHGs and MFIs are important to achieve financial inclusion. This requires new regulatory procedures and depoliticisation of the financial system.

Kochhar (2009:19) adds that financial inclusion should not only be confined to aspects such as accessibility of the entire range of financial products and services. It must also be appropriate, fair and transparent. His study identifies the need for simplifying the Know Your Customer (KYC) norms, promoting 'no-frills accounts', remittances and payments, insurance facilities and offers key recommendations to the banking sector for extending financial services to the unbanked population. These include the setting up of a National Mission on Financial Inclusion comprising representatives from all the stakeholders to achieve universal financial inclusion. Such a mission should be given the responsibility to manage and disburse the allocated funds for developmental and promotional activities among those who are being excluded from the formal banking system. It emphasises the need for promoting financial literacy for a sustained and appropriate access to various financial services and products by the rural people. Having recognised the importance of Business Correspondent (BC) model in furthering the process of financial inclusion, the study also examines the viability and cost-effectiveness of the said model and offers few suggestions to make the model financially viable and customer-friendly. It also argues for the promotion of SHGs and linking those with banks, the role of MFIs and post offices are imperative, which have a presence in rural areas, to achieve the said objective.

Ananth and Sabri (2013) analyse the key challenges being faced by the banking sector in the process of ensuring financial inclusion. Despite the efforts have been made by the banking sector in India, they argue, the challenges to financial inclusion remain formidable. Using AP as a case study, the challenges to financial inclusion are primarily attributed to structural economic peculiarities such as the nature of the informal economy, internal migration, and financial literacy. Migration forced the people into a large informal economy and left them unable to access any of the formal structures pertaining to government schemes or banking services, as they usually lack legal documents such as identity cards. The authors also argue that the inability of formal financial institutions to meet the specific needs of the poor has enabled private financial institutions to adroitly fill the vacuum. They believe that an optimal strategy to expand financial inclusion would be through the expansion of the formal banking sector, especially public sector banks (PSBs). These banks must play a pivotal role in government sponsored schemes, especially those that are subsidy-linked. However, the success of this expansion would depend on the ability of the banks to introduce suitable and appropriate financial products and services to the needy.

As far as the functioning of SHGs in relation to financial inclusion is concerned, A. Vaidyanathan (2014) highlights the importance of delivering credit for successful financial inclusion, with a main focus on SHG model as an intermediary. The author believes that the provision of lending subsidized credit is the key to ensure financial inclusion. The study recommends SHGs as possibly the best avenue to improve credit inclusion by adhering to prudential discipline. However, as the study finds, SHGs in relation to credit disbursement has succeeded only in some areas of the country, in particular Southern India, but somehow do not get successfully replicated everywhere.

A recent study by Kochhar (2014) argues that one of the reasons why the poor have not been able to come out of vicious cycle of poverty is their complete financial exclusion in India. This has been more pronounced in rural areas where the outreach of formal banking sector has been poor. He suggests that financial inclusion must be integrated with other poverty alleviation programmes as it cannot be a standalone exercise. The study analyses the recent initiative in the realm of banking sector, that is, Pradhan Mantri Jan Dhan Yojana (PMJDY) launched on August 28, 2014. The scheme primarily aims at ensuring access to various financial services like availability of basic savings bank account, access to need-based credit, remittances facility, insurance and pension to the excluded sections. The author is of the view that given the financial landscape, the PMJDY will have to overcome several challenges: to bring more households into the banking system; to make the whole exercise meaningful for the banking institutions; and to make bank transaction meaningful for the millions of poor people. In this regard, author believes that financial literacy will play a deciding role in meeting the objective of financial inclusion. The study also recommends that in order to achieve complete financial inclusion, SHGs must be encouraged to form federations and operating banking transactions including borrowing collectively for its members. The SBLP has to play a greater role and institutions like NABARD should be revamped and reoriented. The study suggests ways for PMJDY to be financially viable, self sustaining and emerge as one of the best means to alleviate poverty and ensure financial inclusion.

These arguments highlight the need of bringing the hitherto financially excluded sections into the domain of formal banking. The studies succeeded identify and analyse the key challenges in this direction and offer policy suggestions to address the issue. The role of Self-Help Groups (SHGs), Business Correspondent (BC) model and active participation of the local bodies in the process of financial inclusion have received greater attention. Addressing the microfinance crisis in Andhra Pradesh as a subject of concern, the literature highlights the need for further research on this subject.

The following section is central to this chapter as it provides theoretical framework to the study. Amartya Sen (1999) and Nussbaum's (2000) construction of 'Capability Approach' becomes the theoretical base of the study. In particular, Sen's idea of 'Poverty as Capability Deprivation' and Nussbaum's projection of 'Central Human Capabilities' have gained significance in this study and in fact, these find reflection in all the chapters. Further, the section also attempts to introduce the concept of 'social exclusion' and discusses the correlation between 'poverty' and 'social exclusion'. With the concept of 'social exclusion' as a subject of research concern, this exercise aims at understanding how poverty and deprivation in multiple capabilities exclude the poor and other disadvantaged sections in socio-economic and political spheres.

SECTION III

Theoretical Framework of the Study

Development as Freedom: Amartya Sen (1999)

Feminist scholars such as Kabeer (1999), Sen (1999) and Nussbaum (2000) argue in favour of women's freedom, including the freedom of women from patriarchy, from oppression and from exploitation in the public as well as the private sphere. Freedom of women is an essential element in the process of women's empowerment. Sen in his book *Development as Freedom* (1999: xii) emphasised the importance of 'human freedom'. The main thrust of his book is on the "expansion of freedom both as the primary end and as the principal means of development".

Generally, development is conceived as an all-round development of any society or increase of nation's growth. However, according to Sen, development is altogether different as it means expanding people's freedoms rather than merely achieving economic growth. In support of the argument, he cites the examples of countries such as China, Costa Rica and one of the Indian States of Kerala that have achieved significant increase in life expectancy of people despite low per capita GDP in their economies (pp. 21-22). Sen defines development "as a process of expanding the real freedoms that people enjoy" (1999:3). To substantiate the argument, he puts forward two concepts: human freedoms and unfreedoms. He argues, "development requires the removal of 'unfreedoms' such as poverty, tyranny, poor economic opportunities, social deprivation, neglect of public facilities and intolerance or over activity of repressive states" (p. 3). However, Sen does not deny the importance of economic growth and free markets, which play an imperative role in removing these unfreedoms. Indeed, the freedom to engage in market transactions is one of the freedoms that Sen observes as central to the promotion of development (pp.112-18). According to the author, unemployment is one of the major unfreedoms that leads to scarcity of income and restraints "individual freedom, initiative and skills". Furthermore, it contributes to the "social exclusion" of some groups; consequently, it leads to "losses of self-reliance, self-confidence and psychological and physical health" (p. 21).

Poverty as Capability Deprivation

Another major concern for Sen is poverty. He characterises poverty as "deprivation of the basic capabilities rather than merely as lowness of incomes". He adds that poverty is nothing but the absence of a wide range of capabilities, including security and the ability to participate in economic and political systems (1999:87). A person's well-being depends on his/her capabilities or freedoms to achieve certain valuable 'doings and beings', called functionings. Therefore, expanding people's capabilities should be the prime objective of development (Anand and Sen, 2000). Sen (1999) highlights the significance of the expansion of the capabilities of all human beings, and emphasises that it is one of the vital components to achieve the goal of development. In addition to the avoidance of unfreedoms and expansion of human freedoms, Sen also mentions the importance of providing education to women.

As a whole, Sen's projection of 'poverty as capability deprivation' highlights the idea that expansion of capabilities or freedoms is viewed as one of the central principles of (human) development that endorses well-being and quality of life for every individual. While distinguishing capabilities from functionings, he emphasises that the former can be seen as choices or the means one faces in life and the latter as the outcomes or the ends. Further, his insights on women's development, particularly with regard to the provision of social, economic and political opportunities and basic education are a major contribution. These freedoms are imperative as they enable women to lead a dignified life. By adopting the core elements from Sen's theory, the SBLP and BC models and in some aspects MFI models appear as banking strategies that can promote some of the above human freedoms in the process of human (women's) development. This research takes insights from Sen's approach in order to understand how various microfinance models provide self-employment opportunities, improve the awareness levels of women and their economic opportunities.

Besides, Martha Nussbaum's (2000) elaboration of Sen's theory of capabilities also rightly fits in this study. Nussbaum also emphasises human development for women by highlighting some particular capabilities. The following section delineates Nussbaum's theory on women and human development.

The Capability Approach

Nussbaum (2000) systematically developed the capability approach by building on Sen's notion of 'capability'. However, the author criticised Sen on the ground that though Sen's capability approach emphasises "capabilities are central to human well-being", he never made a list of the central capabilities. While Sen observes capability as an assessment of 'quality of life' or 'standard of living', Nussbaum's concept of capability goes beyond it. She refers to human development, particularly with a focus on women's development by highlighting 'central human capabilities'. According to her, 'human capabilities' means "what people are actually able to do and to be" (2000:5). Capabilities of people can provide a basis for central constitutional principles that citizens have a right to demand from their governments. These capabilities are indispensable for the development of people in order to discharge their errands and to attain the state of well-being efficiently. Nussbaum proposes ten capabilities that provide a basis for determining a decent social minimum in a variety of areas. These are a search to find solutions for human dignity, in which women are the main focus (p.75). In fact, the ten human capabilities listed below differentiate Nussbaum from Sen.

Nussbaum's central human capabilities are as follows (pp.78-80):

- **Life:** Being able to live to the end of a human life of expected length.
- **Bodily Health:** Being able to have good health.
- **Bodily Integrity:** Being able to move freely from place to place, secure from assault, including sexual assault, child sexual abuse, and domestic violence; having opportunities for sexual satisfaction and for choice in matters of reproduction.
- **Sense, Imagination and Thought:** Being able to use the sense to imagine, reason and think; and being able to use one's mind in ways protected by guarantees of freedom of expression and religious exercise.
- **Emotions:** Being able to have attachments to things and people, to love those who love and care for us, not blighted by fear and anxiety.
- **Practical Reason:** Being able to form a conception of the good and to engage in critical reflection about the planning of one's life.
- **Affiliation:**

  A. Being able to live with others engages in forms of social interaction and to have the capability for both justice and friendship.

  B. Having the social bases of self-respect and non-humiliation; being able to be treated as a dignified being whose worth is equal to that of others.

- **Other Species:** Being able to live with a concern for nature.
- **Play:** Being able to laugh and enjoy recreational activities.
- **Political and Material Control over one's Environment:** Being able to participate in political choices, being able to hold property (land and movable goods) and seek employment on an equal basis with others.

From the above-mentioned capabilities, one can understand Nussbaum's concern for human development, in particular for women. All elements in this list are imperative for the all-round development of a human being. However, if a woman wants to develop and utilise her capabilities efficiently, she should maintain good control over her life. If a woman seeks employment outside her home, she will have more consciousness and resources to speak out about her own needs. She will also able to protect her bodily integrity within the family. Nussbaum's approach to human capabilities is very relevant in the case of the poor women who have little control over the most fundamental aspects of their lives.

Above all, the capabilities in the list, in particular, 'bodily integrity', 'affiliation' and 'political and material control over one's environment' could play a very positive role in a woman's life to protect her from sexual abuse and domestic violence; give her control over reproductive choices; and enable her to relate to others in the public sphere. Nussbaum (2000:289) also argues, "the single most effective way for government to promote women's sense of their worth and their entitlements is to promote women's collectives". She argues that the collective action by women is imperative in building the social and political pressures and claiming entitlements. The institution of the SHG serves the same purpose as it functions as a group approach and provides a platform for the poor and marginalised women and offers a sense of collectivity.

In light of the above arguments, it can be affirmed that some of the capabilities in Nussbaum's list are appropriate to the functioning of SHGs through the SBLP model whose main priority is to enhance the rural women economically. Further, SHGs help women to develop their capabilities and their rational thinking power. Nussbaum's capability approach provides an analytical framework to understand how women attain capabilities to develop a voice in decision-making, and reduce inequalities in the society. As a group approach, SHGs potentially promote uniformity between the members. Nussbaum also argues that if the government endorses women's welfare and encourages their entitlements, it should support a sense of collectivity. Thus, an understanding of the impact of SBLP model through SHGs in alleviating poverty and empowering women can be enhanced through adopting Sen's theory of 'development as freedom' and Nubussam's 'capabilities approach'.

The following section is an attempt to under the concept of 'social exclusion' and brings out the correlation between poverty and social exclusion.

Understating Social Exclusion

The term 'social exclusion' is a relatively recent phenomenon in the realm of academics, first coined by Rene Lenoir, a French scholar in 1974. Subsequently, this notion has made substantial inroads into the discussions and writings on poverty and deprivation (Sen, 2004:2). The term 'excluded' was initially coined to denote the acute unemployment that was prevailed during the late 60s and early 70s in Europe, particularly in France (Brien, Wilkes, De Haan and Maxwell, 1997). It implied that unemployment had become grave concern for individuals to attain their freedoms; on the contrary, the welfare state had failed to protect and promote the interests of those who were affected by this social disaster. This unemployment had not only thrown the people into the poverty trap but had also virtually crippled the other socio-economic activities of the society. It was these factors, which propelled Lenoir to coin the term 'social exclusion' (Arjan de Haan and Kabeer, 2008). Later on, this concept has come to encapsulate multi-dimensional perspective on socio-economic problems (Sen, 2004).

Social exclusion is being unable to enjoy levels of participation that mainstream society takes for granted. It is a complex, multi-dimensional, multi-layered and dynamic concept. According to Sen (2000), the process of social exclusion eliminates people's participation in all socio-economic and political spheres of the society. It also perpetuates the disadvantages and deprivations of the people. As a corollary, he argues that when affected by social exclusion, people fail to avail the benefits provided by the government as well as the society.[6]

Similarly, Silver opines that social exclusion precludes full participation in a given society. 'It denies access to information, resources, sociability, recognition, and identity, eroding self-respect and reducing capabilities to achieve personal goals' (2011:2).

Given the wide-raging debates over the definition of social exclusion, this study is confined to the definition put forward by European Commission; and accordingly, the understanding of social exclusion is as follows:

> Social Exclusion is a process whereby certain individuals are pushed to the edge of society and prevented from participating fully by virtue of their poverty, or lack of basic competencies and lifelong learning opportunities, or as a result of discrimination. This distances them from job, income and education and training opportunities, as well as social and community networks and activities. They have little access to power and decision making bodies and thus feel powerless and unable to take control over the decisions that affect their day-to-day lives (European Commission; 2004:23).

In accordance with the definition, the process of social exclusion does have debilitating effects on the marginalised sections of the society by relegating them to the backseat. Moreover, the vicious circle of poverty coupled with the existing deprivations scuttles the life chances of the poor. Thus, the marginalised cannot become active participants in society and cannot tap their potential to the optimum level. Given these limitations and constraints, the disadvantaged sections are also politically excluded. They are rendered powerless and are deprived of political participation thus hindering political decision-making capabilities in their day-to-day lives.

Poverty and Social Exclusion: Understanding the Correlation

In view of the importance of the new concept of social exclusion, it is essential to understand the correlation between poverty and social exclusion. Sliver and Miller (2003) emphasise that exclusion is a broader term, which encompass poverty. Similarly, Haan (1997) makes it clear that people who are socially excluded need not be poor, but all the poor are socially excluded. However, Walker and Walker[7] distinguish the idea of social exclusion from the similar notion of poverty and provide a comprehensive meaning to the concept of social exclusion. In their words:

Poverty as a lack of the material resources, especially income, necessary to participate, and social exclusion as a more comprehensive formulation which refers to the dynamic process of being shout out, fully or partially, from any of the social, economic or cultural systems which determine the social integration of a person in society. Social exclusion, therefore, be seen as the denial of the civil, political and social rights of citizenship (1997:8).

Similarly, the Department for International Development (DFID) (2005) holds that social exclusion causes poverty for particular people. The report argues that the process of social exclusion hurts them materially by restricting them to the edges of society with low level of incomes, where access to basic services is restricted for them. It can also hurt them emotionally, by shutting them out of the life of their community. Socially excluded people are often denied the opportunities available to others to increase their income and escape from poverty by their own efforts. Therefore, even though the economy may grow and general income levels may rise, excluded people are likely to be left behind, and may make up an increasing proportion of those who remain in poverty. Poverty alleviation policies often fail to reach them unless they are specifically designed to do so.

Applying Theory to the Present Study

The concept of social exclusion assumes greater significance in understanding and unraveling various forms of social deprivations exist in the present society. The rural poor, women and other marginalised sections of the society are still reeling under the clutches of exclusion due to various types of disadvantages and multiple deprivations. For instance, in the context of rural economy, deficient access to institutional credit, lack of employment opportunities and absence of innovative approach in on-farm and off-farm sectors destabilise the livelihood of the rural community, which in turn results in the deprivation of their capabilities. Therefore, inadequate financial resources or financial dependence restricts their ability to take initiatives to improve their living conditions and further marginalise them from the mainstream financial sphere. In particular, the plight of women among the above segments is even worse as most of them are economically dependent on their spouses for support.

In the case of financial exclusion, due to deficient access to formal credit and other financial services, large numbers of groups have been excluded in the financial sector. These excluded sections are primarily the small and marginal farmers, workers in the unorganised sector including artisans and self-employed people, and women etc. In view of the above, to address financial exclusion, the Indian government has come up with the idea of 'financial inclusion', which aims at providing basic financial services at affordable cost to the above-targeted sections in order to create livelihood opportunities to ensure them with decent material living standards. On other words, helping the unbanked population with adequate institutional finance to enable them to become self-employed and ensure a stable income. In this context, some of the important microfinance models such as SHG-Bank Linkage Programme (SBLP) and Business Correspondent (BC) models aim at achieving the said objective. In fact, these models have received greater recognition due to the bottom-up approach that ensures active participation of the people and connects them with institutional banking. Thus, financial inclusion leads to social inclusion by accommodating socially excluded communities into the mainstream society. The present study aims to understand the correlation between poverty, social exclusion and financial inclusion.

References

1. The Programme of Action of the World Summit for Social Development (United Nations, 2006, resolution 1, annex II).
2. Mahajan *et al.,* (2008).
3. Sen's idea of 'poverty as capability deprivation' would be discussed in detail in the theoretical section of this chapter.
4. According to Sen, functioning is "an achievement of a person; what he manages to do or to be" (2000:75).
5. Though the Tendulkar Committee submitted its report on November 2009, the Planning Commission, by adopting the Tendulkar Committee methodology, estimated poverty levels for 2011-12 and released through a press note on 2013.
6. For more details see Amartya Sen (2000), "Social Exclusion: Concept, Application, and Scrutiny", Social Development Papers No.1, Asian Development Bank, pp. 1-60.
7. Cited in David Byrne (2009), "Social Exclusion", Rawat Publications, New Delhi, p. 2.

Chapter III

Microfinance: A Theoretical Framework

Introduction

The concept of microfinance has become a significant aspect of development phenomenon in the international arena over the last three decades. When it was first conceived, the idea of microfinance was invoked as a "grass root small-scale philanthropic movement". The primary aim of the microfinance intervention was to provide tiny loans for the unbanked poor households, particularly women. Later on, this practice matured into a "sustainable development finance approach", and efforts were made to break gender barriers in accessing credit services. It is believed that this approach has helped the poor and unemployed, and provided them with adequate amount of credit that was restricted in the formal banking system (Chiu, 2014 and Silvia, 2012:48). In recent times, owing to its popularity, there is a growing acceptance of the fact that microfinance approach has the ability to address the problems of credit accessibility and unemployment. There are two important contributing factors that have put microfinance on the map of development agenda in the developing countries. First, it has controlled conventional moneylenders in rural economies from charging exorbitant interest rates due to the inability of the poor to access institutional loans. Second, it has succeeded in emerging as a key alternative strategy in alleviating poverty through creating small-scale, self employment opportunities (Knight *et al.,* 2009, Maulick, 2012 and Singh, 2014).

The emergence of microfinance at the international level came at a time when the "neo liberal economic order"[1] had started to establish itself as the dominant framework of development paradigm. A significant effect of the coming of this order, it is pointed out, has been in the steady increase of poverty levels and inequality in the developing countries. Together with this challenge, the failure of the government to meet the demand for financial services, particularly for credit, has facilitated a space for new approaches to emerge and provide a direction to counter the problem of poverty. In this context, poverty reduction through the promotion of subsidized credit has become an important policy strategy in many countries. The policy-makers have searched for various alternatives to mitigate poverty, one of which has come in the form of microcredit (Weber, 2004). Over a period of time, most of the developing countries have adopted microfinance practice not only to alleviate poverty but also to promote micro and small-scale enterprise development (Hisako, 2009 and Singh, 2009). Thus, the microfinance movement has become a key alternative towards helping the poor in many of the developing countries (Campbell, 2010; John and Montgomery, 2005).

The idea of microfinance intervention has been given effect through numerous ways. MFI is recognised as an important approach in this regard. Mark and Gabriel (2010) are of the view that although traditional money lending existed for centuries together, it is only recently that a banking-like industry in the informal sector has been established through Microfinance Institution (MFI). These institutions have been playing the role of intermediaries between the financiers and borrowers. Within few years of its inception, microfinance industry has expanded its outreach at a rapid pace in many developing countries. The success of MFI is attributed to many factors. Primarily, MFIs are considered to be of great help to low-income groups or households who are normally excluded by conventional financial institutions, and these institutions provide substantial credit to them (Campbell, 2010; and John and Montgomery, 2005). Women's World Banking (WWB), a non-state actor, in its Annual Report (2010:5) states that "the pioneering MFIs sought to provide credit to poor people who had no assets to pledge as collateral and were denied access to capital by the formal banking sector". While comparing MFIs with formal banks, it is pointed out that MFIs raise funds, evaluate clients, offer loans and other financial services, and collect payments with interest; all of these services are also offered by the banks. However, the lending procedures, the client bases, the sources of funds, mode of repayment and the organisational structure of MFIs are quite different from those of rural banks in developing countries (Mark and Gabriel, 2010).

Microfinance: A Theoretical Framework

This section provides an overview of the microcredit and microfinance movement by spelling out the major features and manifest advantages attached to these initiatives. Sections 3.3 traces the emergence of microcredit in the backdrop of neo-liberal agenda. It elucidates how donor agencies promote microcredit approach as a strategy to reduce and eliminate poverty. Section 3.4 and 3.5 offer a detailed explanation on definitions of microfinance and the difference between the concepts of microcredit and microfinance. Sections 3.6 and 3.7 discuss the features of microfinance and its scope. Sections 3.8 highlights two important approaches to microfinance and sections 3.9 summarises different perspectives on microfinance, including women empowerment and poverty reduction; financial inclusion and Millennium Development Goals (MDGs). Section 3.10 explains the microfinance experience at the global level in general and India in particular. Critical arguments pertaining to microfinance vis-à-vis women empowerment, poverty reduction and financial inclusion are delineated in Section 3.11. The final section ends up with concluding observations.

Neoliberalism, Microcredit Intervention and Poverty Alleviation

The concept of neo-liberalism has become widespread in political and academic circles since late 1980s and early 1990s. Wagh (2009) suggests that neo-liberalism has had two-fold effects. While, on the one hand, it has allowed for a minimalist role of the state, free working of the market and a belief that it will solve the problems of poverty, the neo-liberal ideology is also alleged to have resulted in the loss of livelihoods, reinforcement of social inequalities and marginalisation of people, on the other. In similar vein, Bandhyopadhyay (2000) and Nair (2011) argue that neoliberal policies leading to the retreat of the state in its funding and support in the form of credit, subsidies and provision of support prices, the rural communities have been adversely affected. Thus, the vacuum created by the state as a major credit facilitator has been filled by the private sector.

Similarly, Sengupta (2013) locates the emergence of microfinance within the neoliberal agenda. He believes that in the 1990s, under the rubric of the 'Washington Consensus', the 'third world' countries have moved from a state regulated model of development to a free market economy. This paradigm shift translated into dismantling or rolling back of the state from its welfare functions, and privatisation of public sector, liberalisation of trade and cuts in fiscal spending. Much like other countries, India has also embraced the change brought by the new world order. The adoption of neo-liberal policies in India, beginning in 1990s, unleashed all the major vectors of a free market ideology that led to liberalisation, privatisation and globalisation (LPG) of its economy, accompanied by major cuts in subsidy and social sector spending by the government. Interestingly, Sengupta (2013) also points out that at the same period, women came to be considered as the new agents of change than just mere beneficiaries of development programmes, and efforts have been made to recognise them as partners in the process of development.[2] The achievement of women empowerment and poverty reduction for the World Bank and IMF is, in fact, to be carried out through such projects as microfinance. Thus, the idea of empowerment through the promotion of small-scale, income-generating activities or various lending microfinance services has assumed greater attention not only in India but also elsewhere. The emergence and popularity of microfinance needs to be situated within this context. Scully (1997) is of the view that microcredit emerged as an economic and political consequence of globalisation, trade liberalisation, and more specifically as the impact of structural adjustment programmes (SAPs). Giles (2009) adds to the argument by saying that in the age of neo-liberalism and financial liberalisation, the deregulated financial sector at the international level lowered interest rates and allowed the flow of funds in and out of countries that made credit easier to access.

On the other hand, the idea and practice of microfinance can also be located with the pioneering efforts of Professor Muhammad Yunus through the initiation of Grameen Bank. (for example, see Ahmad, 2008; Leach and Sitaram, 2002; and Rahman, 1999). Initially, Yunus began providing microcredit facilities to 42 bamboo workers to buy raw materials for their work on an experimental basis in 1976 (Ahmad, 2008). Acknowledging the importance of credit, Yunus subsequently established Grameen Bank in 1983, and accordingly initiated the process of lending microcredit to rural poor in a full-fledged manner (Rahman, 1999). Influenced by his initiative, microcredit became a widely favoured intervention for poverty alleviation (Leach and Sitaram, 2002). It has been endorsed and adopted by various financial institutions such as World Bank, Regional Development Banks, Multilateral Development Agencies and United Nations agencies and so on (Weber, 2002). During the post-liberalisation era, the donor agencies have acknowledged the need of the people for microcredit and its role in alleviating poverty in developing countries (Hermes and Lensink, 2007). This is also evident in the words of Preston, the former President of the World Bank, who endorsed the main objectives of microcredit during his speech in the 1993 Conference on Actions to Reduce Hunger Worldwide[3]:

> Micro-level credit schemes, such as those undertaken by Grameen Bank of Bangladesh, the Badan Credit Bank of Indonesia, and the International Fund for Agricultural Development have proven to be highly effective at the grassroots level. The basic idea behind these schemes is to help small-scale income generation projects and businesses. They are a particularly effective way of reaching women, thereby helping to improve the incomes and well-being of their children and families. (2010: 359)

Subsequently, several summits at international level took up the concept of microcredit and acknowledged its significance. The 1997 Washington D.C. Micro-Credit Summit projected microfinance as the provision of delivering credit for self-employment and other financial and business services to poor people. The declaration of the summit reiterated the urgency for recognising the concept of microcredit in relation to poverty alleviation. The Declaration and Plan of Action (1997) read: "The time has come to acknowledge microcredit as a powerful tool in the struggle to end poverty and economic dependence" (Micro-Credit Summit, Declaration and Plan of Action, 1997: 9).

At the global level, the concept of microcredit has also been championed by other international agencies. Kofi Annan, the former

United Nations (UN) Secretary General, for instance, in 1997 stated that "microcredit is a critical anti-poverty tool- a wise investment in human capital". In addition to this, non-state actors like Consultative Group of Assist the Poorest (CGAP) too started advocating microfinance. The Group considered microfinance as a "powerful tool to fight poverty that can help poor people to raise income, build their assets and cushion themselves against external shocks" (CGAP, 2004a: 1). Interestingly, Hanan and Steffen (2004) and Weber (2010) advocate adopting the model advanced by donor agencies to developing and underdeveloped countries. They are of the view that the poor in these countries have inadequate access to credit and other financial services, as commercial banks do not trust their creditworthiness. Therefore, some of the developing countries in Asia and Africa have started realising that the anti-poverty programmes run by the government cannot make a serious dent on poverty, in particular, the kind of poverty caused by the absence of strong rural banking infrastructure (Maulick, 2012).

From the foregoing discussion, it can be argued that the emergence of microfinance can be located from two accounts. First account is an attempt to understand the ideological circumstances in which microfinance emerged. It situates the microfinance intervention in neoliberal policies in the early 1990s, whereby the governments in different countries have encouraged private (non-state) financial institutions to provide credit facilities to poor. It is evident that before the advent of neo-liberalism, the state had been the major player in steering the economy and providing credit and subsidies to rural community. The neo-liberal framework altered the role of the state by shrinking its space, which has now come to be assumed by the market and private institutions. A significant change brought by this shift has been in the area of credit availability which is marked by initiatives like microcredit. The second account is recognition of a new alternative mechanism for poverty alleviation by Professor Muhammad Yunus through the establishment of Grameen Bank in 1984. As a result of the success and popularity of the Grameen Bank model, the concept of microcredit has been recognised as an important and effective strategy to alleviate poverty in many of the developing countries. Later, the concept gained broader acceptance due to the World Bank's attempts to authorise microcredit as a poverty alleviation project. During the 1990s, the World Bank and other international agencies have officially adopted and promoted microcredit schemes to poverty reduction in the developing countries, particularly in Asia, Africa and Latin America.

The following section provides various definitions of microfinance and attempts to highlight the core elements from one definition to the other.

Definition of Microfinance

As Rhyne defines:

> Microfinance refers to the provision of credit and other small-scale financial services to low-income individuals, particularly women, through a group lending methodology. The term microfinance signifies the broad range of small-scale financial services targeting low-income individuals worldwide. (2001: 325)

This definition primarily focuses on two important dimensions: First, providing credit and other financial services to low-income individuals and women. The second dimension is group lending approach. In fact, these two elements are considered as the key factors of microfinance. In particular, the group lending method enables the borrowers to become collectively responsible and ensure guarantees for the loan amount they borrow rather than for individual collateral.

Similarly, George defines:

> Microfinance as a provision of thrift, credit and other financial services (loans) and products of very small amount to the poor in rural, semi-urban and urban areas for enabling them to raise their income levels, improve living standards and empower them in different spheres. (2008: 62)

This definition expands the outreach of microfinance to poor people in rural, semi-urban and urban areas who are in need of tiny loans. It also emphasises that the provision of microfinance and promotion of income-generating activities increase their income levels and in turn improve their living standards.

Comprehensively, Pethiya and Teki define:

> Microfinance as a loan fund especially meant for micro-enterprises (including agricultural, forestry, agro-forestry, horticultural, animal husbandry, handicrafts, fisheries, bamboo and jute crafting,

> mushroom cultivation, etc.) to provide required startup capital to needy local people in an organised manner. (2000: 56)

In similar vein, the Women's World Banking Annual Report (2010) put forward purpose of microfinance as follows:

> Microfinance is the provision of financial services to poor people who have been excluded from the formal banking sector. Most often, the term is used to refer to the practice of giving small loans to poor clients, to be used to start small businesses. Customers use these loans in different ways: some purchase a bicycle to transport vegetables to a market, or use the money to buy fertiliser for their crops, or a sewing machine to start a tailoring business. However, they all have one goal: to make a decent living and support their families' basic needs. (2010: 5)

Features of Microfinance

Grameen Bank (2002), the pioneer in the microcredit intervention, has put forward five defining features of microfinance and similar private lending ventures. These features distinguish microfinance from other credits supplied by the conventional financial institutions: the loan is small in size, averaging about hundred dollars; the primary customers of these loans are the rural poor, women in particular, who have little access to conventional banking facilities; the purpose of these loans is to create income-generating activities in the rural non-formal sectors through self-employment; tangible collateral is not required for taking this kind of loan, meaning that microcredit is collateral-free; and the micro lending ventures have integrated loan and savings mobilisation functions.

These features broadly highlight the meaning, nature, purpose and functions of microfinance. First, the usual average loan-size provided by the microfinance institutions in general and Grameen Bank in particular is assumed to be of a certain amount that is not too large. It is, however, found that the amount differs from one country to another, and depends upon the nature of the employment activity and also affordability to the borrowers. Second, the target population includes not only the poor, but more importantly women. It also underscores the inaccessibility to institutional loans by poor borrowers due to various supply and demand side constraints. Third, the purpose of lending money to the poor and unemployed people can be understood in terms of the productive and unproductive binary. Fourth, the group members assure guarantee collectively rather than individually. For this, regular savings by the group members is a pre-condition for availing loans from the Grameen Bank. In fact, this feature is being adopted by many countries to which India is not an exception. The SHG-Bank Linkage Programme (SBLP) in India, for instance, made 'savings' by the Self-Help Group (SHG) members as one of the pre-conditions for availing loans from rural banks. However, as far as the microfinance institutions (MFI) in India are concerned, collateral is necessary for borrowing money from these institutions and savings facility is not available in this microfinance model (Basu and Srivastava, 2005 and Schreiner, 2003).

Approaches to Microfinance

Microfinance movement is built on two broad objectives: first, to provide credit to the poor and disadvantaged sections; and second, to improve their income levels and living standards. It is meant for promoting financial sustainability to the concerned communities. The concept of microfinance has come to be analysed in terms of two broad perspectives: the institutionist and the welfarist approach (Morduch, 1998). Gary *et al.,* (1999: 1) state that "these two approaches have implications for the future of microfinance – it's guiding principles, objectives, its clients, and impact on the poor and poverty in general". The understanding of these two different approaches is key to identifying the philosophical underpinning of the concept of microfinance, and to examine the debates revolving around it.

The Institutionist Approach

The institutionist approach focuses on creating financial institutions to serve the people who either are not served or are considered underserved by the formal financial system including public sector banks. The goal of this approach is to achieve institutional sustainability through achieving financial self-sufficiency. The basic unit, within this approach, is the 'institution' (microfinance institutions) (Hulme and Mosley, 1996). According to Woller *et al.* (1999), the prime objective of microfinance is financial deepening, and creation of a separate system of sustainable financial intermediation for the poor. MFIs inevitably focus on the breadth of outreach – measured in terms of the number of people – and its (positive) impact on them. The basic premise of this approach is that the institutions are central in providing credit to the rural poor, and institutional success is determined by the institution's progress toward achieving financial sustainability.

Highlighting the need for sustainability of MFIs, Manroth (2001) argues that financial sustainability is critical for any financial institution, which reduces its dependency on donor funding and ensures the long-term existence of the same to serve the financial needs of the poor. Nanayakkara (2012), likewise, believes that financial sustainability is the ability of a financial institution to continue its operations in a long-term basis. The author is of the view that if an MFI is not sustainable, it will fail to achieve its objective of alleviating poverty. The issue of sustainability, therefore, is considered as an important dimension to assess the performance of any financial institutions. As a caution, Nanayakkara (2012) emphasises the need for MFIs to be transparent and to prove its efficiency in delivering services to the poor. The leading examples of the institutionist approach are Bank Rakayat Indonesia in Indonesia and Banco Solidario (Banco Sol) in Bolivia.

There are, however, certain drawbacks associated with this approach. Morduch (1998) questions the very existence and motive of the MFIs. He argues that most of the MFIs are profit seeking. To substantiate his argument, Morduch (1998) adds that although they are committed to serve the poor clients, they are simultaneously earning high returns on their investment. Further, he states that financial sustainability is crucial but not an end in itself. Another important criticism labeled against the institutionist approach is that the institutions often work for their institutions' self-sufficiency at the cost of the betterment of their beneficiaries. Ashim (2010: iii) states that MFIs have dual operational objectives: to serve the poor (social commitment); and, to attain financial sustainability. These two objectives are, however, mutually exclusive and often responsible for mission drift. The author argues that the main aim of institutionist approach is to ensure institutional sustainability through achieving financial self-sufficiency, which subsequently goes against serving their targeted population.

While highlighting the reasons for MFIs turning into profit seeking institutions, Flores (2014) argues that during the late 1980s and early 1990s, the basic objective of the MFIs were 'outreach' that is to reach as many poor people as possible. In the course of time, however, organisational sustainability has become the prime objective of some of the MFIs. Flores identifies two key reasons for this shift. First, the success of microfinance sector in most of the developing countries has attracted other new entrants to this sector, and accordingly profit-seeking has become the main motive for these institutions. This specially has been the case of some commercial banks and certain MFIs recently created with lucrative purposes. Second, it is becoming increasingly difficult for some of the conventional MFIs to obtain financial resources. They usually depend on international aid and foreign investors which could become scarce in times of financial crisis. It is, therefore, in cases of funding provided by the foreign investors that the MFIs try to maximise their returns from their investments. As a result, it has led them to focus mainly on their 'organisational sustainability' rather than on the 'outreach' of their services or reducing the poverty levels of their beneficiaries.

Welfarist Approach

The second major approach to understand the practice of microfinance has come from a welfarist stance. This perspective primarily aims at reducing the incidence of poverty through credit, often provided together with complementary services such as skill training and teaching of financial literacy, health, nutrition, family planning (Ledgerwood, 1999). Gary *et al.* (1999) are of the view that while the institutionist approach focuses on financial sustainability, the welfarist approach emphasises depth of outreach. This approach focuses on promoting self-employment of the poor, particularly women, and improving their income and saving levels. The basic unit of analysis, within this approach, is the family. Polanco (2005) believes that the performance of any financial institution should be assessed in terms of its impact on the welfare of poor. He adds that the welfarist approach is concerned with the poverty levels of the clients before and after borrowing credit.

Robinson (2001) is of the view that, within this approach, credit is provided to poor borrowers, generally at below market interest rates. The objective of this approach is to reach the poorest sections with credit to help them overcome poverty by improving their living conditions. Woller *et al.* (1999) point out that the important objective of this approach tends to be self-employment of women. It is assumed that the modest increases in income and savings will enable the poor to improve their social and economic conditions on their own, without any external help. A prime example of this line of thought could be found in the work of Grameen Bank in Bangladesh and other similar initiatives adopted in Asia and Africa.

Comparatively, both the approaches have different orientations and modus operandi. The institutionist approach, it is seen, places a greater weight on reaching out to the maximum number of beneficiaries with a main focus on organisational sustainability. The welfarist approach, on the other, primarily concentrates on the depth of outreach, which implies the capacity of the microfinance intervention to improve the living standards of the poor. Although both the approaches are different in their style of functioning and management practices, the overarching focus is on minimising poverty and to improve the prospects of the poor. Robinson (2001) points out that the two approaches have substantially contributed to the development of institutional microfinance. The welfarist approach has successfully reached the poor people with the assistance of both donor and government-subsidized credit services.

Keeping in view the present status of microfinance as one of the key strategies to help counter the incidence of poverty, Huff (2011) and Flores (2014) suggest a new framework for the microfinance sector. They believe that for a successful functioning of this sector, MFIs should try to synchronise both the institutionist and welfarist approach. In other words, both the 'organisational sustainability', manifest in the institutionist orientation, and the 'depth of outreach', focus of the welfarist stance, should go hand-in-hand. They are of the view that 'organisational sustainability' would encourage the entry of new investors which would stimulate the growth of microfinance sector. This growth, subsequently, could be focused on the depth of outreach with the purpose of making credit and other financial services accessible to the targeted population.

Three Aspects of Microfinance

Recent crises in microfinance sector in India, particularly in the state of Andhra Pradesh, have compelled academicians and policy-makers to re-examine the concept of microfinance (Nair, 2011). In the following section, three aspects of microfinance are briefly examined. First, the phenomenon of microfinance, and its relationship vis-à-vis women empowerment and poverty reduction is interrogated. Second, the impact of microfinance on financial inclusion is examined. Third, the ability of microfinance services to address the issue of poverty reduction, among others, keeping in view the Millennium Development Goals (MDGs) is investigated.

Microfinance for Women's Empowerment and Poverty Reduction

The problem of unemployment, along with inadequate access to institutional credit, is considered to be a major obstacle for the betterment of rural households in India (Das, 2005 and Vatta, 2003). In order to resolve the twin issues of poverty and unemployment, microfinance intervention has emerged as a key strategy (Niranjana, 2010). With the growing realisation of the nexus between women's empowerment and economic growth, there is today a considerable literature on the subject that examines different dimensions of this relationship. Beteille (1999), Kabeer (1990), Mayoux (2008), Nussbaum (2000), Sen (2000) and Vaidyanathan (2014), for instance, argue that in order to facilitate women empowerment and higher economic growth, it is necessary to create opportunities for the overall development of women. Singh (2009) is of the view that rural women, especially those belonging to the weaker sections, have limited access to resources and face considerable challenges in terms of employment. In this context, providing loans to the needy in areas with no or minimum banking services has been thought of as generating necessary opportunities for empowering women who are perennially entrapped in the vicious cycle of poverty. This belief gained further momentum in the post-liberalisation era, with increased attention to microfinance (Hermes and Lensink, 2007). Microfinance initiatives, it is believed, have a great bearing on achieving the goal of women's empowerment by promoting their saving habits, and extending bank loans to them to start various income-generating activities.

On the relationship between microfinance and its impact on poverty reduction, John and Montgomery (2005) argue that microfinance is advantageous to the poor. According to them, poor people with access to credit can finance productive activities that will generate income growth, provided that there are no other binding constraints like debts, financial risks and others. In common with this view, Campbell (2010) emphasises that when credit is extended directly to individuals and rural poor communities, their ability to access or purchase goods, farming techniques and digitised information is made possible. For instance, accessing technology provides various livelihood opportunities to the poor and microfinance is a proven method in that direction. Campbell (2010) and Montgomery (2005) project microfinance as a means for self-employment and improving the income levels. Besides, microfinance services also enhance their awareness in accessing technology to develop income generating activities.

Recently, the International Fund for Agricultural Development (IFAD, 2009) in its report highlighted the fact that the expansion of micro-finance since the 1990s has significantly increased women's access to facilities for small loans and savings, thereby contributing to poverty reduction and financial sustainability, besides empowering the women. The following diagram portrays microfinance as a means to women empowerment and poverty reduction.

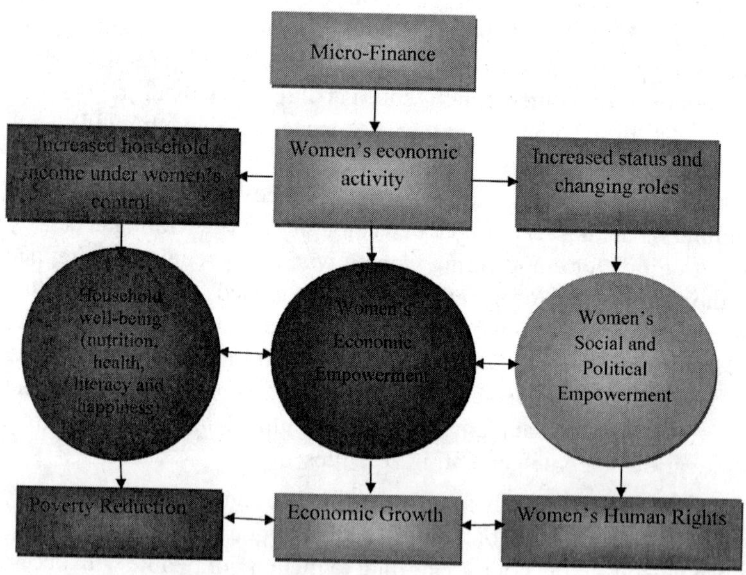

Source: International Fund for Agricultural Development Report (IFAD, 2009). p. 9.

Figure 3.1: Microfinance and Women Empowerment: Virtuous Spirals.

The above diagram illustrates the contribution of microfinance to different spheres of women's lives, such as financial sustainability, reduction of poverty and empowerment in socio-economic and political spheres. The figure shows that loan facilities (microfinance) in general enable women to take up income-generating activities, and start small-scale businesses, which in turn augments women's household income and their command over household affairs. It hypothesises that with access to microfinance, women over a period show positive results with regard to well-being of the family in terms of nutrition, health, education, happiness and so on. On the other hand, the economic empowerment of women further leads to their social and political empowerment. Realising the significance of education, the women tend to encourage their children to get education and enroll them in schools. This may help to reduce the extent of the male domination in the family and bring awareness on social atrocities. On the political front, women vote on their own, contest in the elections, participate in campaigning, and attend gram sabha meetings. Empowerment in different spheres enhances women's confidence through gaining knowledge on various issues pertaining to women. Importantly, this will enable women to lead a dignified life in the society.

Microfinance and Financial Inclusion

In recent times, financial inclusion has become a matter of great deliberation in developing countries. In fact, the very idea of financial inclusion was built on the provision of lending credit and the outreach of various microfinance services to a maximum number of people. The Rangarajan Committee Report on Financial Inclusion (2008:5) defines financial inclusion as "the process of ensuring access to financial services and timely and adequate credit when needed by vulnerable groups such as weaker sections and low income groups at an affordable cost". This definition makes it clear that access to credit and other financial services is a first step in the process of promoting financial inclusion. It also emphasises the availability of the basic financial services at a reasonable price without time lags. Adding to the above Report (2008), Kamath *et al.* (2010) suggest that in addition to a bank account and adequate credit, financial inclusion should also include affordable insurance and remittance facilities, credit counseling and financial education to the needy. Thus, financial inclusion is nothing but providing financial services starting from basic credit services to insurance and remittance facilities along with promoting financial literacy.

The United Nations Capital Development Fund (UNCDF), (2006) identifies key features for inclusive finance. These features, in general, state how microfinance enables financial inclusion of the poor. First, adequate access to various financial services including savings or deposit services, payment and transfer services, credit and insurance at a reasonable cost for all households. This feature reflects the core objective of financial inclusion. Second, sound and safe financial institutions governed by proper regulation and industry performance standards. This feature indicates government's responsibility to have a proper regulating and monitoring mechanism over financial institutions for its proper functioning. Further, it also emphasises that the same institution itself maintains standards for better performance. This seems to be relevant in the case of Andhra Pradesh where there are no proper regulative mechanisms by the government on MFIs[4] (Nair, 2014). This may compel the government to take necessary punitive measures to protect the microfinance consumers against the exorbitant interest rates and illicit practices adopted by the MFIs. Financial and institutional sustainability of the institutions to ensure continuity and certainty of investment is the third feature of inclusive finance. It emphasises accountability and sustainability of the financial institutions in the process of serving the poor. These institutions need to promote awareness among the beneficiaries about various financial services and its usage. The last feature is healthy competition among the financial players to ensure choice and affordability for the beneficiaries. It enables for positive competition within the microfinance industry, in which the borrowers' safety is the prime concern.

It is, however, argued that despite the huge banking system, over three billion people around the world do not have access to formal sources of banking and financial services of which about 90 per cent live in developing countries. This has led to a considerable demand from the developing countries for a more inclusive financial system that would cater to the demands of the poor in these regions (Consultative Group to Assist the Poor, 2012 and John *et al.,* 2009). In case of India, the data of NSSO 59th round survey report reveals that of the 89.3 million farmer households in the country, 45.9 million households (51.4 per cent) do not have access to credit, either from institutional or non-institutional sources. The banking system has proven ineffective in providing universal access to credit. Many financial and infrastructural issues prohibit banks from reaching out to the poor.

Against this backdrop, the Reserve Bank of India (RBI) initiated the idea of 'financial inclusion' in 2005. Since then, it has been promoting financial inclusion through a campaign aimed at providing 'unbanked' households with a bank account (Kamath *et al.,* 2010). Further, through the Eleventh Five Year Plan (2007-2012), the Government of India and RBI have come up with a number of initiatives to promote the process of financial inclusion (Rangarajan, 2008). Before these initiatives, most of the people did not have access to credit and other financial services. Following the recommendations of Rangarajan Committee Report (2008), the government and RBI have taken proper measures to deepen financial inclusion. In fact, having realised the contributions of microfinance institutions in relation to access to credit for the poor, the report emphasises that MFIs could play a significant role in facilitating financial inclusion, as they have a greater understanding of the issues specific to the rural poor. They enjoy greater acceptability amongst the rural poor and have flexibility in operations providing a level of comfort to their clientele (2008). Recently, the Government of India has come up with a socio-economic initiative in the realm of Indian banking sector, named as the Pradhan Mantri Jan-Dhan Yojana (PMJDY) on 28 August, 2014. The main objective of the scheme is to "ensure access to various financial services like availability of basic savings bank account, access to need-based credit, remittances facility, insurance and pension to the low income groups" (Report on Pradhan Mantri Jan-Dhan Yojana: A National Mission on Financial Inclusion, Government of India, 2014: 1). In other words, the scheme also emphasised that access to microcredit and other basic financial services are pertinent to ensure financial inclusion.

Microfinance and the Millennium Development Goals (MDGs)

The third set of arguments attempts to establish a link between access to microfinance and achieving some of the important Millennium Development Goals (MDGs). The United Nations declared 2005 as the International Year of Microcredit and states that the provision of delivering credit and other financial services is seen as an important strategy to achieve one of the key millennium development goals of halving poverty by 2015 (UNCDF, 2005). Singh and Srivastava (2009) believe that microfinance has emerged as the most effective mechanism to minimise the incidence of poverty and to promote inclusive growth. Similarly, the Report on Financial Inclusion Strategy: 2010-2015 (2010), Australian Agency for International Development (AusAID), emphasises that through careful and context-specific implementation, microfinance can make an important contribution in the lives of the poor. The interpretation of the Report on Financial Inclusion Strategy in terms of MDGs is as follows:

Table 3.1: Microfinance and Millennium Development Goals (MDGs)

MDG	*How can microfinance help to achieve these goals?*
Eradicate Extreme hunger and poverty	By borrowing, saving and purchasing insurance, the poor can build and diversify income sources, invest in assets and reduce their vulnerability. When shocks hit – such as a natural disaster, a sudden rise in prices or illness within the household – the poor can use microfinance products to smooth consumption, curbing the intergenerational effects of shocks. Furthermore, by using microfinance to invest in business opportunities, the poor often have more stable income flows, reducing the incidence and impact of shocks.
Achieve universal primary education	Evidence indicates that households with access to microfinance are more likely to send their children to school and those children are more likely to stay in school for longer. Improvements in income and better access to credit, savings and insurance services can reduce the need to rely on children as labourers.
Promote gender equality and empower women	Microfinance clients are overwhelmingly female, and the contribution of microfinance to empowerment of women is widely recognised. Microfinance can help to build women's self-confidence and assertiveness, often resulting in women obtaining greater decision-making power, control over assets, and mobility within both the household and the broader community.
Reduce child mortality, improve maternal health and combat HIV/AIDs, malaria and other diseases	Access to finance can contribute to improved nutrition, housing and health, especially among female clients. Health education programmes delivered in conjunction with microfinance can lead to improved health outcomes, including more timely use of healthcare, greater awareness of health issues and prevention methods, and higher rates of child immunisation in client families compared with non-client

(*Contd...*)

	families. There are an increasing number of institutions offering microfinance services that also offer health insurance products, thus providing mechanisms for the poor to deal with sickness when it occurs.
Ensure environ-mental Sustainability	Microfinance can be used to promote environmentally sustainable business and household practices. The provision of microcredit to purchase sustainable energy products, for example solar powered lamps, is becoming more widespread. With considerable amounts of microcredit being provided for agricultural purposes, there is scope for financial service providers to take a lead in advocating environmentally sustainable farming practices.

Source: Report on Financial Inclusion Strategy: 2010-2015 (2010), Australian Agency for International Development (AusAID). p. 2.

Table 3.1 explains how microfinance can be of help in achieving the MDGs. The report discusses the vision of microfinance in order to achieve the MDGs. With reference to the first goal, adequate and affordable credit is an important element in the creation of various income-generating activities. Further, the savings habit enables the beneficiaries to become financially independent and encourages them to diversify income sources. In particular, insurance services can minimise the borrower's vulnerability towards economic shocks. As far as achieving universal primary education is concerned, the report believes that improvement in income levels and increased access to credit reduces poor household's need to rely on child labour. The increased income levels encourage beneficiaries of microfinance to send their children to school. The third goal: promoting gender equality and empower women is important as it deals with the issue of women's empowerment. In fact, an extensive research has been done on this subject and most of the studies have proved that there is a positive correlation between microfinance and women empowerment (Galab and Rao, 2003; Khandker, 2005; Misra, 2010; Mosley, 2001; Roy, 2008 and Vaidyanathan, 2014). The report reiterates that increased access to credit and promotion of income-generating activities enhances their confidence and decision-making power, control over assets and improves their mobility within and outside the family.

However, considering the microfinance crisis in Andhra Pradesh, several questions have arisen doubting the very objective of microfinance – women's empowerment and poverty reduction through microfinance institutions. Some recent studies strengthened the claim (Hulme and Mairot, 2014; Nair, 2014 and SERP, 2010). From Table 3.1, it can be argued that the role and impact of microfinance in achieving the last two goals is, however, minimal. The role of microfinance is very limited in most of the developing countries, in which microfinance institutions or rural banks primarily concentrate on savings, deposits, and insurances but not on healthcare or health insurance and further environmental sustainability. Importantly, the state actors in any country have to play a crucial role in promoting, regulating and monitoring the microfinance through various models (Nair, 2014).

Microfinance Movement: An Overview of International Experience

Microfinance intervention in Asian Countries: Grameen Bank Model in Bangladesh

Bangladesh was the first country which adopted the concept of microcredit through the rural Grameen Bank movement, by giving support to village entrepreneurs (Higinbothan, 1995). Muhammad Yunus, a renowned economist, acclaimed as the 'father of microfinance' is credited as the main brain behind Grameen Bank.[5] In the aftermath of the 1974 famine in Bangladesh, Yunus carried out a research titled the *Grameen Project* for seven years. His findings concluded that the poor are capable of generating enough income from small enterprises if they are provided with small scale lending. This realisation became a cornerstone for the establishment of Grameen Bank in 1983 (Ahmad, 2008:234). Yunus's aim was to provide financial services, including loans and financial advice to the poor. He found that the poor needed finance for livestock rearing, trading, production in cottage industries, and services (Sadegh, 2006). He also believed that these tiny loans enabled the poor to use their personal skills to start small-scale business ventures. Those who repaid promptly were able to acquire bigger loans and reap profits in different ventures (Ahmed *et al.*, 2013).

In its operations, Grameen Bank follows the group lending approach while delivering credit to the poor. Jung (2008) briefly illustrates how group lending approach works in the Grameen Bank model. In the beginning, a small number of individual borrowers, who do not possess collateral, form a group of five members with the aim of obtaining tiny loans, and the members of the same group cross-guarantee each other's loan. This five-member JLGs (Joint Liability Group, some documents refer to Solidarity Group) gets together with six to nine other such groups from the same village to form a village organisation, and accordingly approach the Grameen Bank for loan. In each group, peer pressure is said to be the key factor in ensuring repayment. This credit worthiness enables JLGs to qualify for a larger loan in the next cycle. Another important factor in this group lending approach is 'savings'. It is a compulsory component of the loan repayment schedule; however, it does not determine the magnitude or timing of the loan. Jung (2008) is of the view that the group lending approach opened up possibilities for the private firms in lending loan to the borrowers. It is claimed that "Grameen Bank today serves more than six million poor families with loans, savings, insurance and other services. The bank is fully owned by its clients and has been a model of microfinance institutions around the world."[6] By now the Grameen Bank has evolved itself as a well-known 'charitable MFI' (Ahmed *et al.,* 2013 and Jessica, 2006). In fact, this model has been replicated in many other countries both by the government and non-government organisations. In particular, microfinance institutions (MFIs) in India started lending credit to the borrowers by following the same model (Elango, 2010).

There is, however, no unanimity over either the success or failure of the Grameen Bank model. Tammen (1990:48), for instance, argues that Grameen's success is often exaggerated, maintaining the criterion that cost cannot be recovered on a sustainable basis. In her words, "Grameen Bank itself is not self-sustaining, but heavily dependent on foreign aid". The author states that accessible credit is not the answer to poverty, but reform in property rights, limited liability and easy licensing are also required.[7] Osmani (1998) examines the impact of credit on women's relative well-being in Bangladesh. The study observes that by providing access to credit, the Grameen Bank has partially succeeded in improving women's relative well-being. The study also indicates that although the Grameen Bank model records partial improvement in the lives of women, it could not have positive impact on women's overall control over decision-making. Another study by Hassan (2001) examines the extent to which microcredit reduces poverty and vulnerability through Bangladesh Rural Advancement Committee (BRAC), in Bangladesh. The data collected from 1072 households found that there are several channels by which microcredit services can reduce vulnerability and poverty. In a recent study, Hulme and Maitrot (2014) argue that microfinance institutions, in recent times, are increasingly focusing on institutions' financial sustainability and neglecting their declared objective of alleviation of poverty and economic empowerment of women. While highlighting the nature of functioning of some of the MFIs, the authors state that loan officers, in the process of achieving individual financial targets, are under enormous pressure, and as a result, they are often mistreating the borrowers, especially poor women. This is quite evident in the villages of Bangladesh and India.

Bank Rakyat Indonesia (BRI)

The Indonesian microfinance industry is one of the oldest commercial entities in terms of its provision of microfinance with large-scale and sustainable outreach (Marguerites and Robinson, 1997 and Jani, 2009). Bank Rakyat Indonesia (BRI) is considered as an important microfinance provider in the country (Stephanie *et al.,* 2004 and Rosengard *et al.,* 2007). A government commercial bank, BRI began as an agricultural development bank. In fact, BRI is the only bank that has spread its outreach not only in urban areas but also in rural regions as well. It is responsible for providing banking services to the rural areas of Indonesia through its 'unit desa system' (branches) with particular emphasis on agricultural credit (Sadegh, 2006). In the early 1970s, BRI developed its 'unit desa system' in order to provide subsidized government credit to the farmers (Marguerite and Robinson, 1997). An important step took by the Indonesian policy-makers was to provide a conducive operating environment for commercial MFIs in terms of interest rates that made MFIs to charge cost-recovery rates and allowed for profitability (Stephanie *et al.,* 2004). The initiation of the microfinance programme helped Indonesia to reduce poverty from about 40 per cent in mid-70s to about 11 percent by 1996 with 98 per cent recovery of money lent so far (BRI, 2005). It has a vast network of village banks to deliver subsidized credit to microenterprises in the rural areas, mainly farmers. It is documented that the BRI has more than 30 million savings accounts and specialises in providing small-scale finance using its network of more than 4000 branches (Kochhar, 2014).

A 1996 report by the World Bank[8] states the reasons for the success of BRI's unit banks.

> The programme succeeded in Indonesia because the banks loaned at market rates, used income to finance their operations, kept operating costs low and devised appropriate savings instruments to attract depositors. By mobilising rural savings, (the unit banking system) was not only provided with a stable source of funds, it also kept financial savings in rural areas, thus helping development growth in the countryside. Other reasons for success included; the simplicity of loan designs, which enabled the banks to keep costs down, effective management at the unit level, backed by close supervision and monitoring by the centre; and appropriate staff training and performance incentives. (1997: 25-26).

It is understood that first, due to market interest rates, low operating costs and appropriate savings, the BRI unit banks in a success mode. Second, its success can be attributed to conducting its financial transactions in rural areas through unit banks that in turn attracted the hitherto rural unbanked population who had been excluded by the banking system. Third, providing suitable financial services at an affordable price, effective management at the bank units, and proper regulatory mechanism, appropriate staff training and performance incentives made the BRI bank units a successful microfinance model in reaching out to the poor and the marginalised sections.

As far as the client's assurance is concerned, it is observed that BRI's microfinance unit demands collateral from the borrowers. However, it is far more flexible than the conventional banks that operate in Indonesia. It is also said that the bank units seldom take possession of borrower's assets, except in cases of suspected fraud. In fact, the loan officers of the bank units are fairly flexible in what they accept as collateral. They are also flexible about required ownership documents (Johnston and Morduch, 2008). From the foregoing discussion, it can be argued that though the BRI bank units are flexible in accepting collateral from the borrowers, the poorest households, who are unable to pledge collateral, are deemed ineligible to avail any credit from the bank units. In other words, BRI unit banks are excluding the poor people despite their creditworthiness.

Robinson (1992) argues that BRI microfinance model does not see itself as a social organisation and accordingly, it does not provide clients with training or guidance facility. Given its profit-oriented approach, BRI treats microfinance as a lucrative business.[9] This argument makes it clear that the BRI model falls under the practice of institutionist approach, which primarily aims at achieving financial self-sufficiency of the organisation and accordingly, places its concern on 'breadth of outreach', in other words, reaching the maximum number of people. While highlighting the operating mechanism of the bank units, Morduch (1999) argues that unlike Banco Sol and Grameen Bank, BRI does not follow group lending approach. It prefers lending money to individual borrowers; therefore, the BRI banking system excludes the very poorest borrowers. However, the bank operations remain small-scale, collateral and with simple procedures. It is also argued that majority of MFIs in Indonesia are characterised by poor portfolio, weak management skills, lack of efficient system, and lack of effective supervision or support structures. It is also observed that rural areas in Indonesia are still largely devoid of financial services for low-income populations, particularly outside of Java and Bali. It is estimated that 40 million people in Indonesia still lack access to financial services. Much of this is the result of a lack of capacity to design products and efficient delivery systems to make microfinance a robust financial alternative in rural areas (Shrader *et al.,* 2006).

Microfinance intervention in Latin America: Banco Solidario in Bolivia

In Latin America, Bolivia is one of the countries that adopted microfinance approach to improve the socio-economic conditions of rural poor. The government officials and development analysts of Bolivia have enthusiastically embraced microfinance approach as a primary strategy for encouraging economic revitalisation in the country's poorest areas and among the poorest population (Mosley, 2001). The idea and practice of microfinance was introduced in this country in the late 1980s following the Structural Adjustment Programme (SAP). However, SAP had a negative impact on low-income groups in the country. Throughout the 1980s, thousands of male workers were pushed out of primary sector work, particularly in the mining and agricultural sectors, resulting in sharp increases in unemployment. Such dramatic shift has propelled an urgent need for such programmes that manifestly support self-employment activities for the unemployed poor, including facilitating their access to loans (Beth, 2011).

In this context, Banco Sol, the first commercial bank of its kind in Bolivia, was launched in February 1992 to serve the unemployed youth, particularly with a focus on urban poor with microenterprise market. This development has marked the beginning of commercial microfinance in the country. It is said that this financial institution is different from the Grameen Bank model since the Banco Sol was to be a completely commercial and regulated financial institution. However, this financial institution has a fiduciary responsibility toward depositors and investors. Initially it was begun as PRODEM, an NGO (also called as Banco Sol-NGO) in 1987 established by the American organisation ACCION and the recipient of large initial investments from USAID. Later on 'Banco Sol-NGO' launched 'Banco Sol' in 1992 under the leadership of Fernando Romero and Pancho Otero (Mosley, 2001 and Dorado, 2013). Since its inception, it has served over 650,000 clients with strong social focus (Ledgerwood and White, 2006: xxvi). However, it is argued that the Bolivian intervention was typically urban rather than rural, less concerned with poverty and more focused on micro-enterprise (Rutherford, 2003).

The Bolivian National Institutes of Statistics Household survey[10] reports that people who were excluded from formal credit instruments are more likely to participate in Rotating Savings and Credit Associations (ROSCAs). It also highlights that unemployed women, holding less stable jobs, which reduce the ability to borrow formal credit, use ROSCAs as a mechanism to enforce savings on the household. Interestingly, the survey observes that ROSCAs are working as a consumption driven phenomenon in Bolivia and mostly middle-income families and higher consumption families are more likely to join ROSCAs. On the whole, in the last 15 years, microfinance in Bolivia has become a profitable and sustainable development project for the NGOs involved. As of 2003, the estimated total value of Bolivian microfinance portfolios was \$326.2 million US (Beth, 2011: 28). Rozycki (2006) believes that the progress of microfinance programme has been impressive. The microfinance practitioners in Bolivia focus on how to design innovative products beyond basic lending and savings services.

Morduch (1999) argues that Banco Sol success has generated an unhealthy competition among the private and government run financial institutions in offering loans to the low-income clients. It is, therefore, the mushrooming of private financial institutions that has flooded the borrowers with excessive loan supply resulting in the non-repayment of loans and long run indebtedness. In a similar vein, Sriram (2010) states that the client poaching approach of MFIs, coupled with the unhealthy competition, reckless lending, and over-indebtedness of the clients, among others, has eventually debilitated the otherwise efficient credit delivery mechanism in Bolivia.

Microfinance in India

Post-independence India has initiated numerous measures in providing credit facilities to the rural poor. The rural credit structure in India has been set up gradually over a long period of time starting from 1947 to 1980s such as state cooperative banks (1955), the Reserve Bank of India (RBI) in banking policies (since1955) and creation of Regional Rural Banks (RRBs) in 1976 and so on (Mihir *et al.,* 2007 and Misra, 2006). The 1980s witnessed a significant shift in the Indian rural credit structure. The formal banking sector took the initiative to develop a supplementary credit delivery mechanism through the establishment of National Bank for Agricultural and Rural Development (NABARD). This period was marked with the active involvement of RBI and NABARD in providing microcredit to the rural poor. These initiatives gained momentum when the RBI with the help of NABARD approved a pilot project linking SHGs to banks in 1992, which eventually led to the 'Self-Help Group-Bank Linkage Programme, (SBLP) in 1996 (Mohan, 2008). Under SBLP model, women in a village are encouraged to form a group of ten to fifteen members each called Self-Help Group (SHG). All the members of the group regularly contribute small savings to the group. These savings are later supplemented by loans provided by rural banks for various income-generating activities. The group conducts monthly meetings; and the members save money and also repay the borrowed amount through monthly installments. The formation of SHGs and providing credit and other microfinance services to the group members is an important feature of SBLP model (Mukhopadhyay and Rath, 2011).

The SBLP model received key policy and promotional support, both from the central and various state governments, in particular, Andhra Pradesh. Of late, it has emerged as an important microfinance programme in the country, being implemented by commercial banks, Regional Rural Banks (RRBs), and co-operative banks (Thakur, 2010; Vaish and Agarwal, 2010). The recent report of NABARD reveals that as on 31st March, 2013 there are 7.3 million savings-linked SHGs covering 970 million poor households under microfinance programme. The report further states that though this phenomenon was impressive in Andhra Pradesh and Karnataka, later on, the movement has widely spread to various parts of India (The Status of Microfinance in India, 2012-13).

Running parallel to the SBLP model is the Microfinance Institutions (MFI) model. This model is an internationally established one that appears to be increasingly favoured strategy to poverty alleviation (Thakur, 2010). It made its entry in India largely in the form of non-bank financial companies (NBFCs) and primarily aimed at financial sustainability. Under this model, MFIs encourage villagers to form a group of four to six individuals (male and female), called joint liability group (JLG). After the formation, MFI offer loans to the individuals who are members of the JLG. The loans are individually and collectively guaranteed by the other members of the group. In other words, members of the JLG ensure mutual guarantee of each other's loan that makes them jointly liable for interest payment and principal amount obtained from MFI (Schreiner, 2003; Basu and Srivastava, 2005). Under this model, MFI primarily offers a variety of loans for agriculture, animal husbandry and non-farm activities as well as for housing needs, however, these institutions do not provide 'savings' service (Crombrugghe *et al.*, 2008). These institutions usually get funds by commercial banks like Industrial Credit and Investment Corporation of India (ICICI), development banks like Industrial Development Bank of India (IDBI) and other overseas investors. It is observed that many of the MFIs initially started providing credit and other financial services as 'non-profit entities', however, in the course of time, they found difficult to raise funds for their financial operations largely due to rapid growth of the microfinance sector and breadth of outreach. These institutions, therefore, converted themselves into for-profit financial institutions (Malegam, 2011). One among such institutions in India is Swayam Krushi Sangam (SKS) microfinance led by Vikram Akula, who transformed the organisation from a non-profit to a for-profit venture in the year 2005.

Advocates of MFI model Ross and Savanti (2005), and Johnson and Sushmita (2010) emphasise that the MFI model is the second best option for the poor, both in terms of interest rates and financial services after the SBLP model in India. These institutions, though mainly concerned with rural women, have also expanded their outreach to the rural farmers and other disadvantaged segments. Private financial institutions now command the largest share of the market after public microfinance programmes like SBLP. By the year 2010, the growth of the MFIs in India had reached its peak growing at 80 per cent per annum and the outreach had reached around 27 million (Sengupta, 2013).

As far as the breadth of outreach is concerned, it is reported that MFIs have become the most important channels in Indian microfinance, with a market share of almost 47 per cent and growing rapidly compared to the SBLP model (International Finance Corporation, World Bank Group, 2008). According to Sa-Dhan, a network body of India's Microfinance Institutions, there are about a total of 264 MFIs in India with a total loan outstanding of Rs 18,343.9 crores from 2.67 crore active borrowers (2010). However, between the years of 2010 and 2013, the MFIs have lost almost 40 lakh borrowers; the main reason for which is believed to be the microfinance crisis in Andhra Pradesh (Kochhar, 2014).

Critics like Kumar (2006), Shylendra (2008), and Sinha and Matin (1998) argue that the overwhelming dependency of the rural poor on MFIs has resulted in charging exorbitant interest rates in order to make more profits. With reference to microfinance crisis in Andhra Pradesh, it is argued that these institutions have not been adequately controlled by the government and this has caused a tremendous set back in achieving the goals and objectives of the programme. The number of these institutions has grown at a frantic pace and this has resulted in a major crisis in the microfinance sector. It is alleged that the strict and often coercive debt recovery methods adopted by some of the MFIs, and the exorbitant interest rates have caused some of the hapless borrowers to end their lives (Nair, 2014). Immediately after this incidence, the state government of Andhra Pradesh initiated stringent measures to put a halt on the loan recovery process of the MFIs. This step also made public sector banks stop lending finance to MFIs. As a result, many of the MFIs went bankrupt. At the central level, the government has come up with a microfinance bill, which is yet to be passed in the parliament. A salient feature of the bill is compulsory registration for all MFIs under Reserve Bank of India (RBI) guidelines. In the meantime, the RBI came up with some necessary measures to put a cap on the limit of the chargeable interest rates (Mohanty, 2013).

It is understood that in recent times, microfinance and other financial services have received greater recognition as a strategy for poverty reduction and for economic upliftment by expanding their livelihood opportunities. Notably, some of the developing countries in Asia, Africa and Latin America have succeeded in utilising the microfinance services through various models in a modest way. For instance, Grameen Bank model in Bangladesh; SBLP and MFI models in India; Bank Rakyat model in Indonesia and Banco Sol in Bolivia stood at the forefront in microfinance lending operations. As far as the Grameen Bank in Bangladesh is concerned, scholars have highlighted that the bank primarily aims at providing microcredit and other financial services to the poor women and encourages them to start small-scale income-earning activities. An important factor identified in the Grameen Bank model is the 'group lending approach' as it not only eliminates the problem of collateral but also enables a sense of collectiveness among the group members. Two other factors which deserve appreciation in Grameen Bank model are: group pressure and savings. Group pressure ensures proper repayments and savings encourages the borrowers to cultivate savings habit among them that are in turn critical for improving the financial status of an individual. In fact, these two factors made the Grameen Bank model to sustain in a longer run.

Examining Microfinance: A Critical Perspective

While some authors advocate microfinance in favour of poor women and their upliftment from the poverty trap by promoting income-generating activities (Campbell, 2010, Chiu; 2014; Das, 2005;

Montgomery, 2005 and Silvia, 2012), others emphasise its contributions in relation to financial inclusion (Ananth and Sabri, 2013; Dev, 2006; Frost and Sullivan, 2009; Kamat *et al.*, 2010; Rangarajan, 2008 and Vaidyanathan, 2014). However, there are a few skeptics who argue that the very usage of microfinance has its own adverse effects on the rural community, particularly on women. A study by Milgram and Weber (2006), for instance, argues that the very foundation of microfinance is based on a neoliberal approach to poverty, interpreting it as a mere lack of unfulfilled market potential. The authors claim that microfinance hardly addresses the problem of poverty and broader socio-economic issues such as the societal relations of power and domination. Critics contend that this type of credit does not empower women (Casper, 1994; Goetz and Gupta, 1994). On the other hand, Johnson (1998) makes it clear that although microfinance targets women, the product design and some financial services rarely address gender-specific issues.

Critics also question and assert that the availability of credit is not sufficient for poverty alleviation, as credit alone does not ensure income generation or decision-making on the use of the income (Temba and Kihombo, 2005). Khandker (2005) argues that along with the provision of lending microcredit, the borrower also requires both entrepreneurial skill and a favourable local market. Without them, the returns to the investments provided under microfinance are likely to be small, and hardly effect any reductions in overall poverty. In similar vein, Lamben and Targett (1990) and Kaganda (1991) assert that though credit is a key element in the productivity of the enterprise, it may fail to empower women entrepreneurs for several reasons, viz, mismanagement or lack of infrastructure, agricultural subsidies and supportive services.

Hulme (2007) believes that not all microcredit interventions produce favourable results. Especially for those poor people who are working in low-return activities, environmental and economic shocks are not uncommon. He goes on to say that when the circumstances are beyond their control (sickness, flood, drought, theft and so on), lack of skills and knowledge or taking bad decisions, a proportion of poor borrowers encounter great difficulties in repaying loans. Hudon (2009) identifies two barriers that the poor face for approaching banks for loans: first, the poor usually feel reluctant to approach banks, as they do not have enough courage because lack of education and poor lifestyle, and second, traditionally, banks have not considered poor people to be a viable market. The author adds that microcredit and other financial services can be implemented on a large scale in order to respond to urgent needs of the world's poorest, as it focuses on the moral consequences of financial exclusion as well.

As far as the MFIs are concerned, they have come under adverse criticism. Harper (1998), for instance, is of the view that the concept of micro-finance is a business programme and is organised in a business-minded way. This is true in a situation where the NGOs and MFIs begin to take part in it and start providing loans to the rural poor. Loganath (2006) raises a concern that although the microfinance scheme was started in an efficient manner initially by the professionalised NGOs and MFIs, they have been diluted in the course of time for several reasons. One of them is the mushrooming of MFIs that paved the way for their establishment without being registered with RBI. It leads to duplication of activities that causes the beneficiaries to be indebted. Another criticism against these MFIs is that they charge high rates of interest with zero tolerance for repayment delays, coercive methods of recovery of loans, low coverage of the poorest and non-transparent ways of functioning (Aloysius, 2007; Gate, 2006; Hulme and Thankom, 2011; and Shylendra, 2008).

A recent anthropological study carried out by Kalpana (2011) reports on the unintended consequences of the MFIs in terms of suicides. The study shows how the crisis led to skepticism regarding microfinance's claims about poverty reduction and social empowerment of women. Karim's (2011) empirical study on microfinance intervention in Bangladesh highlights the challenges posed by the MFIs. The author argues that the NGO-sponsored microfinance has not eliminated rural money-lending, but has, in fact, ended up in pushing the borrowers in a debt trap. In other words, the borrowers who failed in creating income-generating activities with the borrowed money, fell into a severe debt trap. These are some glaring examples of the negative impact of microfinance in relation to the claims of poverty alleviation.

Summary

On the whole, it appears that in the late 1970s and early 1980s, the microcredit intervention in Bangladesh and elsewhere contributed greatly to our understanding of various dimensions of rural poverty and unemployment and feasibility of reducing the same with the creation of small-scale income generating activities. The international donor agencies like World Bank have come to recognise that acute poverty is a potential threat to human development. Donor agencies, therefore, have initiated several poverty alleviation measures and strategies, and experimented with different models in different countries (Weber, 2010). In this process, the phenomenon of microcredit has also been recognised as a key poverty alleviation strategy. Gradually, the microfinance industry has developed into a microfinance movement all over the world. It has made inroads into most of the developing countries either led by the government through its banks or by non-governmental or private organisation through MFIs.

While analysing the purpose and usage of microfinance services through the formal banking system, it is believed that the provision of extending credit and other financial services to the poor in rural areas will not only lead to their socio-economic betterment but also integrate them in the overall development process. SHG-Bank Linkage Programme (SBLP) model in India, for instance, showed that the microcredit intervention is a successful strategy in the rural credit market. Apparently, the governments in most developing countries have given prominence to extending banking facilities to rural people through the rural bank units. In recent times, the scope of microfinance has also widened. Beside providing credit and savings facilities, the public and private sector financial institutions are promoting other financial services such as house loans, educational loans, insurance facilities, remittance services, and other modes of payment services. Such initiatives have attracted the attention of hitherto unbanked people, and encouraged them to be a part of the financial system. However, few of the microfinance services are yet to materialise in practice.

The growing literature on the subject of microfinance succeeded in developing two different approaches to understand the practice of microfinance models in various countries. It is believed that institutionist approach and welfarist approach are central to understand the main motive of any financial institution. While the institutionist approach focused on breadth of outreach with a main focus on organisational sustainability, the welfarist approach primarily concentrated on depth of outreach, that is, how effectively the microfinance intervention can improve the living standard of the poor.

The microfinance models which are in operation in various countries fall under either of the approaches. This chapter has made an attempt to examine microfinance contributions in relation to women's empowerment and poverty reduction; ensuring financial inclusion and achieving the Millennium Development Goals (MDGs). The chapter also highlighted some of the main arguments in the literature related to its negative repercussions. It is argued that even after the two decades of microfinance intervention, many scholars remain skeptical about its scope and validity. In fact, the most acclaimed countries in successful implementation of microfinance such as Bangladesh and India have come under severe scrutiny.

References

1. Neo-liberal economic order is based on a set of neo-liberal economic principles that were first practiced in a number of developed countries during 1970s and later being exported to the developing world that in turn witnessed a mixed result. In the due course, the implementation of neo-liberal economic policies in the developing world forced both international advisers and national economic policy-makers to attempt to impose a standard set of policy recommendations on the economies of the developing countries. Indeed, as a part of the structural adjustment policies, the economies of these third world countries were opened up and the states reduced their social spending; thus providing a conducive environment for Multinational Companies and also released huge finances for debt repayment of the developing countries. For more details see, Weber, Heloise (2004). The 'New Economy' and Social Risk: Banking on the Poor?, *Review of International Political Economy*, 11 (2), 356-386.
2. It is argued that with the initiation of liberalisation, privatisation and globalisation (LPG) in the 1990s, the focus shifted to growth and production, modernisation of technology and economic development, to which India is not an exception. Indian government has tried to develop new economic policies to accelerate growth and enhancement of the production process, which opens the way to socio-economic development. Interestingly, along with the stress on growth and production, a commitment towards what is called the 'empowerment' of the people (particularly women) is usually affirmed. Hence, there was a shift taken place from 'growth with social justice' to 'development with empowerment'. For more details on empowerment of women, see Mohanty (1995:1434).
3. Cited in Weber, 2010:359.
4. The reasons of microfinance crisis in Andhra Pradesh and its consequences on the rural communities would be dealt systematically with empirical evidences in the later chapters.

5. Grameen Bank is the largest non-governmental organisation operating in Bangladesh. By 1991 Grameen Bank operated 808 branches in 19,984 villages of Bangladesh, serving more than 8,84,000 members. By May 1994, Grameen Bank had 1,915,000 members in 34,243 villages served by 1,042 bank branches. As of 2009, it had nearly 8 million depositors and 6.4 million active borrowers, with 2564 branches covering 83,458 (99 per cent) villages in Bangladesh. For more details, see Higinbothan (1995), Tisell (2000), Grameen Bank (2010) and Rahman and Qiang (2011). Over time, Grameen Bank evolved into Grameen Bank II, a model offering more flexibility in types of loans and services offered to meet the needs of borrowers (Sengupta and Aubuchon, 2008). This phenomenal growth was due to the diverse product range, and more significantly, the element of flexibility built into the Grameen Bank. For more details, see Hulme (2009). It is worth noting that today at least 43 countries around the world have adopted some version of the Grameen Bank model (Campbell, 2010:1084)
6. http://www.grameenbank.org (2009).
7. Cited in Higinbothan Susan Holcombe (1995), 'Managing to Empower: The Grameen Bank's Experience of Poverty Alleviation' p. 48.
8. The World Bank report (1996) is cited in Marguerite and Robinson (1997), Microfinance in Indonesia, pp.25-26.
9. Cited in Morduch (1999), 'The Microfinance Promise', *Journal of Economic Literature*. p.1577.
10. The survey report quoted in Ambec and Treich (2007).

Chapter IV

Financial Inclusion in India: A Conceptual Analysis

Introduction

Financial inclusion is a global phenomenon in the banking system that has gained wider currency in the development literature in contemporary times. Given the magnitude of poverty in the Third World economies, wherein a large segment of the population do not have access to basic financial services, the idea of financial inclusion – commonly understood as 'banking to all'– has become conspicuous in these economies. A recent United Nations (UN) study observes that financial inclusion of the poor is a global challenge to the achievement of the Millennium Development Goals (MDGs) (2006:5). This report draws attention to a plethora of problems that are being faced by poor in accessing financial services, and reveals the stark reality that a large number of people are not in a state of saving money as formal banking services are not within their 'reach'. According to this report, structural barriers prevent the poor from accessing banking facilities, thereby resulting in financial exclusion. The study further argues that the poor do not have savings bank accounts, let alone insurance policies *(ibid)*.

An increasing body of literature delves into the causes of financial exclusion. A recurring theme is here to lack of 'access to institutional finance', which not only leads to income inequality but also results in slower economic growth. Lack of access to adequate institutional credit and other financial services compel poor individuals and small enterprises to depend on their own limited savings and earnings. This restricts their choice to investing in small business enterprises and taking advantage of growth opportunities (Ellis, 2007; Thorsten, Kunt and Patrick, 2009; World Bank, 2012: ix). Outlining the causes of financial exclusion, Arora (2012) points out that poor human development, high illiteracy and poor awareness levels prevent a large sections of the population, particularly women, from accessing basic financial services that prevent them from reaping the benefits of formal financial institutions. Recent estimates show that, globally, over three billion people lack access to basic financial services, of which about 90 per cent are from Africa, Asia, Latin America and the Middle East. This has led to considerable demand from the developing countries for a more inclusive financial system that would cater to the demands of the poor in these regions (Consultative Group to Assist the Poor, 2012; and John, Julius and Worapot, 2009).

The absence or lack of formal institutional arrangements to provide sustainable financial services is believed to be one of the basic causes that force the poor to increasingly turn to and depend upon informal financial institutions. The United Nations (2006) and CGAP (2012) reports assert that poor households with inadequate access to finance largely depend upon semi-formal or informal financial providers, such as private microfinance institutions (MFIs), pawnshops, conventional moneylenders, and other rotating savings and credit associations. However, these informal financial institutions are less reliable and insecure, and also more expensive than the formal financial institutions. Inadequate access to financial services, along with the overarching dominance of the informal financial providers, may impede the decision-making capability of the poor as they are restrained from making a rational choice while deciding on investments.

Given this background, financial inclusion is increasingly becoming a major focus of research, and the recent literature on the subject focuses on emphasising the possibilities and prospects of well-designed financial arrangements. Scholars note that better financial services lead to the social and economic development of the rural population. With a view to economic development, scholars argue, a 'well-functioning financial system' with access to adequate institutional finance enables the poor to start investing money in various income-generating activities and maximise the returns, and reduces their vulnerability to the financial risks that they encounter in their daily lives. It helps to bring poor people into the mainstream of the economy, and allows them to contribute more actively to their personal economic development. It enhances mobilisation of savings and contributes to economic growth by supporting capital accumulation. While correlating access to banking in terms of savings with social development, it is argued that savings in banks enable the poor to invest in education and health that facilitate a better living standard, along with marked social development. Having a bank account and access to other financial services through formal financial institutions helps the low-income segments to accumulate funds in a secure place. This, in turn, will have a sobering influence on the informal sector, hence benefiting those who were otherwise excluded from it (Arora and Leach, 2005; Beck, *et al.,* 2009, Biju, *et al.,* 2013; Ellis, 2007; Kirkpatrick, 2000, and United Nations, 2006).

Combining the banking services with access to market offers all participants to take advantage of their investments by channeling funds to productive uses resulting in improving income-levels, reducing poverty and protection against economic shocks (Honohan, 2004; Kanther and Nagabhushan 2012; Ramji, 2009 and United Nations, 2006). Thus, given its ability to promote social and economic development, the idea of promoting financial inclusion is no longer a policy choice but a policy compulsion in developing economies. India is not an exception to this trend, and has adopted financial inclusion as a potential strategy for financial development since 2005. It is to be noted that attempts are continuously being made to enlarge the financial system across India in order to achieve the goals of inclusive governance.

This chapter is organised as follows. Section 4.2 briefly discusses the concept of financial exclusion, and gives an overview of financial exclusion in India, highlighting the supply and demand side causes of financial exclusion. Section 4.3, central to this chapter, provides a conceptual framework for the study of financial inclusion, which captures various perspectives on the concept and its importance, and attempts to illustrate the financial inclusion life cycle. Section 4.4 traces the evolution of banking system in India. Section 4.5 discusses the 'Index of Financial Inclusion' (IFI) and attempts to measure the statewide financial inclusion in India through this Index. Section 4.6

reviews some of the recent policy initiatives implemented by Government of India (GoI), Reserve Bank of India (RBI), and National Bank for Agricultural and Rural Development (NABARD) to promote financial inclusion in India. Section 4.7 looks at the relationship between Self-Help Group-Bank Linkage Programme (SBLP) and Financial Inclusion. The final section summarises the review of literature.

Financial Exclusion

Scholars tend to view financial exclusion in terms of accessibility. Accordingly, financial exclusion is broadly defined in terms of lack of adequate access to a range of financial services. People belonging to the lower income strata are unlikely to get access to mainstream financial services and products, and reap the benefits of it. Further, it prevents the poor and disadvantaged segments from taking key decisions regarding human and physical capital accumulation. Given the above, the repercussions of financial exclusion could be far-reaching, which not only destabilise livelihood opportunities but also push them into the complex phenomenon of the 'poverty trap' (Joshi, 2011; Leyshon and Thrift, 1995; Mahmoud *et al.,* 2011; and Sinclair, 2001). There is another stream of scholars, who extend this argument beyond the accessibility dimension by relating financial exclusion to the income status of the poor. Income levels of an individual in any country determine the propensity to save. Underlining this view, Joshi (2011) observes that majority of population in India neither has savings accounts nor receives credit from formal financial institutions. They seldom make or receive payments through formal financial institutions. Apart from the access and income dimensions, Sharma (2008) shows that exclusion can be due to geographical conditions, transaction costs, lack of experience in marketing or self-exclusion in response to negative experiences or perceptions. It is thus clear that financial exclusion is primarily due to lack of income, access and limited exposure to the financial sphere. These constraints invariably have serious repercussions on the living standards of the poor.

Financial Exclusion in India

Despite a well-developed banking system in India, a large number of groups remain excluded from the basic opportunities and services provided by the financial sector for a variety of supply and demand side reasons. In a major and first of its kind document, the All India Rural Credit Survey (AIRCS) in 1954 showed that the credit needs of the financially excluded population are often met by the informal, non-institutional sources rather than the formal institutions. The excluded sections were from the small and marginal farmers, women, unorganised sector workers including artisans, the self-employed and pensioners.[1] The 59th round survey of National Sample Survey Organisation (NSSO) (2003) shows that of the 89.3 million farmer households, 45.9 million (51.4 per cent) do not have access to credit, either from institutional or non-institutional sources. Among the excluded, the plight of financial exclusion of the dalit households is deplorable. The All India Debt and Investment Survey (AIDIS) (2002-03) claims that dalit households in rural India obtained more than half of their total debt from informal sources. The share of formal sources in the total debt of these households was only 44.8 per cent, lower than the corresponding share of 59 per cent for non-dalit households. Among informal sources, conventional moneylenders were the predominant sources of debt for these households.[2] This strengthens the fact that financial exclusion in India is high in general, and it also varies widely across regions in India.

In terms of region, the Report of the Committee on Financial Inclusion, Government of India (2008) observes a geographical dimension to understanding the extent of financial exclusion. The report cites inaccessibility, distance and lack of proper infrastructure as the reasons for financial exclusion in a country with a large rural population. Therefore, the above data emphasises the need for an expansion of geographical coverage for ensuring the outreach of various financial services to the entire population without any demand and supply constraints. It also highlights the need to expedite the process of financial inclusion that ensures poor and disadvantaged sections to be a part of formal financial system. The following paragraphs discuss the causes for financial exclusion from both supply and demand sides and the consequences of such exclusion.

Causes for Financial Exclusion

The Financial Access Task Force Report (2011:14) identifies the following causes for financial exclusion. They are categorised into both supply side constraints as well as demand side constraints.

Supply side Constraints

(i) **Outreach:** The companies intending to provide financial services in the low-density areas and low-income populations cannot find the business for the provision of financial services attractive. Moreover they may not be financially sustainable. In such cases provision of the financial services to the needy is unthinkable.

(ii) **Regulation:** The report states that regulatory frameworks are not always adapted to local contexts. It implies that rules and regulations that regulate the financial services do not consider the local context in terms of geography and culture.

(iii) **Business models:** Implementation of the business models to provide financial services are costly.

(iv) **Providers:** If the number of services as well as the types of financial service providers are limited in scope, then it may not serve the objective of financial inclusion.

(v) **Services:** If at all the financial services are provided to the beneficiaries they are non-adapted products and services to meet the requirements of the low-income populations.

Demand side Constraints

Coupled with the supply side barriers, the Financial Access Task Force Report (2011:14) also identifies demand side constraints which lead to financial exclusion. The barriers include: low and irregular income, cumbersome banking procedures, literacy level and lack of awareness on financial products, lack of trust in formal banking institutions and cultural obstacles (for instance, gender and cultural values). These constraints emphasise the socio-economic and cultural conditions of the customers in relation to accessing banking services. For instance, opening a bank account and operating financial transactions from the account is very much dependent on the income levels of the client. According to the report, in rural and semi-urban areas, a large chunk of the people live with meager incomes earned at irregular intervals, resulting in voluntary exclusion from accessing financial services. A second constraint relates to complicated banking procedures, which become difficult for the poor customers right from opening bank account to availing various financial services. This is also related to the issue of financial literacy. Lack of proper financial education on how to deal with financial matters and choosing appropriate financial products and lack of cooperation from the bank staff create distrust among the customers. In addition, cultural obstacles compound the situation and push them to rely upon informal financial institutions and conventional moneylenders.

While emphasising the problem of financial exclusion of women, the German Federal Ministry for Economic Cooperation and Development's Report (2013) also put forward some of the supply and demand side constraints that particularly affect women in accessing basic financial services. The supply-side constraints for women are: first, collateral requirements exclude women who often lack land/ property rights. In other words, bank rules and regulations do not permit them to open a bank account without any guarantee. Second, limited physical outreach and typical bank opening hours affect women more than men because they are less mobile than men. Third, documentation requirements pre-empt women from accessing financial services, as most of them often lack proof of identity. It has become a serious constraint that prevents rural women from being a part of formal banking system. Fourth, product features of financial services may not meet women's requirements. For instance, eligibility criteria and loan term may discourage women from applying for financial benefits. As far as the demand side constraints in accessing banking services for women are concerned, the Report observes that women have lower incomes than men, often because of the kind of work they do. Women's low levels of education than men also affect their financial capability and mobility. Low levels of income and lack of education also restricts their access to information regarding various financial services and benefits of the bank. Financial exclusion is, therefore, a consequence of both the supply (formal financial institutions) and demand (people) side constraints and it is especially high in the case of women. The following section attempts to provide a conceptual understanding of financial inclusion.

Financial Inclusion: A Conceptual Framework

Over the years, the extant literature has defined financial inclusion in several ways. The concept of financial inclusion is typically approached from three different perspectives in this literature: (i) global perspective; (ii) national perspective with specific reference to India, and (iii) financial inclusion in relation to women's empowerment in India. While looking at the concept from global perspective, the United Nations Report documents financial inclusion from the 'customer' point of view. It encompasses two important elements. First, financial inclusion means a customer having access to a variety of formal financial services and products, from simple credit and savings to more complex services such as insurance, pensions and remittances. Second, customer is accessing more than one formal financial service provider, wherein it ensures a variety of competitive options (2006). Thus, the report brings the 'customer' centre stage and emphasises that the goal of promoting financial inclusion could become a reality when the customer is able to access various financial services, and have mobility to approach various financial service providers.

A World Bank Report (2008:11) defines financial inclusion as "broad access to financial services". It explains that the promotion of financial inclusion means "the absence of price or non-price barriers in the use of financial services". The Report primarily emphasises two things; greater access to financial services and absence of various barriers in utilising those services. The Micro-Credit Ratings International Limited (M-CRIL) an International Non-Governmental Organisation on microfinance (2009) has a different perspective on understanding financial inclusion, which goes beyond providing various financial products and services to the excluded population. It underlines the need for providing financial services in a responsible manner. Being responsible means providing various financial products and services to the unbanked population by considering six basic principles, which primarily emphasise client's protection. Those are as follows: prevention over-indebtedness, transport pricing, appropriate collection practice, ethical staff behaviour and privacy of client data. These principles suggest that the goal of financial inclusion can be achieved only when the financial service provider, whether it is formal, semi-formal or informal, considers the protection of customers while providing the financial services.

This perspective of understanding the promotion of financial inclusion in terms of client's protection is very much relevant to an analysis of the microfinance crisis during 2009-10 in Andhra Pradesh, in which major allegations were made against the (private) microfinance intuitions (MFIs). Shylendra (2011) and Nair (2012) argue that MFIs have grown at a frantic pace, and have not been adequately controlled by the government. These institutions have collected exorbitant interest rates from the borrowers. Lack of transparency regarding their interest rate practices and unethical ways of recovering loans have placed a huge burden on the poor. Instead of helping them to come out of the poverty trap, it has further pushed them into a vicious cycle of debt, poverty and even deaths.[3] These shady business practices have put at stake the goal of poverty alleviation and further financial inclusion.

With a view to understanding financial inclusion in a national perspective, the Rangarajan Report on Financial Inclusion in India provides a very broad and inclusive definition of financial inclusion. It defines financial inclusion as "the process of ensuring access to financial services and timely and adequate credit when needed by vulnerable groups such as weaker sections and low income groups at an affordable cost" (2008:5). This view broadens the scope of financial inclusion beyond a bank account by emphasising access to credit and other financial services, at an affordable price without time lapse. In the same year, the Planning Commission constituted a High Level Committee on Financial Sector Reforms under the Chairmanship of Dr Raghuram Rajan, primarily aimed at identifying the emerging challenges in meeting the financial needs of the poor. The Committee defines financial inclusion as "universal access to a wide range of financial services at a reasonable cost". These services include not only banking products but also other financial services like insurance and equity products (2008:3). In a nutshell, though the committee's definition of financial inclusion is similar to the Rangarajan committee's report, the term universal access places emphasis on the availability of various financial services in all parts of India, at a reasonable price. Both the definitions, however, identify the financial vacuum in the banking sector to cater to the financial needs of the low-income and other disadvantaged sections, and significantly emphasise the importance of delivering all the required financial services and products in a subsidised manner to these groups.

In contrast to the reports, Sarma defines financial inclusion as "a process that ensures the ease of access, availability and usage of the formal financial system for all members of an economy" (2008:3). She also observes that the process of financial inclusion can be achieved with three important dimensions viz., accessibility, availability and usage of the formal financial system. The author has developed an Index of Financial Inclusion (IFI) in order to measure the level of financial inclusion of a country or region by considering the three dimensions. While analysing the promotion of financial inclusion with reference to developed and developing countries, Chakrabarthy, Deputy Governor of RBI, asserts that in developed economies, accelerating financial inclusion is more about promoting financial literacy and transparency in their services and products, whereas in developing economies like India, access to basic financial services and products also holds considerable significance (2012). He is of the view that in most of the developing countries, the banking system is still in an incipient stage, wherein a major chunk of population is still left untouched by the basic banking services. As such, providing basic financial services and products to these sections assume greater priority to achieve financial inclusion.

In recent years, the literature on this subject has significantly emphasised the inclusion of women in the ambit of the formal banking system. In this regard, international and national agencies along with academicians have put forward different views on various problems and prospects of financial exclusion/inclusion of women. The German Federal Ministry for Economic Cooperation and Development's report (2013) holds that the goal of financial inclusion of women could be achieved only when they have easy access to a variety of financial services and products in a sustainable manner. It caters to their small-scale business and household needs. Highlighting the possibilities of access to financial services by women, the report notes that this can help improve women's opportunities to earn income or control assets outside the household. It also enables their bargaining power within and outside the family and increases their influence over how money and other resources can be efficiently used. By having access to insurance services, they can reduce the element of risk in their day-to-day businesses such as unexpected expenses or losses in business.

The report rightly emphasises the financial inclusion of women and highlights its significant contribution to women's social and economic development. The report, however, underestimates some critical issues, which remain as major obstacles in the path of economic development, and need to be addressed. First, given a patriarchal society and poor economic conditions, it is difficult for an individual woman to open a bank account, as she faces resistance from her family members. Second, household responsibilities restrict her ability to go to bank frequently. Beside these two issues, financial illiteracy is a major barrier for any women to get access and optimally utilise various financial services. Without achieving financial literacy, women cannot avail those services in a full-fledged manner, and hence, the objective of ensuring financial inclusion of women remains a distant reality.

The three perspectives have advanced different understandings of the strategy of promoting financial inclusion. At the international level, the definitions of financial inclusion largely place the 'customer' centre stage. Customers' ability to easy access to financial services and mobility to approach various financial service providers could significantly determine the possibility of accelerating the process of financial inclusion. Second, the supply and demand side constrictions are seem to severely hinder the process of financial inclusion, and accordingly necessary efforts need to be made. Third, public and private sector financial service providers must consider client's protection while delivering a variety of financial services. At the national level, the arguments largely revolve around developing countries. With reference to India in particular, the targeted population is the economically marginalised and financially excluded sections. The definitions are primarily aimed at bringing these sections into the ambit of formal banking system. Thus, ensuring universal access to financial services at an affordable price becomes the focus. The third perspective primarily focuses on financial inclusion of women, and highlights the positive aspects of giving women easy access to various financial services.

Evolution of Banking System in India: An Overview

The banking sector in India forms the fulcrum of financial system since Independence. Beginning with early national plans, successive governments in India emphasised the role of finance in promoting equitable growth. Accordingly, banking policies were formulated in order to expand the scope of formal financial services to the unbanked population. These policies envisaged 'social and development banking' to meet the credit needs of the rural people as well as to reduce the role of the informal sector in the provision of credit (Dev, 2006). Indeed, financial inclusion was not an alien concept in the development trajectory of India. As a concept, it was adopted and embedded in credit policies since the early period, though in a disguised form and not in the nomenclature that the term has come to assume today (Rao, 2007). The evolution of the banking sector in India can be divided into three distinct phases: 1951 to 1969; 1969 to 1991-92; and post-1992 onwards. A brief discussion of the two phases as well as detailed description of the third phase of Indian banking system are in order.

First Phase (1951 to 1969)

In the initial years following independence, non-institutional sources, particularly moneylenders used to play important role in meeting the financial needs of the rural communities (Rao, 2007). Since these private informal sources were not sustainable for the borrowers, the government set up cooperative banks in 1955. The objective of this initiative was to have broad-based financial development that would allow financial institutions to mobilise savings throughout the economy, and allocate them to agriculture and small industry, particularly in the countryside. In the course of time, these cooperative banks being limited in number and proved inadequate to serve the growing financial needs of the people, leading to the failure of banks in the early 1960s. Subsequently, it also affected the flow of credit to agriculture and small-scale industries (Basu, 2008). In addition to this, the banks followed stringent and rigid structural procedures to render financial services to the beneficiaries, which hindered the flow of subsidised finance to agriculture and allied sectors. Besley (1995) documents the unsatisfactory performance of the banking system to meet the needs of its targeted sections, leading the government to opt for nationalisation of banks in 1969.

Scholars note that in order to meet the policy goals, the Indira Gandhi government in 1969, embarked on nationalising commercial banks in the private sector. As has been mentioned, nationalisation of banks focused on social banking to meet the needs of a developing economy. A major concern of nationalisation was to make banking facilities accessible to all the people, including the remote areas. Special emphasis was laid on the provision of delivering adequate and sustainable credit to agriculture and allied sectors (Besley, 1995; Deodhar and Abhyankar, 2001; and Mohan, 2008). Basu (2008) in her study highlights two important goals of nationalisation of banks: first, to mobilise the savings of the public through a massive programme of expansion of bank branches in rural and semi-urban areas, and second, to ensure adequate and cost-effective financial assistance to the priority sectors of the economy. The motivating force behind this drive was the belief that a better banking system with widespread bank branches (with customer-friendly) and flexible procedures of lending loans to rural and semi-urban regions would instigate growth and help the rural economy to grow. To sum up, the first phase saw a series of experiments. It witnessed a shift from informal credit to public or government ownership of financial institutions; and from a rigid structural process to customer-friendly and flexible procedures, that gave the banking system a direction to help the rural economy.

Second Phase (1969 to 1990)

During the second phase of banking (1969 to 1990) the policy of social and development banking remained a priority of the Government of India. The government attempted to further expand the geographical and functional outreach of the banking system through establishment of Regional Rural Banks (RRBs) (1975) in areas that had an underdeveloped banking infrastructure (Dev, 2006 and Chavan, 2007). The RRBs were envisaged to fill the gap that was left by the commercial banks and cooperative credit societies. The latter were not able to provide subsidised credit to the small and marginal farmers, agricultural labourers and artisans in the rural areas. It was, therefore believed that RRBs would operate exclusively in rural areas with a view to developing the rural economy by providing cost effective credit and other financial facilities, particularly to small and marginal farmers, agricultural labourers, artisans and small entrepreneurs (Deodhar and Abhyankar, 2001, and Misra, 2006). Between 1969 and 1980, thousands of new bank branches were established across rural India. In addition to cooperative and commercial banks, the RRBs have, since the mid-1970s, been inducted into the ambit of financing in agriculture and other priority sectors and holding a major share in institutional finance (Rao, 2007). Throughout this period, the strategy for banking was shaped by the goal of "serving better the needs of the development of the economy" (Basu, 2008:20). Deodhar and Abhyankar (2001) in their study observe that there has been a significant rise in the mobilisation of deposits by the commercial banks in the post-nationalisation era.

Total outstanding deposits of the commercial banks on 31st March 1999 were INR. 7,37,003 crore as against INR. 4,665 crore in July 1969. As far as bank lending is concerned, there was also a remarkable rise in the bank credit. Total advances of these banks increased from INR. 3,399 crore in 1969 to INR. 3,21,813 crore by March 27, 1998.

The establishment of National Bank for Agricultural and Rural Development (NABARD) in 1982 was a landmark in the evolution of banking system in India. Reserve Bank of India (RBI), an apex institution in the financial system joined NABARD in providing microcredit to the rural poor. This active involvement of RBI and NABARD led to credit planning that includes quantitative credit targets and subsidised credit. Banks allocated large proportions of credit to priority sectors, including agriculture, small-scale industries and other sectors; and identified them as critical for bringing about economic and social change in rural areas (Basu, 2008). Despite these efforts to structure rural credit, Biswa and Raut, (2008) observe that banking facilities in rural areas have not been able to cater to the growing credit needs of agriculture and allied sector.

Third Phase (1991-92 onwards)

The third phase of banking sector begins with the early 1990s, in the backdrop of the liberalisation of the Indian economy. This is the period in which the banking system in India underwent profound transformation in its scope and functioning. In addition to this, financial reforms were initiated in the banking sector in the early 1990s as part of the economic reforms. The main objectives of these reforms were twofold: "to create an efficient, competitive and stable financial sector" and "to enhance the efficiency and profitability of the banking system". Towards this direction, RBI, set up a Committee under the chairmanship of M. Narasimham to look into the Indian Financial System in 1991.The Committee on Banking Sector Reforms was entrusted with the responsibility of bringing about significant changes in the institutional structures of the banking system. The Committee recommended two important measures to revamp the financial sector in India. They are: to provide autonomy and flexibility for the banks in their operations and to "delayer the cooperative credit system". The committee suggested reduction in the transaction costs in the provision of lending credit by removing the intermediaries, and make the credit cheaper to the ultimate borrowers (Government of India, 1998:61).

Under the influence of liberalisation and privatisation agenda, the financial sector reforms sought to encourage the entry of new financial institutions into the ambit of the banking sector. Besides, many of the regulations were relaxed to allow a market-based operation of the banking system. The distinction between the banks and non-banking financial institutions was thus blurred (Deodhar and Abhyankar, 2001; and Ratti, 2012). The other recommendations of the Committee on Banking Reforms included reducing of the interest rates, allowing the public sector banks to have the freedom to determine deposit and lending rates. A remarkable shift occurred in the evolution of the Indian financial system from a 'highly regulated to more market-oriented banking system' (Bhide *et al.,* 2002 and Chavan, 2007).

During the same phase, the banking sector had introduced two innovations in the rural credit structure. These included the initiation of microfinance scheme by the NABARD (1992) and launching of the Kisan Credit Cards (KCC) scheme (1998) by the RBI. Both innovations aimed at the provision of lending timely and cost-effective credit to the beneficiaries. They were exclusively targeted to cater the financial needs of the farmers, the poor and women to improve their socio-economic conditions. KCCs are issued to the farmers by the rural banks to purchase agricultural equipments for the farm production. The amount of credit under the KCC scheme is primarily based on the landholdings of the farmers (Rao, 2007).

From the above historical survey, it is clear that the evolution of the banking system can broadly be categorised into three phases. It indicates that a large number of rural poor, particularly farmers have been left out of the ambit of the banking sector during the first phase, in spite of the existence of cooperative banks. The development banking system was largely concentrated on the industrial sector, and provision of adequate credit to the agricultural sector was given the least consideration. This vacuum was expected to be filled up by the nationalisation of banks, through 'social banking' and stronger institutional arrangements with emphasis on the agricultural and allied sectors. Since the nationalisation of banks, the Indian banking sector realised that the financial institutions had to go deeper in the rural, semi-urban and other unbanked areas. In the second phase, the scope of banking services was expanded by the setting up of Commercial Banks, RRBs and cooperative credit institutions in the mid-1970s. These efforts were augmented by the establishment of NABARD in 1982, which is primarily concerned with agriculture. This financial institution occupied a significant position in the sphere of rural and agricultural finance and was recognised as a potential contributor in delivering sustainable credit to promote income-generating activities in rural areas.

The third phase is characterised by the initiation of financial sector reforms in 1991 to bring some significant reforms in the Indian financial system. It is apparent that the reforms mainly emphasised autonomy and flexibility for the banks in their operations and in reducing transaction costs in the provision of lending credit by removing the intermediaries. A significant trend was the order to facilitate the entry of private sector in the financial domain. It is evident that the state has allowed the market to operate in the financial sphere, which later gave room for the inception of private microfinance institutions. It was believed that these private players have the potential to cater to the needs of the low-income sections with new financial products and services, and apply technology to reduce the service cost of reaching the poor. Against this backdrop, providing a variety of financial products and services to the unbanked has become a major area of concern for policy makers. Over the past few years, various attempts have been made to bring the idea of financial inclusion centrally to the policy-making and efforts have been made in the banking sector to expand its scope and functioning.

Critics argue that despite the expansion of the banking sector right from the 1950s, a large number of social groups have been excluded from the basic opportunities and services provided by the formal financial sector. According to them, although the performance of the banking system was impressive, it suffered from poor infrastructure in rural areas and its unsatisfactory performance. The Federation of Indian Chamber of Commerce and Industry (FICCI) (2012) in one of its reports, noted that the main purpose of the establishment of RRBs was to deliver small-scale credit to the unbanked population in the remote regions, and to accelerate the agenda of financial inclusion. However, the absence of customer-friendly products that suited the needs of the marginal poor was also cited as one of the key reasons for the failure of the RRBs (Frost and Sullivan, 2009).

The growth of bank branch network had been uneven and largely concentrated in metropolitan and urban regions. A sizable portion of the population of the country, especially farming and underprivileged sections, were not brought under the ambit of banking system. The farm production was effectively constrained by lack of access to formal or government controlled credit (Ananth and Sabri, 2013; Kochhar, 1997; Leeladhar, 2005; Mujumdar, 1999; and Shivamaggi, 2000). Thakur (2009) observes that the growth of the banking network slowed after the financial reforms in 1991. The share of rural credit had fallen continuously from a peak of 15.3 per cent in 1990 to 8.4 per cent in 2006. The share of rural deposits had also fallen steadily from a peak of 15.5 per cent in 1990 to 10.8 per cent in 2006. These figures indicate that the efforts of RBI, with the help of Indian government, in expanding the scope of banking system across the regions through financial reforms were inadequate. Bagli and Dutta (2102) suggest that the geographical distance from bank, financial illiteracy, gender-inequality, paucity of income and collateral assets, and lack of proof of identity of the disadvantaged people are the main causes of the exclusion of the low-income segments from the formal financial fold. On the other hand, shortage of staff, high transaction cost and economic viability of the extension of bank branches are cited as common problems of the financial institutions in extending financial services to such groups.

Financial Inclusion in India: Recent Policy Initiatives

Provision of delivering credit and other financial services to the people has been emphasised by the government since the independence. As already discussed, parallel to the early national plans, the Government of India has also given importance to the development of banking system in India. For instance, creation of cooperative banks in 1955 allowed financial institutions to mobilise savings and allocate them to agriculture and small-scale industry. Nationalisation of banks in 1969 made banking facilities accessible to all the people and laid emphasis on the provision of delivering adequate and sustainable credit to agriculture and allied sectors in rural areas. Further, establishment of Regional Rural Banks (RRBs) in 1975 expanded the geographical and functional outreach of the banking system throughout the country.

It also provided cost-effective credit and other financial services to the small and marginal farmers, artisans and small entrepreneurs. In addition, the establishment of NABARD (1982) and SIDBI (1990), which aimed at providing subsidised credit to the rural populace, particularly farmers, and small and medium enterprises are the major initiatives in the realm of Indian banking system (Dev, 2006; Rao, 2007; and Kamath, 2007). However, in the post-1990s, with the launch of banking sector reforms, a distinct shift took place in banking policy. RBI and NABARD were regarded the prime institutions to provide policy impetus and execute new policies and programmes. These efforts were further intensified by RBI with a target on rural populace, in particular farmers and poor women (Ratti, 2012). This is reflected in the policy initiatives taken over the last few years, briefly reviewed in the following section.

Kisan Credit Card (KCC)

The Kisan Credit Card (KCC) scheme is considered as an important credit facility for farmers that has been providing from the public sector banking system in India since August 1998 (Sinha and Patole, 2003). The scheme primarily aims at delivering adequate and timely credit in a flexible and cost-effective manner to farmers by catering to their cultivation needs, including the purchase of seeds, fertilisers, pesticides and livestock (Frost and Sullivan, 2009). It is believed that in relation to a traditional banking system, the KCC is seen as an important financial product in meeting the short-term credit needs of farmers (Sinha and Patole, 2003). This credit facility is also meant to mitigate the difficulties faced by farmers in accessing timely and hassle-free credit to meet their production credit needs. To make it comprehensive and user friendly, NABARD has further enlarged the scope of the Scheme to cover long-term loans and consumption loans along with crop loans (Karmakar, 2009). This credit facility is currently being implemented by all the District Central Cooperative Banks, Regional Rural Banks (RRBs) and Public Sector Commercial Banks throughout the country. As on 31 March 2012, the banking system has issued 11.39 crore KCCs and the total amount sanctioned under this scheme is INR. 5,72,617 crore (NABARD Annual Report, 2011-12: 63).

However, Frost and Sullivan (2009) observe gaps in the implementation of Kisan Credit Card (KCC) scheme. According to them, absence of record of accomplishment, complex processes, inaccessibility of the services to the poor, ignoring the landless and marginal farmers as well as non-cultivating households are bottlenecks in the implement this programme. They argue that the activities in implementing the scheme have not been recorded properly. Further, due to cumbersome banking procedures and financially illiteracy, the customers find it difficult to apply for the Kisan Credit Card. These cumbersome procedures compel them to depend on local moneylenders instead of approaching banks. In addition to this, although the loans are meant for the small and marginal farmers, the benefits are reaching the privileged farmers, who are financially in a better position.

Know Your Customer (KYC) norms

Simplified norms facilitate the opening of a bank account without hassles. With a view to simplifying the application procedures for customers, the RBI introduced Know Your Customer (KYC) norms in August 2005. According to the RBI norms, banks can accept any evidence to their satisfaction for establishing the identity and address proof of the customer. In other words, these KYC norms simplified the procedures to open an account for those whose financial transactions are of modest amounts (Bhatia and Chatterjee, 2010; and Ramji, 2007).

The difficulty in meeting the identity requirements under Know Your Customer (KYC) is supported by the Unique Identification (UID) Project, undertaken by the Unique Identification Authority of India (UIDAI). The UIDAI proposes to furnish an identity card that will satisfy the KYC norms of banks. The 'Aadhaar' (the unique identification Number) card aims to provide a Unique Identification in the form of 12-digit unique number with some basic demographic and biometrics information to every citizen of India. As the UID numbers are acceptable for complying with the KYC norms, UIDAI can act as a major facilitator for financial inclusion through opening of bank accounts. Further UID number would provide a strict check on the customer's identity through biometric authentication. In addition to this, the costs and time required by the customer for opening accounts would be reduced substantially (Joshi, 2011). It is understood that the KYC norms are primarily targeted at low-income groups and rural illiterate people. The objective of KYC norms is that persons belonging to low-income groups both in urban and rural areas do not face difficulty in opening the bank accounts. The Aadhar Card takes care of the identity proof of the illiterate and poor people to open a bank account. A combination of these two factors is expected to encourage the hitherto financially excluded sections to come under the ambit of banking system.

No-Frills Accounts (NFA)

The Reserve Bank of India in its Annual Policy Statement of 2005-06 directed banks to provide banking services to all segments of the population on an equitable basis. It came up with an initiative called 'no-frills' account to expand the outreach of banking services. The 'no-frills account' (NFA) allows financially excluded individuals to access banking services with low or zero balances; and also with either low or no charges. NFA encourages the poor people to save more by providing credit in the form of overdraft facility. The services provided by NFA include "deposit and withdrawal of cash at the bank branches as well as ATMs, receipt/credit of money through electronic payment channels or by means of deposit/collection of cheques drawn by Central/ State Government agencies and departments" (Khan, 2012:1452). Ramji (2009) explains the rationale behind introducing no-frills account: to inculcate the habit of saving among the poor and disadvantaged segments and ensure basic banking facilities to them in a uniform manner. According to Majumdar and Gupta (2013), the idea of introducing NFA is to ensure credit and other financial services easily accessible to all sections of society and to make them as part of formal banking system. As on June 2011, 7.91 crores No-frills accounts have been opened by banks with outstanding balance of Rs 5,944.73 crores. These figures respectively, were 4.93 crores and Rs 4,257.07 crores in March 2010 (Subash, 2013).

However, no-frills accounts (NFAs) have drawn criticism from scholars. Frost and Sullivan (2009) argue that NFAs are still in a dormant stage and the frequency of access to this facility in most cases are negligible. They are of the view that NFAs do not have linkages with other financial services, that is, people cannot avail other financial service through this no-frills account. In similar vein, the Federation of Indian Chamber of Commerce and Industry (FICCI) Report (2012) observes that although NFAs are expected to cater to the basic financial needs of the low-income and vulnerable groups, they are still not actively used by most of the NFA account holders. The report identifies the bottlenecks in availing the NFAs by the poor, such as distance from banks, lack of dissemination of information about NFAs, irregular and uncertain flow of income and on.

Financial Literacy

Financial illiteracy is frequently cited as a significant constraint on financial inclusion. It leads to the voluntary self-exclusion of people from accessing basic financial services. According to Robson (2012:4), financial literacy is "having the knowledge, skills and confidence to make responsible financial decisions". It inculcates the habit of savings among customers and provides the knowledge on how to access financial products and services, management of accounts, operation and so on are essential for financial inclusion (Rana *et al.,* 2012). If consumers are illiterate, they may not make rational choices in selecting and utilising financial products in financial transactions. This gives an opportunity for the lenders to take advantage of the illiteracy of such customers. Providing financial literacy to the needy sections is, therefore, recognised as a key aspect in promoting "financial inclusion, consumer protection and financial stability" (RBI Bulletin, 2012:1291, and United Nations, 2006). The United Nations Report on Building Inclusive Financial Sectors for Development (2006:18) states that "providing financial literacy increases access as well as the ability of customers to get the financial services they need on appropriate terms".

Echoing this argument, the National Foundation for Educational Resource (NFER) (1992:45) defines financial literacy as "the ability to make informed judgements and to take effective decisions regarding the use and management of money". It is also about using the skills to access financial services. The RBI defines financial literacy as "a set of skills that allow people to manage their money wisely along with some understanding of essential financial concepts. It is also about markets and investing, but also savings, budgeting, financial planning, basics of banking and, most importantly, about being financially smart" (RBI Bulletin, 2012:1291).

Leopald *et al.* (2012) examine financial literacy from the view of the knowledge of basic financial concepts and the skills on the assumption that financial literacy is instrumental in translating this knowledge into improved financial behaviours. They affirm that financial literacy programmes enable people to have an increased awareness and comprehension of financial concepts, particularly savings. Moreover, providing training in financial matters and enabling them to understand the basics of banking system will have a significant impact on altering the economic conditions of the poor. Referring to Indian context, the RBI broadly categorises the users into three strata: the poor; the lower and middle-income groups; and high net-worth individuals. Providing access to financial literacy to the poor and low-income segments in turn addresses the major barriers obstructing them to participate in the financial system (RBI Bulletin, 2012).

Business Correspondent (BC) Model

In order to provide an alternative banking structure to branch-based banking services, the RBI in the year of 2006 adopted the technology-based agent bank model through business facilitators (BFs)/ business correspondents (BCs) model. The model is intended to reach out to a geographically diverse population, particularly those who are financially excluded from the mainstream banking services (Khan, 2012). It is also aimed at developing and strengthening the relationship between unbanked people and the formal financial system. The salient features of this model include: identifying the borrowers, collection and verification of loan applications, creating awareness on various financial services, products and transactions, and post-sanction monitoring and so on. Important financial services available under the BC model such as opening bank accounts, fixed cash deposits, savings, cash withdrawals, balance enquiries, money transfer on a small-scale basis, receipt, and delivery of small value remittances/other payments. However, a maximum limit is imposed on every financial service (Anath and Sabri, 2014, A Report on the Pradhan Mantri Jan-Dhan Yojana (PMJDY), 2014, and Bhargava, 2009). As of 31 March, 2014 there are more than 1.4 lakh business correspondents (BCs) of public sector banks and Regional Rural Banks (RRBs) in the rural areas (A Report on the Pradhan Mantri Jan-Dhan Yojana (PMJDY, 2014: i).

Under the BC model, banks undertake financial transactions with the help of the business correspondent and permits branchless banking. In other words, banks allow private employees to provide financial services in the villages where bank branches are not available. This model is increasingly aided by technology such as point of service handheld devices, mobile phones and biometric scanners (Karmakar, 2009). The best advantage through the BC model is, on the one hand, banks get vast exposure to the rural population without its physical presence in terms of branches, and on the other hand, the rural unbanked people get easy access to basic banking facilities at their doorstep by the person among themselves. It also promotes and nurtures SHGs/JLGs wherever relevant and works as potential contributors in creating awareness about various financial operations. The BC model is, therefore, recognised as an economically feasible and customer-friendly banking model for the poor (Bhargava, 2009). It also helps the people to overcome regional barriers of language and culture, and inadequate infrastructure in rural areas (Frost and Sullivan, 2009). This model can also bridge the gap between the service providers (the banks) and the service seekers (people) who are under-served and unbanked. The BC model was evolved to counter the lack of required manpower to reach all people in the current banking system (Khan, 2012).

Pradhan Mantri Jan-Dhan Yojana (PMJDY)

In the light of achieving comprehensive financial inclusion, the Government of India has come up with a recent socio-economic initiative in the realm of Indian banking sector, named as the Pradhan Mantri Jan-Dhan Yojana (PMJDY). The scheme was announced by the Prime Minister of India on 15 August, 2014 and it was officially launched on 28 August, 2014. It is primarily intended to financially empower the people by opening bank accounts and providing basic banking services. The main objective of the scheme is "ensuring access to various financial services like availability of basic savings bank account, access to needs based credit, remittances facility, insurance and pension to the excluded sections such as low income groups and disadvantaged sections" (A Report on Pradhan Mantri Jan-Dhan Yojana: A National Mission on Financial Inclusion, 2014: 1). The Scheme emphasises that every household in our country must have a bank account and he/she is in a position to avail credit and other banking facilities and get benefit out of it. The report believes that having a bank account and availing banking services will enable them to come out of the grip of moneylenders and financially helps them from emergencies.

The Report (2014:11) mentioned six important components to bring about comprehensive financial inclusion for all the households in the country. These are: universal access to banking facilities, provision of basic banking accounts, financial literacy programme, access to credit, access to insurance and pension facility. The first three components are targeted to reach in the first phase, that is, from 15 August, 2014 to 14 August 2015. The remaining three components would be achieved in the second phase, that is, from 15 August, 2015 to 14 August 2018. Under this scheme, every account holder gets a 'RuPay debit card' with Rs 1 lakh accident coverage, life insurance coverage of Rs 30000 and an overdraft facility of Rs 5000. As of 31 December, 2014 there are 10.44 crore basic bank accounts opened and 8.46 crore RuPay debit cards issued under PMJDY in the country.[4]

Since the scheme was initiated very recently, there are few studies on the evaluation of the scheme. A study by Kochhar (2014), the first of its kind, argues that opening a bank accounts under Jan Dhan Yojana scheme is a significant step in the process of achieving complete financial inclusion; however, it may not lead to empowerment of all the poor unless some of the important issues are addressed. Indeed, most of the bank accounts opened under this scheme became dormant. In fact, the Report on Pradhan Mantri Jan-Dhan Yojana: A National Mission on Financial Inclusion, Government of India (2014) points out that of the 10.44 crore basic bank accounts opened under the Jan Dhan Yojana, 6.68 crore accounts continue to be dormant. The said figures, on the one hand, emphasise the government and bankers efforts in providing bank accounts to the hitherto financial excluded sections, however, on the other hand, the inactivity of bank accounts highlight the lackadaisical approach of the bankers in propelling the scheme. In a similar vein, the RBI governor Raghuram Rajan raised concern over this scheme by saying that "the scheme will be a waste, if it leads to duplication of accounts and if no transaction happens on the new accounts."[5]

From the discussion, it is clear that under the agenda of financial inclusion, various policies initiated by the government aimed for an inclusive banking system. In the rural credit structure, the KCC scheme provided loans to farmers at subsidized interest rates to purchase agricultural inputs and livestock. Simplified Know Your Customer (KYC) norms and no-frills accounts enhanced the accessibility of the poor, illiterate and disadvantaged segments of population to various financial services and products at an affordable cost. The financial literacy and financial counselling campaigns serve to address the demand side constraints of financial inclusion. It is evident that financial literacy contributes to the habit of savings among the bank customers and provides knowledge on how to access financial products and services, and manage bank accounts. In other words, it enables the poor to understand the needs and benefits of the products and services being offered by the formal financial institutions. Financial illiteracy, however, proves to be a major obstacle to achieve the objective of financial inclusion. Business Correspondent (BC) model primarily targeted to reach the geographically diverse population, who are being left out from the banking system. The other recent initiative in the realm of banking system is the Pradhan Mantri Jan Dhan Yojana (PMJDY). As mentioned, the scheme is aimed at providing bank account and access to banking facilities to all households in the country. In order to encourage people to start using banking facilities, the Government of India is providing RuPay debit card with Rs 5000 overdraft facility. It is evident that the report on Jan Dhan Yojana (2014) considered that the Business Correspondent (BC) model is an important strategy to implement the scheme successfully.

The Relationship between Self-Help Group-Bank Linkage Programme (SBLP) and Financial Inclusion

The Indian model of microfinance, Self-Help Group-Bank Linkage Programme (SBLP), is increasingly recognised as the largest and most successful model of its kind in the world. This model primarily aims at enhancing rural poor's access to the formal financial system in a cost-effective and sustainable manner by making use of SHGs (Rajeev and Mahija, 2013). In this regard, SHGs in India are increasingly seen as potential intermediaries between women and banks. In order to understand the relationship between SHGs and financial inclusion, it is pertinent to understand the concept of SHG, and its functioning, with a focus on India.

The idea of Self-Help Groups (SHGs) surfaced as a social phenomenon in 1970s in developing economies. As an approach, it gradually transformed into a unique form of help that was believed to enhance effective coping skills, improve self-esteem, promote personal growth and enhance collective mobilisation for social change. These groups have been the focus of development discourse in the Third World economies as they aim at delivering credit and other financial services through banks at subsidized interest rates for the poor, particularly women, to start small-scale business enterprise (Hasenfeld and Gidron, 1993). In India, NABARD began to promote SHGs formally since 1992 under the SHG-Bank Linkage Programme (SBLP) model as a pilot programme (Sylendra, 2008). The model is recognised as a "decentralised, cost-effective and fastest growing microfinance initiative" that continues to enable over 103 million poor households to access a variety of sustainable financial services from the banking system as its member (NABARD, Report on States of Microfinance in India, 2011-12: 3). Thanka (2012) is of the view that ensuring access to adequate institutional credit in rural areas augments agricultural production and increases the percentage of bank customers. Such a trend is seen as a potential sign for furthering financial inclusion. In this context, as far as SHGs linkage to financial inclusion is concerned, Vaidyanathan (2014) believes that the provision of lending subsidized credit is the key issue in ensuring the process of financial inclusion. The potentialities of SHGs in disbursing tiny loans to the rural unbanked sections, particularly women, are critical.

By increasing the bank membership and expanding the outreach of banking system, SHGs become one among the important actors in the process of promoting financial inclusion. The empirical studies show that as an SHG member, a woman can successfully conduct financial transactions and avail required financial services. Corroborating this observation, a recent study by Thanka (2012) observes that the SBLP has brought millions of poor into contact with the formal banking, which eventually reduced their dependency on the informal sector, particularly conventional moneylenders. In one of NABARD's Annual Reports titled, 'Status of Microfinance in India' (2012-13:1) reveals that as on 31st March, 2013 there are 73.18 lakh savings-linked SHGs covering 9.7 crore poor households under microfinance programme. However, Vaidyanathan (2014) argues that the functioning of SHGs has succeeded only in some areas of the country, in particular Southern India, but somehow do not get successfully replicated everywhere. The study urges that the Reserve Bank should play a more proactive role in highlighting the critical importance of credit cooperatives, including SHGs, for successful financial inclusion.

Summary

This chapter has reviewed various concepts related to financial inclusion and its significance, beside identifying the problems inherent in it. People's continued exclusion from the formal financial sphere makes them dependent on their own limited savings, which in turn restricts their choice of investment. Further, the people are compelled to depend on informal financial sources, which in the long run, trap them into a cycle of perpetual debt and poverty. Given these conditions, financial inclusion has assumed growing significance. The chapter has emphasised that access to adequate institutional finance enables the poor to start investing in various small-scale, income-generating activities that in turn contribute to their personal economic development. It is also recognised that a well-established financial system with a goal of financial inclusion helps the people to secure a sustainable income of their own, enhances their mobilisation of savings and enables them to stay within the ambit of a formal banking system. The chapter has also highlighted some of the important stages, various actors and variety of models involved in Indian context. It is held that holding a bank account, promoting financial literacy and facilitating technological assistance in accessing various financial services to the low-income sections are seen as important stages in order to achieve greater financial inclusion. The individuals, SHGs, MFIs, rural banks and the government are some of the important agencies involved in encouraging people to adopt and accept formal financial institution goods and services. In this regard, SHG-Bank Linkage Programme (SBLP) model and Business Correspondent (BC) model have emerged as favoured delivery channels to promote financial services to remote regions.

With reference to India, the chapter has attempted to trace the evolution of the banking sector and analyse the policies and programmes initiated by the RBI and NABARD with the help of the Government of India since 1950s. Especially in the post-liberalisation era, the banking sector underwent a paradigm shift in the realm of policies, and made remarkable changes in the provision of credit and other financial services to the needy. During this phase, the initiation of SBLP model by the NABARD (1992) and the launching of the Kisan Credit Cards (KCC) scheme (1998) by the RBI were exclusively targeted to cater to the financial needs of the farmers, the poor and the women to improve their socio-economic conditions. Since 2000, the banking sector in India has transformed from traditional structure to technology-oriented operations in matter of financial services and transactions. Some noteworthy initiatives in recent years have been the schemes like know your customer (KYC) norms, no-frills accounts (NFAs), financial literacy, business correspondent (BC) model, Pradhan Mantri Jan-Dhan Yojana (PMJDY) among many others, aim at establishing an inclusive financial system.

References

1. Cited in Dev, Mahendra S. (2006), 'Financial Inclusion: Issues and Challenges', *Economic and Political Weekly,* p. 4310.
2. Cited in Chavan, Pallavi (2007), Access to Bank Credit: Implication for Dalit Rural Households, *Economic and Political Weekly,* August 4, 2007. p. 3219.
3. Recently a fact-finding report prepared by the Gender Unit of Society for Elimination of Rural Poverty (SERP) (2010) viewed that 54 people have committed suicides due to the high interest rates and coercive recovery methods practiced by the MFIs.
4. Ministry of Finance, Government of India.
5. Cited in Kochhar (2014), Defeating Poverty: Jan Dhan and Beyond, pp. 21-22.

Chapter V

SHG-Bank Linkage Programme (SBLP) Model on Poverty Alleviation: Findings from Andhra Pradesh and Telangana

The field survey is divided into two chapters. The first chapter primarily attempts to examine the impact of India's largest public sector microfinance model, that is, 'SHG-Bank Linkage Programme (SBLP)' on poverty alleviation of rural women in undivided Andhra Pradesh. This chapter examines two hypotheses of the study. First, access to subsidized credit and other financial services through SBLP model have a positive impact in terms of alleviating poverty levels and promoting the process of financial inclusion of the poor women. Second, the easy accessibility of microcredit may lead to over dependency on the MFIs that lead to serious repercussions for the rural poor. To test the same, this study reports the findings of field research in three villages from the undivided state of Andhra Pradesh. Given the regional variation in the state, for a balanced understanding, three villages were selected from three districts covering three regions of the undivided state[1]. The field research targets women members in the selected villages, who were members of SHGs and part of SHG-Bank Linkage Programme (SBLP) model. A sample of 150 respondents has been selected by using stratified random sampling method. The data was collected through four stages: (i) through a structured questionnaire to the respondents (ii) semi-structured interviews to provide a fuller narrative account of the field (iii) key-informant interviews with the group presidents and bank officials and (iv) Focus

Group Discussions (FGDs) with the group members. The collected data is analysed by using frequency distribution and cross tabulation.

Introduction

The recent developments in the Indian banking system emphasise access to basic financial services for the poor households. In particular, the Reserve Bank of India's (RBI) policy towards ensuring financial inclusion of rural women through SHG-Bank Linkage Programme (SBLP) has assumed critical importance. The idea of SBLP was initiated to provide subsidized credit to the members of Self-Help Group (SHG) in rural areas who had no access earlier to formal institutional credit due to the lack of collateral. In the course of time, this model led to the formalisation of Bank Linkage Programme under which every SHG was required to be linked to banking system to meet the financial requirements of the group members. Gradually, the practice of group lending approach received appreciation as a microfinance model in the country (SERP Repot, 2013). NABARD's annual report of 2012, titled, Status of Microfinance in India (2012-13:1) showed that as on 31st March, 2013 there are 73.18 lakh savings-linked SHGs covering 9.7 crore poor households under microfinance programme. The report further states that though this phenomenon was impressive in Andhra Pradesh (AP) and Karnataka, later on, the movement spread widely to various rural areas of India.

In scripting the success of SHG movement, the case of AP has become noteworthy. The state has been at the forefront of microfinance interventions through the SBLP model in India since the late 1990s. The public sector banks in the state have given priority to the SBLP model and encouraged rural women to be part of the financial inclusion programme (Status of Microfinance in India, 2012-13). In fact, the penetration of credit intervention through SHGs is greater than any other state in India. According to the Annual Report of the Society for Elimination of Rural Poverty, Government of Andhra Pradesh (GoAP) (2013-14), the implementation of SBLP model has been taken up on a larger scale since 2005, covering all 1098 mandals in the 22 rural districts. As of 31st January 2014, there are a total of 10,59,777 SHGs with 1,16,08,418 members. These members have organised and formed into 44,433 village organisations (VOs). Geographically, these VOs were spread into 1098 Mandal Samakhyas (MSs).

Table 5.1 shows the year-wise progress of SHG-Bank linkage from 2004-05 to March 2013-14.

Table 5.1: SHG-Bank Linkage

Year	*Coverage of SHGs in number*	*Amount of Loan (Rs Crores)*	*Per Group Finance (Rs)*
2004-05	2,61,254	1,017.7	38,954
2005-06	2,88,711	2,001.4	69,322
2006-07	3,66,489	3,063.87	83,601
2007-08	4,31,515	5,882.79	1,36,329
2008-09	4,83,601	6,684.07	1,37,498
2009-10	4,13,625	6,501.35	1,57,180
2010-11	3,89,444	7,092.71	1,82,123
2011-12	3,52,485	8,084.16	2,29,347
2012-13	4,42,032	10,651.00	2,40,955
2013-14	3,58,940	10,724.81	2,98,791

Source: Annual Report of the Society for Elimination of Rural Poverty, Government of Andhra Pradesh (2013-14:7).

Table 5.1 demonstrates the ten years progress of the SHG-Bank Linkage Programme (SBLP) model in relation to loan disbursement to the SHGs. The state government of Andhra Pradesh introduced 'Pavala Vaddi Scheme'[2] (interest subsidy: 0.25 paisa per Rs 100 per month) on 1st July, 2004. Since then, the SBLP model has become popular in providing subsidized loan to the SHG members. From Table 5.1, it is observed that there has been a gradual increase in the coverage of SHGs every year and the loan disbursement. It is also evident in per group loan disbursement. During the year 2004-05 there were 2, 61, 254 SHGs and its size increased to 3,58,940 in the year of 2013-14 (increased by 13.73 per cent). Similarly, in the year of 2004-05, on an average each group has received Rs 38, 954, whereas it was Rs 2,98, 791 per group in the year of 2013-14 (increased by 13.03 per cent). These figures reflect the government's efforts in developing this model year by year. However, there are ups and downs in the coverage of the SHGs. It is observed that from 2004-05 to 2007-08, the coverage of SHGs has been increasing continuously. Since then, it started declining up to 2011-12. In contrast to this, both Per Group Finance and Amount of Loan disbursed have increased.

The Government of Andhra Pradesh also launched two more initiatives to supplement the credit needs of the Self-Help Groups (SHGs): Vaddileni Runalu (interest free loans) and Sthree Nidhi Credit Cooperation.[3] Veddilini Runalu (interest free loans) was launched on 1st December 2012 to reduce the financial burden on the SHGs. Under this initiative, banks provide interest free loans to the SHGs which can repay monthly loan installments promptly under 'Pavala Vaddi' scheme (25 paisa interest per Rs 100). A sum of Rs 955.55 lakh was disbursed to 983301 SHGs up to December 2013. 'Sthree Nidhi Credit Cooperation Federation was established to address the problem of inadequate and untimely availability loan for meeting financial emergencies of poor women SHGs. As of January, 2014 Rs 852.09 crores were disbursed to 471761 SHG members (Report of the Society for Elimination of Rural Poverty, Government of Andhra Pradesh, 2013-14:3). Though both the initiatives assumed importance in the context of providing subsidized loan and addressing immediate credit needs of the SHG members, it is too early to gauge the success of these two initiatives.

However, the success story of microfinance sector has, of late, been marred by certain financial upheavals in Andhra Pradesh. For instance, the exorbitant interest rates and coercive recovery practices adopted by Microfinance Institutions (MFIs) resulted in spate of suicides by the hapless borrowers in the year 2010. These events led to a sudden crisis in the state, which in turn eroded the credibility of the microfinance industry (Nair, 2013). In the immediate aftermath of the crisis, the Andhra Pradesh Microfinance Institutions (Regulation of Money Lending) Act, 2010 by the state government of Andhra Pradesh and various committees appointed by the RBI have drawn critical attention to the objectives and functioning of private microfinance sector. Before the eruption of this crisis, MFIs had played a predominant role in delivering microfinance to the unbanked rural segments. However, the crisis has drastically altered the current situation. With the enactment of AP MFI (Regulation of Money Lending) Act, 2010, the activities of MFIs in general have come to a virtual standstill (Kaur and Dey, 2013). In the absence of MFIs, the public sector banks have tried to fill up the vacuum. In this context, the present study assumes critical importance as to how far the SBLP model has been successful in alleviating poverty and promoting financial inclusion in

Andhra Pradesh and Telangana. Further, the study also critically examines the current crisis and its structural constraints in the functioning of MFIs in both the states.

Profile of Andhra Pradesh

After the bifurcation of the erstwhile Andhra Pradesh (AP) state into Andhra Pradesh and Telangana on 2nd June, 2014, the Andhra Pradesh remains with 13 districts and the newly formed state of Telangana consists of 10 districts. Though the geographical extent of Andhra Pradesh has been reduced, it has still its prominence with high population and rich natural resources. It shares common boundaries with Telangana and Odisha in the North, the Bay of Bengal in the East, Karnataka in the West and Tamil Nadu in the South. Geographically, the state is divided into two distinct regions such as Coastal Andhra and Rayalaseema. Out of thirteen districts, nine districts fall under Coastal Andhra region and the remaining four districts fall under Rayalaseema region. The climate of state varies considerably and depends on the geographical region and monsoon play a major role in determining its climate. The state receives greater rainfall from the Southwest Monsoon during August, September and October. About one-third of the total rainfall in Andhra Pradesh is brought by the Northeast Monsoon (Andhra Pradesh State Statistical Abstract, Planning Department, 2014).

The diversity of the topography of the region is responsible for the diversity in agricultural practices. The state is located with two mighty rivers named Krishna and Godavari with fertile agricultural fields. Agriculture is the backbone of Andhra Pradesh's economy. About 70 per cent of the population is engaged in agriculture and the state claims to be one of the main rice producing areas in India. Besides, being a leading producer of paddy, AP also produces commercial crops like Tobacco, Groundnut, Chillies, Turmeric, Cotton, Sugarcane and Banana. The state is also in the forefront of livestock management and poultry production. As many as nine districts of the State have a sea coast along with Bay of Bengal, which created manufacturing and export centric industry. It is one of the storehouses of mineral resources in India which led to large scale exports. It is also listed top in the deposit and production of mica in India. Minerals found in the state include reserves of Oil and natural gas, manganese, asbestos, Iron Ore,

Ball Clay, Fire Clay, graphite, dolomite, quartz, Tungsten, Silica sand and so on. The state has also emerged as a major industrial centre and with major public and private sector establishments producing large scale industrial goods ranging from steel, metals, petroleum, polymers, fertilisers, heavy engineering equipment. It also facilitates ship building, ports and fishing (Andhra Pradesh State Statistical Abstract, Planning Department, 2014).

Table 5.2: Facts and Figures of Andhra Pradesh (2011 Census)

Total Geographical Area	***1,60,200 sq km***
Capital city	Hyderabad
Population of the State	4,93,86,799
Rural Population	3,47,76,389 (70.4 per cent)
Urban Population	1,46,10,410 (29.6 per cent)
Male Population	24,738,068
Female Population	24,648,731
Population density	308 per sq km
Sex Ratio	996 females per 1000 males
Literacy rate	67.41 per cent
Male literacy	74.95 per cent
Female literacy	60.06 per cent
Official Language	Telugu
Total Households (HHs)	1,26,03,872
HHs availing banking services	66,48,222 (52.7 per cent)

Source: Compiled by the researcher by using various sources of state government of Andhra Pradesh.

Profile of East Godavari District

East Godavari district is one of the largest districts of the state of Andhra Pradesh. It has a unique blend of all the three types of geographical formations of forest area, upland, fertile delta lands and a coastline. The boundaries of East Godavari district are Visakhapatnam district in the North, Bay of Bengal in the East and South, and Khammam district in the West. As the name of the district conveys, East Godavari district is closely associated with the river Godavari, occupying a major portion of the delta area. Known as rice bowl of Andhra Pradesh with lush paddy fields, Agriculture is the main occupation in this region. Apart from paddy, the other crops are maize, jowar, groundnut, sugarcane and banana. Coconut production occupies the first place among the horticulture crops. Cattle and poultry constitute the important livestock resources of the district. The climate is comparatively moderate throughout the year. The normal rainfall of the district is 1280.0 mm. The district has forest cover in 3.23 lack hectors, which is about 30 per cent of the total geographical area. The headquarters of the district is located at Kakinada[4].

Profile of Diwancheruvu village of East Godavari District

Diwancheruvu village is a gram panchayat in Rajanagaram mandal of East Godavari district. It comprises six separate habitations viz. Diwancheruvu, Sreerampuram, Raghunadhapuram, Auto Nagar, Industrial Area and Mahalakshmi Nagar, and serves as the headquarters of all the six habitations. It has ten Anganwadi Centres, five Fair Price shops, two Primary Health Centres and one Gram Samakhya. The total agricultural land is 3539.30 acres. The main crops are paddy, cashew, citrus, mango and custard apple. The main occupation of this village is agriculture. Besides cultivation, livestock rearing is also one of the main alternative livelihood sources for many people in this village. Most of the small and marginal farmers depend on selling vegetables and fruits. State Bank of Hyderabad is located in Diwancheruvu gram panchayat. All the SHGs receive loans from this bank under SHG-Bank Linkage model (Rajanagaram Mandal Profile, 2013-2014). One of the habitations of Diwancheruvu gram panchayat, that is, Diwancheruvu has been selected for the field study.

Profile of Chittoor District

Chittoor district is located in the Rayalaseema region of Andhra Pradesh state. The district is surrounded by Kadapa and Anantapur districts in the North, Nellore in the East, Karnataka state in the West, and Tamil Nadu state in the South. For administrative convenience, the district is divided into three Revenue Divisions viz. Chittoor, Tirupati and Madanapalli subdivided into 66 Revenue mandals. The climate of the district is dry and humid with inadequate water supply systems. There are no permanent irrigation and navigation rivers flowing in and around Chittoor district resulting in poor harvesting. The rainfall received during winter and summer is negligible.

The average normal rainfall of the district is 934 mm. Around 30 per cent of the land area in Chittoor is covered by forests. The type of soil that is generally found in the district of Chittoor are red-loamy, red sandy, black clay, black loamy, black sand and red sandy. The economy of Chittoor is mainly agro based. It has a huge market for mango, sugarcane, grain and peanuts. Some of the major crops of the district are paddy, ragi, groundnut, sugar cane, mango, cashew nut, tomato, papaya and tamarind. Cattle rearing are an important livelihood source in Chittoor. The district has around 300,000 milch animals yielding about 18 lakh liters of milk per day. The Headquarters is Chittoor. The important industries of the district include oilseeds, rice milling, and mango pulp manufacturers. The granite industry is also or prime importance in the district of Chittoor.[5]

5.2.2.1. Profile of Taduku village of Chittoor district

Taduku village is located in Puttur mandal of Chittoor district, Andhra Pradesh. It is located 66 km towards East from district head-quarters Chittoor; 4 km from Puttur and 425 km from state capital Hyderabad. Total area of Taduku is 1351 hectares. Tirupati is the nearest town to Taduku. Agriculture and livestock rearing are the main occupations of this village. The main crops are paddy, groundnut and mango. It has one Anganwadi centre, one fair price shop, one primary health centre and one Primary Agriculture Credit Society (PACS). Most of the small and marginal farmers of this village avail loan from PACS. As far as the SHG-Bank Linkage Programme model is concerned, Self-Help Groups in this village initiated and formed under NABARD's SHG-Bank Linkage Programme. SHG women of this village avail loans and other financial services from State Bank of Hyderabad of Puttur Mandal.[6]

Table 5.3: Facts and Figures of two districts of Andhra Pradesh (2011 Census)

	East Godavari	*Chittoor*
Total Geographical Area	10,807 sq km	15,200 sq km
Population	51,51,549	41,70,468
Male	25,69,419	20,83,505
Female	25,82,130	20,86,963
Population (urban)	13,14,597	12,28,887
Population (rural)	38,36,952	29,41,581

(Contd...)

Sex Ratio	1005 per 1000 males	997 per 1000 males
Population Density	477 person/sq.km	275 person/sq.km
Population Growth (decadal)	5.1 per cent	11.33 per cent
Literacy	71.35 per cent	72.36
Male	74.91 per cent	81.15
Female	67.82 per cent	63.65
No. of Revenue Mandals	60	66
No. of Gram Panchayats	1011	1545
No. of Villages	1404	1498
No. of Self-Help Groups (SHGs)	76,176	60,039
No. of. SHG members	8,31,084	6,46,355

Table 5.4: Facts and Figures of Diwancheruvu (East Godavari District) and Taduku (Chittoor district) villages (2011 Census)

	Diwancheruvu (East Godavari District)	*Taduku (Chittoor district)*
Total Geographical Area	24.12 Sq Kms	13.17 Sq.km
Population 2011	11372	2268
Male	5581	1165
Female	5791	1103
S.T. Population	40	93
S.C. Population	2179	732
B.C. Population	5034	957
Others	4119	486
No. of Registered voters	6657	1249
Literacy Rate	58.7 per cent	62 per cent
Farmers	664	238
Agricultural Labourers	1716	427
Non-Agricultural Labourers	7552	851
Self Help Groups	108	42

Source: Compiled by the using various sources of Diwancheruvu and Taduku Gram Panchayat.

Profile of Telangana State

The state of Telangana has come into existence on 2nd June, 2014, is the 29th state of the Indian Republic. K. Chandrasekhar Rao is the first Chief Minister of newly formed state. The state has been divided into 10 districts and shares common boundaries with Maharashtra in the North, Chhattisgarh in the East, Karnataka in the West and

Andhra Pradesh in the South. Agriculture is the main occupation of the state, contributing 17 per cent to the total Gross State Domestic Product (GSDP) at 2013-14 prices. About 55.9 per cent of the population is engaged in agriculture. Some of the major crops in the state are paddy, jowar, maize, red gram, black gram, bengal gram, cotton, turmeric and so on. The development of irrigation in Telangana mostly depends on the utilisation of the water of Godavari and Krishna Rivers and tributaries, tanks and ponds. The state is richly endowed with variety of soils, ranging from highly fertile alluvial to very poor sandy soils. Red soils are also predominant with 48 per cent of the land, while black cotton soils, alluvial, rocks and boulders share 25 per cent, 20 per cent and 7 per cent respectively. The normal annual rainfall of the state is 906 mm. The rain received during the South West Monsoon (June-September) period for 2013-14 was 852 mm as against the normal rainfall of 715 mm, recording an excess of 19 per cent. However, erratic monsoon, untimely availability of inputs and credit, low productivity, depleting ground water, inadequate extension and poor irrigation are the biggest challenges that the state confront. Key industries in the state are cement, chemicals, food processing, paper, textiles, pharma, engineering, automobiles and so on. The GSDP of the State is Rs 3,78,962 crores and per capita income is Rs, 93,151 at 2013-14 prices. As of 31 December, 2014, there are 47,48,633 Self-help Group (SHG) members in 4, 24,936 SHGs organised into 17,914 Village Organisations (VOs), 442 Mandal Samakhyas (MSs) and 9 Zilla Samakhyas (ZSs) in the state (Socio-Economic Outlook, Government of Telangana, 2014).

Table 5.5: Facts and Figures of Telangana (2011 Census)

Total Geographical Area	1,14,840 sq.km
Area under forest	27, 430 sq. km (23.89 per cent)
Capital city	Hyderabad
Population of the State	3,51,93,978
Male Population	1,77,04,078
Female Population	1,74,89,900
Rural Population	2,15,84,986 (61.33 per cent)
Urban Population	1,36,08,992 (38.67 per cent)
Population density	307 per sq km
Sex Ratio	988 females per 1000 males

(Contd...)

Literacy rate	66.46 per cent
Male literacy	74.95 per cent
Female literacy	57.92 per cent
Total Number of Districts	10
Mandals (Blocks)	443
Official Language(s)	Telugu, Urdu

Source: Socio-Economic Outlook, Government of Telangana, 2014.

Profile of Karimnagar District of Telangana State

The Karimnagar district is located in the newly created state of Telangana. In terms of historical and cultural heritage, it occupies an important place in the state. The district stands second in production of paddy in the state. It is endowed with minerals and other natural resources such as coal, limestone, iron ore, granite sand and quartz. It is one of the hottest places in Telangana with the maximum temperature of 49 degrees in summer. The average rainfall in this zone is 967 mm. The district has 21 per cent of forest coverage with 250410 hectors. Manair and Godavari are the two major rivers in the district. Major crops in the district are paddy, green gram, sugar cane, maize, jowar and red gram. Apart from agricultural production, the district has many large-scale companies like NTPC, Kesoram Cements, Ramagundam-Singareni collieries and so on. As far as SHGs are concerned, the SHG women made a significant progress in paddy marketing. Some of the SHG women, who are members of the village organisation, actively participating in purchasing paddy from the farmers at the village level, on behalf of the government, and sell it to the civil suppliers at the district headquarters (Socio-Economic Outlook, Government of Telangana, 2014).

Table 5.6: Facts and Figures of Karimnagar district (2011 Census)

Total Geographical Area	11,800 sq.km
Total Population	38,11,738
Male	18,97,068
Female	19,14,670
Rural Population	28,25,044
Urban Population	9,51,225
Population density	322 per/ sq km

(Contd...)

Sex Ratio	1008 females per 1000 males
Literacy rate	64.87 per cent
Male literacy	74.72 per cent
Female literacy	55.18 per cent
Total SHGs in the District	51222
Total No. of families covered in to SHGs	6,22,872
Mandals	57
Gram Panchayats	1194
District Head Quarter	Karimnagar

Source: Compiled by the researcher by various sources of state government of Telangana.

Profile of Chinabonala village of Karimnagar district

Chinabonala is a gram panchayat situated in Siricilla mandal of Karimnagar district of Telangana. It is located 44 km west of the district headquarters, Karimnagar, 4 km from Siricilla mandal and 136 km from state capital Hyderabad. People of this village are mostly engaged in agricultural and allied activities. The main crops are paddy, cotton, maize, green gram and groundnut. The village has one Anganwadi Centre, one Fair Price shop, and one Village Organisation. There is a government girls' residential school, namely, 'Andhra Pradesh Students Welfare Residential School' located in this village. SHGs in this village were initiated and formed under NABARD's SHG-Bank Linkage Programme and recently some of the SHGs are formed by NGOs, which have been working in Siricilla Mandal. SHG women of this village avail loan and other financial services from Deccan Grameen Bank of Tangallapalli village and State Bank of Hyderabad of Siricilla Mandal (Siricilla Division Profile, 2013-2014).

Table 5.7: Facts and Figures of Chinabonala Village (2011 Census)

Total geographical area	10.02 Sq.km
Population	2279 (2011 Census)
Male	1170
Female	1109
Households	524
Literacy rate	60 per cent
Male	63 per cent
Female	58 per cent

(Contd...)

S.T. Population	153
S.C. population	726
B.C. population	918
Others	482

Source: Siricilla Division Profile, 2013-14.

Demographic and Socio-economic Profile of the Respondents

Before getting into data and analysis of the study, the current section provides an account of the demographic and socio-economic profile of the SHG respondents. The profile of the respondents is divided along the following: (i) Demographic (age), (ii) Social (religion, caste and education) and, (iii) Economic factors (type of occupation, income levels and landholdings). These profile-based indicators are important to understand the respondent's standard of living. Further, these factors also influence the participation levels of the respondents in attending SHG meetings and utilising loans for various purposes.

Demographic Characteristics

(a) Age distribution of the Respondents

Age is one of the important variables in socio-economic analysis of a qualitative study. In this study, it provides an understanding of the participation of women from different age groups in various activities of the SHGs and other activities related to their empowerment both within and outside the village. Table 5.8 gives an idea of age-wise distribution of the respondents from the three villages.

Table 5.8: Age-wise distribution of the respondents

S.No.	*Age*	*Name of the Village and District*			
		Chinabonala (Karimnagar)	*Diwancheruvu (East Godavari)*	*Taduku (Chittoor)*	*Total Respondents*
1.	20-30	12	15	14	41
2.	31-40	20	17	21	58
3.	41-50	10	11	10	31
4.	51 above	8	7	5	20
5.	**Total**	**50**	**50**	**50**	**150**

Source: Primary data.

As Table 5.8 demonstrates, a majority of the respondents (39 per cent) fall under 31-40 whereas 41 (27 per cent) are from the age group of 20-30, while 31 respondents (21 per cent) are in age group of 41-50 and 20 respondents constitute age group of 51 and above. From Table 5.8, it can be inferred that the middle-aged women who are in age group of 31 to 40 years are high in number, followed by the age group of 20-30. It could be seen as a positive sign, as of the 150 respondents, 99 members (66 per cent) fall under the age group of 20-40. It can be also observed that of the 48 women respondents, who are running self-employment activities in all the three villages, 32 fall under the age group of 30-40, and who have more than five years of experience as a group member.[7]

Social Characteristics

The study takes various social characteristics such as religion, caste and education into consideration.

(i) Religion

Table 5.9: Religion-wise distribution of the respondents

S.No	*Religion*	*Name of the Village and District*			
		Chinabonala (Karimnagar)	*Diwancheruvu (East Godavari)*	*Taduku (Chittoor)*	*Total Respondents*
1.	Hindu	39	34	36	109
2.	Muslim	5	5	4	14
3.	Christian	6	11	10	27
4.	Total	50	50	50	150

Source: Primary data.

The study observes that the people belonging to all the major religious groups, viz. Hinduism, Islam and Christianity are found in the three surveyed villages. As far as respondents are concerned, of the 150 respondents, 109 constitute Hindus, 14 per cent are Muslims, while 27 are Christians. Thus, while a maximum of 72 per cent of the respondents are Hindus, about 27 per cent respondents are Muslims and Christians. One of the obvious reasons for the low number of respondents from Muslims and Christians who are registered under SHGs is due to their low proportion of population in all the three villages. In fact, it is found that especially the poor and marginalised sections are converted themselves into Christianity. This phenomenon is particularly high in Diwancheruvu village of East Godavari district.

(ii) Caste

Caste composition is another important feature of the SHGs, which may affect its performance, and the level of participation. For the purpose of the study, the respondents are categorised into various social groups such as Scheduled Castes (SCs), Scheduled Tribes (STs), Backward Castes (BCs) and Forward Caste in accordance to their proportion in SHGs. Table 5.9 figures the social composition of the SHG respondents in three villages.

Table 5.10: Caste-wise distribution of the respondents

S.No.	Caste	*Name of the Village and District*			
		Chinabonala (Karimnagar)	*Diwancheruvu (East Godavari)*	*Taduku (Chittoor)*	*Total Respondents*
1.	SC	14	17	17	48
2.	ST	7	9	4	20
3.	BC	20	16	19	55
4.	Forward Caste	9	8	10	27
5.	**Total**	**50**	**50**	**50**	**150**

Table 5.10 shows that the participation of women from the BC (55 respondents) and SC (32 respondents) as high, followed by women from the OC (27 respondents) and ST (13 respondents) social groups as the proportional representation of women from BC and SC social group together is high in all the SHGs. It is observed that most of the SHGs in three villages were formed on the caste lines, though there were also cases of some mixed caste groups. Although the ST population was low in these villages, they have formed a few SHGs. The membership and participation of SC women in SHGs, however, is reasonably good. They also show a keen interest in mobilising other SC women to join these groups. It is worth noting that some of the BC and OC women formed SHGs within their own community rather than joining or collaborating with other social groups.

(iii) Education

The educational background of the respondents is important to examine whether, if at all, the literacy levels of the SHG women bring any perceptible change in their participation in SHG activities, and in availing loans from the bank and Mandal Samakyas (MS). It was found that education levels of the respondents have indeed encouraged their participation in capacity building programmes, financial literacy workshops and livelihood promotion programmes conducted at the block and district level. It is also said that the educated SHG women have been selected by the officials of the Mandal Samakhya (MS) in order to establish paddy-purchasing centres in their villages. The following Table 5.11 shows the education levels of the selected respondents.

Table 5.10: Educational background and percentage of the respondents

S.No.	*Education*	*Name of the Village and (District)*			
		Chinabonala (Karimnagar)	*Diwancheruvu (East Godavari)*	*Taduku (Chittoor)*	*Total Respondents*
1.	No formal Education	15	8	12	35
2.	Primary	14	15	13	42
3.	Secondary	6	8	8	22
4.	Higher Secondary	11	9	11	31
5.	10th class above	4	10	6	20
6.	**Total**	**50**	**50**	**50**	**150**

Source: Primary data.

The literacy level of the respondents is categorised into five groups. These are: (i) no formal education, (ii) primary, (iii) secondary, (iv) higher secondary and (v) above SSC, which includes intermediate to any higher level of education. The Table 5.11 highlights that of the 150 respondents, 35 respondents (23 per cent) have not received any kind of formal education; 42 (28 per cent) have completed their primary education; 22 (15 per cent) have studied up to secondary (5th to 7th standard) and 31 (21 per cent) have passed higher secondary (7th to 10th class). The remaining 20 respondents (13 per cent) have passed 10th class and above. These findings show that a higher percentage of respondents have received primary education irrespective of their region. However, the percentage is high in Diwancheruvu village of East Godavari district.

Economic Characteristics

(i) Respondent's Occupation

Through applying respondent's occupation as a variable in the analysis, some important observations could be drawn on whether respondent's occupations have any effect on women with regard to their socio-economic development. It is observed that most of the respondents are engaged in more than one occupation. The selected respondents are broadly classified under six categories such as homemakers, daily-wage labourers, farming, livestock rearing, self-employed, and Anganwadi workers and staff of the mid-day meal programme. The following Table 5.12 highlights the occupational representation of the respondents.

Table 5.11: Respondent's Occupation

S.No.	*Respondent's Occupation*	*Name of the Village and District*			
		Chinabonala (Karimnagar)	*Diwancheruvu (East Godavari)*	*Taduku (Chittoor)*	*Total Respondents*
1.	Homemaker	9	8	4	21
2.	Daily wage labour	16	11	8	35
3.	Farming	6	7	6	19
4.	Livestock rearing	5	6	11	22
5.	Self employed	14	15	19	48
6.	Anganwadi worker and staff of mid-day meal programme	–	3	2	5
7.	**Total**	**50**	**50**	**50**	**150**

Agriculture constitutes a major occupation in rural Andhra Pradesh, while livestock rearing is considered as an important alternative source of livelihood. Those who do not have landholdings are largely involved in agricultural and allied labour services. Of the 150 surveyed respondents, 21 are homemakers, 35 respondents work as daily-wage labourers, 19 are involved in farming in their own land and 22 respondents are occupied in livestock rearing. Interestingly, a maximum of 48 of the 150 respondents, are engaged in various small-scale business ventures under the self-employment category. Of this 48, different individuals have taken up different occupations, from opening small business enterprises such as photostat shop or a bangle or vegetable store to beedi-rolling or handloom weaving. It is important to note that although these SHG women are involved in various self-employment opportunities, they are yet to become entrepreneurial in order to fetch benefits. It is said that most of the respondents save money out of their self-employment activities, and repay the loan installments. The homemakers, who do not have income sources, depend upon their family to pay the monthly installments.

As far as livestock rearing is concerned, 22 respondents are involved in this livelihood-generating source, of which a maximum of 11 respondents belong to Taduku village of Chittoor district. Thirty-five respondents are involved in agri-and-allied labour services, and maximum of 16 respondents are from Chinabonala village of Karimnagar district. A respondent from Swayam Krushi SHG in Chinabonala village says:

> I have one acre of land, which is infertile. However, we cultivated cotton crop in 2012, but it failed. I had invested the SHG-Bank loan on that crop. To repay the loan, my husband and I work as a daily wage labour. If I get bank loan again, we would like to buy buffalos and start livestock rearing.

Of the 50 respondents, only five are involved in livestock rearing from Chinabonala village. It can be argued from the above finding that these respondents are yet to know the importance of livestock rearing as an important livelihood source.

Table 5.12: Income levels of the respondent

S. No.	*Respondent's Income (monthly)*	*Name of the Village and District*			
		Chinabonala (Karimnagar)	*Diwancheruvu (East Godavari)*	*Taduku (Chittoor)*	*Total Respondents*
1.	1000-2000	15	14	12	41
2.	2001-3000	17	11	18	46
3.	3001-4000	5	7	9	21
4.	4001-5000	4	7	5	16
5.	5000 above		3	2	5
6.	No earnings (housewives)	9	8	4	21
	Total Respondents	**50**	**50**	**50**	**150**

Source: Primary data.

The Table 5.13 represents the income levels of the respondents. It is observed that of the 150 respondents, 41 are earning between Rs 1000-2000 per month, 46 earn between Rs 2001-3000, 21 between Rs 3001-4000, 16 between 4001-5000 and only five respondents earn Rs 5000 and above. Twenty-one respondents those who settled down as homemakers are left with no earnings of their own. Of the five respondents identified above as the Anganwadi workers and staff of the mid-day meal programme, two are working in Anganwadi centres, while the other three work as cook in the mid-day meal programme.

Impact of SBLP model on Poverty Alleviation: Field-Survey Findings

Table 5.13: Year of Join in SHGs

S.No	*Year of Join*	*Name of the Village and District*			
		Chinabonala (Karimnagar)	*Diwancheruvu (East Godavari)*	*Taduku (Chittoor)*	*Total Respondents*
1.	1996-2000	4	6	3	13
2.	2001-2005	6	13	10	29
3.	2006-2010	15	12	14	41
4.	2011-2013	25	19	23	67
	Total Respondents	**50**	**50**	**50**	**150**

Source: Primary data.

Table 5.15 highlights the year in which the respondents joined the SHGs. The success of a SHG may largely depend upon the maturity of a group, its (formal) interaction with the bank, and the number of times loans were received under SBLP model. It is, therefore, pertinent to document the year of joining of the respondent or the period of attachment with an SHG. It is evident from Table 5.15 that 13 respondents (nine per cent) have joined an SHG between 1999-2000. Between these years, the SBLP model formally started operating in Andhra Pradesh. Of the remaining, 29 respondents (19 per cent) joined one or the other SHG between 2001-2005, while 41 respondents (27 per cent) became a part of SHGs between 2006-2010. It could be argued that of the 150 respondents, 83 became part of SHG-bank linkage by 2010. In fact, it is commonly held that beginning with 2004, SHG movement in AP has received a greater recognition, with some of the important women-oriented development and welfare programmes

Table 5.14: Purpose of availing loan from SHG-Bank Linkage from the three villages: Cross Tabulation

S.No.	*Purpose of Availing Loan*	*Total Respondents*		*Purpose of Utilisation*	*Chinabonala*	*Diwancheruvu*	*Taduku*
1.	Daily Consumption	31	54 (36 per cent)	Non-productive purpose	14	8	9
2.	Ceremonies	6			2	3	1
3.	Emergencies	17			8	4	5
4.	Agriculture and agri equip	26	96 (64 per cent)	Productive purpose (Self-employment)	7	14	5
5.	Livestock rearing	22			5	6	11
6.	Photostat centre	2			1	1	-
7.	Tailoring	5			1	2	2
8.	Weaving	7			7	-	-
9.	Kirana Store	5			2	2	1
10.	Bangle store	6			1	1	4
11.	Chat Bandar	3			-	2	1
12.	Vegetable/fruit shop	6			-	3	3
13.	Basket and Broom Making	6			-	4	2
14.	Beedi-making	8			2	-	6
	Total	**150 (100 per cent)**			**50**	**50**	**50**

Source: Primary data.

Table 5.15: Caste profile and Purpose of availing loan by the SHG members: Cross Tabulation

S.No	*Purpose of Availing Loan*	*Total Respondents*	*Purpose of Utilisation*	*SC*	*ST*	*BC*	*Forward Caste*
1.	Daily Consumption	54 (36 per cent)	Non-productive purpose	13	4	11	3
2.	Ceremonies			2	3	1	–
3.	Emergencies			10	2	5	–
4.	Agriculture and agri equip	96 (64 per cent)	Productive purpose (Self-employment)	4	4	8	10
5.	Livestock rearing			6	2	10	4
6.	Photostat centre			–	–	–	2
7.	Tailoring			1	1	3	–
8.	Weaving			–	–	7	–
9.	Kirana Store			–	–	1	4
10.	Bangle store			2	1	1	2
11.	Chat Bandar			-	1	2	–
12.	Vegetable/fruit shop			1	–	3	2
13.	Basket and Broom Making			4	2	–	–
14.	Beedi-making			5	–	3	–
	Total	**150 (100 per cent)**		**48**	**20**	**55**	**27**

Source: Primary data.

Note: Figures in parentheses represent the number of respondents in percentage.

being channelised through SHGs. The GoAP is of the belief that SHGs in AP have a strong institutional mechanism, which is spread across the villages (Ananth and Sabri, 2013). Having realised the manifest potentialities and benefits of SHGs, rural women in AP have shown greater interest in joining SHGs en masse. In fact, the shift to join SHGs was clearly evident in the field areas as well. Table 5.16 shows that of the 150 respondents, 67 joined during the last three years, that is, from 2011 onwards.

The purpose of availing loan under SHG, as highlighted in the Table 5.16, falls under two categories: (i) productive and (ii) non-productive purposes. Based on their nature of work/occupation and usage, all the respondents have been divided broadly into either of this category. Of the 150 respondents, 96 (64 per cent) have availed bank loan and utilised it for productive purposes. As far as particular occupation/business ventures are concerned, the productive purpose category is divided into 11 sub-categories. Of the 96 respondents in this category, 26 (17 per cent) are utilising their loan to purchase agriculture-related equipments and necessities activities such as seeds, fertilisers, and pesticides. Besides, livestock management is considered to be a valuable alternative source of livelihood in the rural areas of Andhra Pradesh with multiple utility. They purchase cows and buffaloes and sell milk in nearby dairy centres. The remaining 48 respondents (32 per cent) in the productive purpose category utilise their loan for various self-employment activities.

The remaining 54 respondents, which compose 36 per cent in the second category, namely non-productive purpose, use the loan amount in neither off-farm nor on-farm activities. Table 5.16 shows that 31 respondents (21 per cent) use their loan for daily consumption, six (four per cent) put their loan amount for performing various social ceremonies and; 17 (11 per cent) for emergency (medical) purposes. Geographically, Chittoor district in Rayalaseema region is largely drought prone and most of the rural population here depends on single crop cultivation. As a result, their incomes are meager. During the off season, the tenant farmers and seasoned labourers of this district are left with no secure income source. The insecurity gets multiplied in case of women. Left without any option, these women are compelled to depend upon the SHG loan to meet their basic daily necessities and other material needs such as constructing houses, performing social

Table 5.16: Income levels of the respondents before and after joining SHGs

S.No.	Purpose of Availing Loan	Total Respondents		Period of attachment with SHG (in Years)	Before Joining SHG	After joining SHG levels	Change in Income
1.	Daily Consumption	31	54	2-3	1500-2000	—	—
2.	Ceremonies	6		2-3	—	—	—
3.	Emergencies	17		1-2	1000-2000	—	—
4.	Agriculture and agri equip	26	96	4-5	1000-1500	2000-3000	1000-1500
5.	Livestock rearing	22		6-7	1000-1500	2500-3000	1500
6.	Photostat centre	2		1-2	—	2500-3000	2500-3000
7.	Tailoring	5		3-4	1000-2000	3000-4000	2000
8.	Weaving	8		5-6	1000-1500	2000-2500	1000
9.	Kirana Store	5		5-6	—	2500-3000	2500-3000
10.	Bangle store	6		3-4	1000-2000	3000-3500	1500-2000
11.	Chat Bandar	3		2-4	1500-2000	2500-3000	1000
12.	Vegetable/fruit shop	4		5-6	1000-1500	1500-2500	1000
13.	Basket and Broom Making	6		5-6	—	1500-2000	1500-2000
14.	Beedi-making	9		3-4	1000-1500	2000-2500	1000
15.	**Total**	**150**		—	—	—	—

Source: Primary data.

ceremonies and meeting medical and other emergencies. It is noteworthy that the dependency on these loans is particularly high in case of women from Schedule Caste (SC) and Schedule Tribe (ST) background.

A respondent belong to ST category from Taduku village in Chittoor district feels that "if we did not have access to loan under SBLP model, we would have had to depend upon private microfinance companies or conventional moneylenders in the villages to meet the financial needs, who invariably charge high interest rates." From these responses, two inferences can be drawn. First, the basic purpose of obtaining loan under SBLP model, theoretically, is to encourage rural women to start any kind of self-employment activity. However, as the case has often been, most women use their loan for non-productive purposes such as to meet their daily requirements. Second, considering the exploitation at the hands of conventional moneylenders and other informal lending sources, it is comparatively safe for the (poor) women to meet their financial needs with the help of SBLP loan rather than through informal credit facilitators. On the whole, this argument underlines the need of subsidized credit by the poor women to meet their financial needs as well as for self-employment generation.

Table 5.17 is important for a number of reasons as it provides cross-tabulation between caste profile and purpose of availing bank loan by the SHG members. In other words, it provides an insight into how different caste groups utilise the subsidized loan, made available under the SBLP model, and how caste dynamics play a significant role in choosing an income-generating activity. As mentioned before, the purpose of availing bank loan can be divided into broadly two categories, with the respondents falling into either of the two according to the nature of their work/occupation and the purpose of using the loan. Table 5.17 primarily identifies the purpose of availing bank loan by the selected SHG members who come from different ladders of social hierarchy such as SCs, STs, BCs and Forward Castes in order to understand the correlation between caste and purpose of availing loan.

Among all the surveyed SHG members, the respondents who belong to BC community (55 respondents, 37 per cent) are high in number as compared to the other three categories. Among the 55 SHG members, eight use loan for buying agricultural equipment and for other working expenses relating to cultivation, while 10 prefer to use loan for livestock rearing. Of the remaining, 20 members use loan in various income-generating activities. Among the SC community, four SHG members opt to use loan for buying agricultural equipment and other working expenses in relation to cultivation, while six of them use loan for livestock management, with remaining 13 members use loan to start various income-generating activities.

The figures in the Table 5.17 also reveals that using bank loan for the consumption purpose is high in case of SCs (13 respondents) and BCs (11 respondents) members. This is largely due to the fact that a predominant portion of wage labour comes from these social classes. Some of the SHG women hand over their borrowed loan to the male member of their family. If they use it for the financial upliftment of their families, it could be seen as a positive sign. Conversely, however, if the loan amount is spent for consumption purpose, then they confront severe difficulties at the time of repayment.

As mentioned before, of the 150 respondents, 27 belong to Forward Caste. Of these, 10 members use loan for buying agricultural equipments and other working expenses in relation to cultivation, while 4 members use it for livestock rearing. The remaining 10 respondents avail loan to start various income-generating activities. Interestingly, only 3 respondents use loan for consumption purpose. It shows that of the 27 respondents from the OC community, 24 members are using their loan for productive purpose, which increases their income levels. The basic reason for such investment is that most of the SHG members of this community possess landholdings ranging from 1 to 5 acres and above. Of the 150 respondents, 20 (13 per cent) represent ST community. Of these, only four respondents use loan for buying agricultural equipment and other working expenses in relation to cultivation, four for livestock rearing, and five members to start various income-generating activities. The remaining nine respondents use their borrowed amount on non-productive purposes.

Table 5.18 explains the income levels of the surveyed respondents before and after joining SHG, and accordingly identifies the manifestly improved income levels. As already discussed, the year of attachment of the respondent with a SHG and number of times loan received by a member through bank influence the nature of occupation and income levels of a respondent. Table 5.18 is divided along the four themes: (i) purpose of availing loan, (ii) period of attachment with a SHG, (iii) income levels of the respondents before and after joining SHG and (iv) monthly change in income levels of the respondents. As mentioned in previous tables, most of the respondents who have remained homemakers and work as wage labourers in agricultural and allied services utilise their loan amount for non-productive purposes such as daily consumption, performing social ceremonies and meeting emergencies. It could be observed that these respondents did not show any progress in their income levels even after joining SHGs.

However, the respondents using their loan for productive purposes such as agriculture related activities, livestock rearing, and various self-employment activities show a steady progress in their income earnings after joining SHGs. A Forward Caste respondent from Diwancheruvu village in East Godavari district observes:

> I borrowed Rs 10000 from the SHG Bank linkage and added another Rs 10000 with which I purchased an iron plough. We offer that equipment on rent for two or three days to other farmers who do not have the similar equipment for which we charge Rs 150-200 per day depending upon the demand. On an average, we earn Rs 1500-2000 per month as a rent during the work seasons. However, this income drastically falls during off-season.

As far as the livestock management is concerned, 22 respondents utilise their amount in purchasing cows and buffaloes. The milk produced thereof is sold in the nearby dairy centres. Of the 22 respondents, 11 members belong to Taduku village of Chittoor district. It was found that income earning through livestock rearing is most preferable option for most of the SHG members.

Of the various self-employment activities, tailoring seems to be the most rewarding income generating business scheme, as the respondents show progress in their income levels after joining SHG. These respondents, after joining SHGs and opening tailoring outlets, were in a position to earn Rs 3000-4000 per month, which was only Rs 1000-2000 before starting the tailoring shop. Interestingly, they joined SHGs some 5-6 years ago, which indicates that they have received loan amount at least three-four times. The second most preferable option under self-employment activity appears to be *chat bandars*. On an average, they earn Rs 2500-3000 per month. Few respondents who have opened *chat bandars* testify this manifest improvement in their income levels. The owner of one such *chat bandar*, a widow from Diwancheruvu village proclaims:

> I borrowed Rs 20000 from VO two years ago, added my own personal savings of Rs 10000, and started a *chat bandar* in my village. On an average, I earn Rs 2500-3000 per month. I have repaid the borrowed amount recently.

This finding highlights an interesting dimension of women empowerment, where the women, through the loan borrowed under SBLP model, is now in a position to run *chat bandars*. However, the above respondent is also quick to point out the difficulties in running her *chat bandar*. She has to work from three to eight in the evening and some-times even till nine in the night as the business runs only in the evening or night time. Working in such odd timing hours definitely is a daunting task for women as it may give rise to safety and security issues. Besides, they have to take care of their daily chores and other household responsibilities as well. Some of the women respondents are also involved in handloom weaving, basket making, beedi-rolling and running vegetable/fruit shop. These categories of income-generating ventures also show progress in their income levels. These observations could be interpreted to imply that the increased income levels of the respondents have considerable impact on their living standards and it certainly affects household income. The following Table 5.19 explains the contribution of their income to the family expenditure, which influences the socio-economic conditions of the family.

Table 5.17: Contributions to Family Expenditure

S.No	*Contribution to Family Expenditure*	*Total Number of Respondents who utilise credit for productive purpose (N=96)*
1.	Basic Food	31
2.	Children's Education	20
3.	Buying electronic goods	15
4.	Health Care	12
5.	Constructing house	7
6.	Repaying old debts	11

Source: Primary data.

Table 5.19 demonstrates the contributions of SHG women who utilise the loan amount for productive purpose from the three villages. It is found that of the 96 respondents, 31 members (32 per cent) contribute their income for purchasing food items, 20 members (21 per cent) contribute their earnings for children's education, and 13 members (15.5 per cent) contribute their income for purchasing electronic goods. 12 respondents (12.5 per cent) who contribute their income for healthcare purpose, 7 (7 per cent) for constructing houses and 11 members (11 per cent) use it for repaying old debts. One respondent, Padmavathi, aged 36 years, from Sai Laxmi SHG of Deewancheruvu village in the East Godavari district says,

> We have one acre of land and we have added another two acres on tenant basis. In addition, we have also bought two buffaloes. We have borrowed Rs 30000 from SHG federation and Rs 20000 from SHG under three per cent interest rates. Now we are able to do farming as well as cattle rearing. I sell three liters of milk everyday and earn Rs 2500-3000 per month. Gradually, I am also repaying the debt amount of Rs 50000. With the savings, my children are able to study in English medium school.

The above observation shows that with the help of savings from income-generating activity, the respondent is able to send her children to an English medium school. Another respondent from Jagruthi SHG of Taduku village in Chittoor district, says:

> I have borrowed Rs 25000 from VO and used the loan for constructing the house. My husband and I work as daily wage labourers. With the income, I used to save Rs 500-700 per month and repay the loan installment. Though we have constructed house with the help of loan amount and other sources, without regular income source, I have been facing difficulty in repaying the borrowed amount in regular installments.

Repaying old debts also appeared as a common phenomenon in most of the households. In this study, 11 respondents use their surplus income in repaying their old debts. The respondents who borrowed loans from the private microfinance sources are often unable to repay their weekly installments. In order to repay these installments, they were compelled to depend upon other financial sources. In fact, it has become one of the basic causes for the alleged microfinance crisis in

Table 5.18: Change in Socio-Economic conditions of the respondents after joining SHG in all the three villages: Respondents' Perceptions

S.No.	*Indicators for change in Socio-economic conditions*	*Highly preferred (Very good)*	*Preferred (Good)*	*Least Preferred (Average)*	*Not considered (No idea)*	*N=150 (100 per cent)*
1.	Social mobility	31 (20.6)	75 (50)	24 (16)	20 (13.3)	150 (100)
2.	Recognition in the family	36 (24)	69 (46)	28 (19)	17 (11)	150 (100)
3.	Construction of house through Indiramma housing loan	15 (10)	57 (38)	42 (28)	36 (24)	150 (100)
4.	Access to health services	18 (12)	50 (32)	66 (44)	16 (10.6)	150 (100)
5.	Access to credit sources	35 (23.3)	81 (54)	23 (15)	11 (7)	150 (100)
6.	Increase in Income levels	24 (19)	75 (50)	31 (20.6)	20 (13.3)	150 (100)
7.	Financial awareness	16 (10.6)	41 (27.3)	79 (52.6)	14 (9)	150 (100)
8.	Awareness Levels on Markets	22 (14.6)	69 (46)	40 (26.6)	19 (12.6)	150 (100)
9.	Awareness and Participation in developmental programmes and other political activities at gram panchayat level	16 (10.6)	77 (51.3)	42 (23)	17 (11)	150 (100)
10.	Encouraging children's education	21 (14)	82 (54.6)	37 (24.6)	10 (7)	150 (100)
11.	Cumulative Percentage	15.6 per cent	45 per cent	27.4 per cent	12 per cent	100 per cent

Source: Primary data.

Note: Figures in parentheses represent the number of respondents in percentage.

Andhra Pradesh. Various studies point out that most of the MFI borrowers often used their loan to buy luxurious and other electronic goods rather than utilising it on some productive purpose. At the time of repayment, they were left with no income and were unable to repay the loan amount, which entrapped them in usurious debt trap (Nair, 2011 and SERP report, 2013).

From Table 5.20, it is evident that of the 150 respondents, half of the respondents' preference on various social indicators such as social mobility, recognition in the family, access to health and encouraging children's education are preferable. In other words, this section show progress in the above mentioned indicators. As far as access to health facilities is concerned, 18 respondents show high preference, 50 show preference, 66 show least preference and the remaining 16 do not show any interest at all.

As far as the economic indicators are concerned, SHG women are lagging behind on financial awareness. Of the 150 respondents, 79 show least preference in various financial matters. In fact, financial awareness of the rural poor has become a critical issue in ensuring financial inclusion. Eighty-one respondents, however, express their satisfaction in accessing credit source from bank, while 75 show progress on their improved income levels. These people largely utilise their loans for productive purposes.

As far as participation of the SHG respondents in various developmental programmes and other political activities at the gram panchayat level is concerned, Amartya Sen's theory of development is very much applicable. According to Sen (2000), 'political freedom', that is the opportunity of the people, particularly women to participate in various political affairs and other developmental programmes, and to cast vote of their own choice ensures accountability in the political system. During the field survey, it was found that of the 150 respondents, 77 express their interest in participating various developmental activities organised at the village level. The participation of women, even at the mandal level is one of the encouraging trends that has come to mark the panchayat meetings.

It can be argued that given the opportunity, women are capable of participating in various political matters at different levels. In fact, when women participate in this meetings as a group, it enhance their confidence and encourage them to participate in a full-fledged manner. This study draws insights from Sen's theory of development in order to understand how SHGs, as a group approach and collective participative mechanism, promote some of the human capabilities listed by Sen and Nussbaum in the process of socio-economic and political development of women.

Drawbacks of SBLP Model and SHG Functioning: Respondents' Perceptions

Despite its potential contributions, the SHG-Bank Linkage Programme suffers from certain limitations. The manifest challenges to the functioning of SBLP model operate from both ends, that of bank officials as well as SHG members. Of the 150 respondents surveyed, 141 express their dissatisfaction in the functioning of SHG. Forty-three respondents (29 per cent) complain that there is no mutual understanding within the group, and 19 (13 per cent) are unhappy at the behaviour of their president. For some in this group, the president is "not so cooperative" in providing information regarding loan and other necessary financial services. Twenty-two (15 per cent) respondents complain about the distribution of the loan. They are of the view that the loan distribution is not transparent. The participation of some respondents was, in some cases, found to be completely lacking. An SC respondent from Chinabonala village expresses her inability to participate in the meetings as: "I seldom participate in the group meetings as nobody bothers about my presence or absence. Even when I do not turn up for the meetings, nobody enquires about my absence in the next meeting." Interestingly, in some SHGs, the group president's spouse or any other male member of her family is involved in the process of receiving the loan amount from the bank and disbursing it to the group members. Such intrusion severely hinders the functioning of the SHGs and severe the relations among the group members. Besides, there is a lot of scope for engaging in fraudulent ways in loan disbursement.

The above problems regarding the functioning of SHG point to the poor governance of the group meetings and lack of effective leadership that evidently have a negative impact on the functioning and sustenance of a group. In view of this, the success or failure of an SHG largely depends on its effective governance. In order to address the alleged anomalies in the functioning of SHGs, the literature on the governance of SHGs point out ways to make foolproof. A study by Suguna (2006) emphasises that effective and committed leadership, active participation of the group members on decision-making, self-discipline of the group members and transparency in group-operations are key determining factors for successful functioning a SHG. Reddy and Sandeep (2005) in their study argue that a strong governance system is needed to ensure accountability in disbursing loans, regular repayments and transparency in bookkeeping. Besides, they are of the view that good relations with bank officials, regular repayments by the group members, problem solving and cooperative approach are also important factors for an effective governance of an SHG. One of the serious impediments in the functioning of the SHGs is the manifest lack of ownership and dynamism of the members because of the stagnant leadership in the SHGs, VOs and even MMSs.

Figure 5.11: Reasons for dependency of SHG women on MFIs and other informal sources

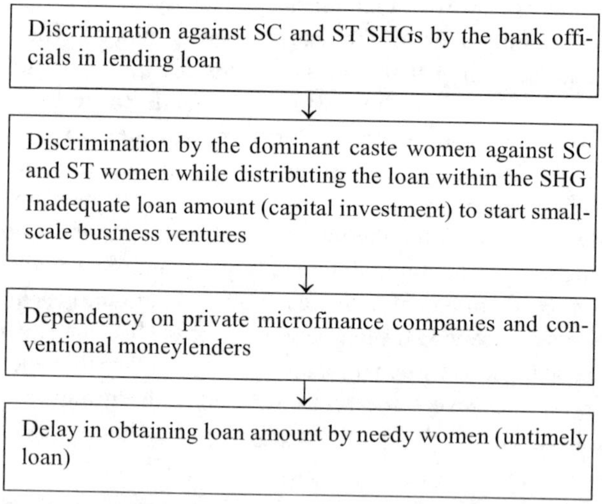

A second set of problems relates to the disbursement of loans. It was found, during the course of study, that some of the SHG women are dissatisfied with the mechanism of loan disbursal. Around 19 respondents (13 per cent) complain about the untimely disbursal of loans, while 11 (7 per cent) from SC and ST communities allege that bank officials often give first preference to the SHGs of the predominant castes in disbursing loans rather than on the basis of the maturity of the group. This finding is corroborated by the observation made by Simanowitz and Walter (2003) who argue that bank loans usually do not reach the poorest strata who are in the urgent need of financial assistance. The reason for such financial exclusion of these sections is alleged to be the discrimination practiced by the dominant caste SHG women as well as by the bank officials.

The third set of arguments relates to SHG vis-à-vis entrepreneurship development. The literature on this subject claims that SHGs are being promoted as a platform for the development of entrepreneurship qualities, and further to start various innovative small-scale business ventures (Nawaz, 2009; and Johnson and Sushmita, 2010). The findings from the field, however, negate this claim, and in fact, point to the negative results in relation to entrepreneurship development. Based on field observations, it could be argued that the major problem of the SHG borrowers is not only small and untimely loans but also lack of entrepreneurial and management skills to initiate and sustain various business undertakings. A respondent, president of Dhanalaxmi SHG from Diwancheruvu village observes:

> We (SHG women) merely receive subsidized loan amount from the banks. However, the bank officials never provide any kind of entrepreneurial training or management skills to start any small-scale business venture. In fact, they hardly bother whether the given loan amount is utilised for productive development or consumption purpose by the SHG women.

In view of the above, Chowdhury (2009) point out the factors that are crucial for making credit more productive, of which the most important is recipient's entrepreneurial skills. Another study by Mahajan (2005) adds some other inputs that are crucial in making credit more worthy such as identification of livelihood opportunities, selection and motivation of the rural women, business and technical training, establishing of market linkages, among others. Drawing insights from both the field and existing literature it could be argued that just providing subsidized credit is not sufficient to bring desired change. It must, alongside, offer adequate and timely credit with effective training programmes on entrepreneurial skills and business management.

The fourth set of arguments relates to the viability of on-farm goods and its purchasing value in the market. It is observed that of the 150 respondents only 32 women utilise their loan amount for producing non-farm goods. They usually depend upon basket-making, broom-making, mat weaving, beedi rolling, bangle store and others. However, the question is how far these non-farm goods have a reasonable sale value in the market, how far these goods will sustain in the longer run, and to what extent these goods compete with the plastic goods, which are available in low prices compared with some of these goods? A study by Madheswaran and Dhamadhikary (2001) claims that the non-farm goods made by the rural women and brought to the urban areas hardly meet the standards of the urban market, thereby affecting their incomes and in turn their capacities to repay the loans. The authors further suggest the need for entrepreneurial training and business skills for the borrowers who obtain loan to start small-scale business firms. The arguments underline the fact that despite providing investment capital either by SBLP model or MFI model, the poor, because of lack of access to entrepreneurial training and business skills, continue to be entrapped in poverty as they are unable to reap profits from their business ventures.

Another set of arguments offer bankers' perceptions of SHGs. In an interview, the bank manager of the State Bank of Hyderabad (SBH), Siricilla branch of Karimnagar district, says, "though we provide low subsidized loan to the SHGs, the repayment of some of the SHGs are not regular and some of them are using loans largely for consumption purpose. By the time of repayment, they usually drop out from SHG and migrate to nearby towns." Another banker, from State Bank of Hyderabad (SBH) Diwancheruvu branch in East Godavari district says, "during the loan sanction period, we experience some kind of domination by the politically influenced SHGs, which is not a good sign for the sustenance of SBLP model. These groups are in the forefront of receiving the loan amount as compared with the other SHGs." The above two observations identify the problems involved in sanctioning the loans by the banks. These include, in particular, irregular repayments, mismanagement in book-keeping, mishandling of loans, using loans for non-productive purposes and political influence of some of the SHGs create distrust among the bankers, which in turn leads to delay in sanctioning loans to the SHGs.

The following section attempts to discuss and analyse another important model of microfinance that has become popular as microfinance institution (MFI) model. In fact, it addresses the second hypothesis of the study, that is, the easy accessibility of microcredit may led to over dependency on the MFIs that lead to serious repercussions for the rural poor. The observations drawn are from the selected SHG women respondents who previously had borrowed loan from MFIs. The section below focuses primarily on some of the important aspects such as the loan size borrowed from MFIs, rate of interest, purpose of borrowing, business advice and entrepreneurial training for MFI borrowers, harassment by the MFI staff and so on. It provides an understanding on functional aspects of MFIs and identifies the reasons for microfinance crisis in Andhra Pradesh and state's intervention in the aftermath of the crisis.

Key Observations on Microfinance Institution (MFI) Model

Apart from the SBLP model, MFIs are considered as good alternative channels for disbursing microfinance to the rural poor. By providing microfinance, these institutions also encourage them to start various small-scale business ventures along with business advice and entrepreneurial training. It is acknowledged that MFIs contribute in financial deepening and remain an important segment of the Indian financial market (Khan, 2012). In recent times, however, there have been quite a few contentious issues have arisen relating to governance and ethics of organising business by some MFIs. The collapse of the microfinance industry in Andhra Pradesh in particular has opened space for practitioners, academicians and policy-makers to re-examine the contribution of MFIs. The present field survey on the impact of microfinance models on poverty alleviation and financial inclusion in rural Andhra Pradesh attempts to draw key observations regarding the functioning of a few MFIs.

Limitation of the Study

During the field study, it was observed that the crisis that has led to suicides of several borrowers from MFIs has dictated a new Act puts many restrictions on the way that the MFIs function. As a result, it is found that no MFI was operating in the selected districts and all the transactions of these institutions have come to a halt in Andhra Pradesh immediately after passing of the Andhra Pradesh Microfinance Institutions (Regulation of Money Lending) Act, 2010. In order to elicit important information regarding MFI functioning and its financial transactions, thus study draws upon the selected SHG respondents (within the selected sample), who had previously borrowed from the MFIs. The researcher found it difficult to assess the impact of MFI borrowings on poverty alleviation from the sample frame, because these respondents are already members of SHG and the productive transformation that they witness in the current context might be attributed to their loans being received under SBLP model. The researcher, however, received significant inputs from the respondents related to issues such as the MFIs operational structure, rate of interest, purpose of lending, reasons for suicides, and other necessary information. This first-hand information helped the researcher to draw some important observations on the functioning of MFIs in Andhra Pradesh. The significant proportion, of about 71 per cent of respondents, has previously borrowed from MFIs. Therefore, the analysis related to MFI functioning here is restricted to the inputs received from 71 per cent or 106 members of the total sample. Table 5.21 provides data related to the responses of the total respondents in relation to their experience with MFIs. Of the 150 selected SHG members, 106 members were previously borrowed from MFIs.

Table 5.19: Have you been a client of any MFI previously?

S.No	*Benefits through Government Schemes*	*Name of the Village and District*			
		Chinabonala (Karimnagar)	*Diwancheruvu (East Godavari)*	*Taduku (Chittoor)*	*Total*
1.	Yes	38 (76)	35 (70)	33 (66)	106 (71)
2.	No	8 (16)	10 (20)	7 (14)	25 (16.5)
3.	No idea	4 (8)	5(10)	10 (20)	19 (12.5)
	Total Respondents	**50 (100)**	**50 (100)**	**50 (100)**	**150 (100)**

Note: Figures in parentheses represent the number of respondents in percentage.

It is interesting to note that despite large borrowings from SHG-bank linkage model, SHG women relied upon private microfinance business companies (MFIs). This is an unexplained paradox of microfinance sector in Andhra Pradesh. The recent SERP report (2012) argues that the poor SHG women were being targeted for lending money by the MFIs with an intention to make profits. This is largely supported by the fact that: SHG women have always shown a strong track record of repayments, and it results in maximising profits for MFIs from large borrowings and repayments on higher rates of interest. The report further alleges that MFI model mainly revolves around coercive recovery practice in order to ensure 100 per cent repayments irrespective of the borrower's socio-economic status. It is learned that MFIs such as Swayam Krishi Sangam (SKS), Spandana, Sphoorthy Financial Ltd, Share, L&T Finance Ltd, Amma NGO and Bhartiya Samruddhi were the major operators before the crisis. Table 5.22 also shows that of the 150 respondents, 25 (16.5 per cent) did not borrow money from any MFI. The remaining 19 respondents (12.5 per cent) were not familiar with MFIs.

Table 5.20: Caste and village-wise MFI borrowers: Cross tabulation

S.No	Caste	*Name of the Village and District*			
		Chinabonala (Karimnagar)	*Diwancheruvu (East Godavari)*	*Taduku (Chittoor)*	*Total*
1.	SC	13 (32)	11 (30)	10 (36)	34 (32)
2.	ST	6 (15)	3 (8)	2 (7)	11 (10)
3.	BC	17 (41)	14 (38)	12 (43)	43 (41)
4.	OC	5 (12)	9 (24)	4 (14)	18 (17)
	Total	**41 (100)**	**37 (100)**	**28 (100)**	**106 (100)**

Table 5.22 represents the caste and village-wise respondents of the MFI borrowers from the three villages. Of the 106 respondents, 34 belong to SC community, 11 belong to ST community, 43 belong to BC community and 18 belong to Forward Caste community. These figures show that the MFI borrowers were high among BC community followed by SC community. During the focus group discussion, it was stated that the loan amount which they usually get from the bank is neither sufficient to start any self-employment activity nor for livestock rearing, which further forced them to depend upon other external sources. The MFIs, with simple paper work and doorstep delivery appeared handy at this juncture. The village level data reveals that

Chinabonala village of Karimnagar has reported high MFI borrowings. It is because, of the 50 respondents, 16 work as daily wage labourers and 9 remain as homemakers (see table 5.12). Since they do not have any other income-source, they were compelled to borrow money from other sources for diverse needs. Siricilla is a nearby town for Chinabonala village where SKS, Spandana and Sharemula were some of the MFIS were active before the crisis.

Table 5.21: Loan size borrowed from MFIs

S.No	*How much do they lend to a client*	*Respondents from the three villages*
1.	10000-20000	16
2.	20001-30000	31
3.	30001-40000	22
4.	40001-50000	12
5.	50000 above	9
6.	No idea	16
7.	**Total Respondents who had borrowed from MFIs**	**106**

Table 5.23 attempts to find the size of the loan provided by the MFIs for rural communities in order to meet their productive and non-productive needs. Of the 106 respondents, 9 are reported to receive a high amount of Rs 50000 or above followed by 12 who claimed to receive between Rs 40001-50000. Among the other respondents, 16 say that they received amount ranging from Rs 10000-20000, 22 say between Rs 30001-40000. Thirty-two per cent stated that they received loan amount between Rs 20001-30000. From the table 5.23 it is inferred that the average loan amount provided by any MFI was Rs 20000-40000 and it went beyond Rs 50000 and above, in some exceptional cases. As stated, MFI borrowings in this sample are in addition to the borrowings from SHGs. Such high aspirations for credit clearly reflect the financial need of the rural poor households. As is argued by the SERP report (2013) sometimes the huge lending (loan size) by the MFIs had exceeded the average annual income of the poor borrowers, which made difficult for them to repay the borrowed amount. This situation further put them into the vicious cycle of a debt trap. During

the focus group discussions, it was found that these private microfinance actors had lent money for both as a 'group' (these groups are called as Joint Liability Group) as well as 'individuals'. MFIs employed collateral business technique, in which the group members used to provide surety to other members of a particular group. At the individual level, these institutions had considered the client's movable (livestock, ornaments and furniture, among others) and immovable property (land, house and so on) as a surety and provided the loan amount. The following Table 5.24 explains the rate of interest and purpose of lending by MFIs.

Table 5.22: Rate of Interest charged by the MFIs

S.No	*Rate of Interest*	*Respondents from the three villages*
1.	16-20 per cent	11 (10)
2.	21-25 per cent	17(16)
3.	26-30 per cent	23(22)
4.	30 per cent above	10 (9)
5.	No idea	45 (43)
	Total Respondents	**106 (100)**

During the crisis, some of the MFIs such as SKS, Spandana, Share and Sphoorthy have been openly criticised by government of Andhra Pradesh, public sector banks and microfinance experts; as these institutions charged exorbitant interest rates and held with predatory collection practices that led to distress deaths by the MFI borrowers in the state. With the help of the lessons learned from the crisis, Andhra Pradesh Microfinance Institution (Regulation of Money Lending) Act (2010) asserts that the MFIs had followed self-regulatory methods in order to fix the interest rates, ignoring the RBI guidelines. In a similar vein, while highlighting the interest rates charged by the public sector banks, SERP report (2011) argues that the interest rates of the banks normally stands between 9-11 per cent per annum for the SHG members under SBLP model, which is very low in comparison with the MFIs. While stating the reasons behind MFI's high interest rates, the report emphasises that some of these institutions imposed extra charges like transaction costs, the cost of documents, and service charges for the field staff.

Table 5.24, it is evident that of the 106 respondents, 11 state that the interest rates range between 16-20 per cent per annum, 17 state 21-25 per cent per annum, while 23 say 26-30 per cent per annum and 10 respondents say 30 per cent above per annum. As far as the repayment period is concerned, the respondents express that these institutions follow weekly repayment method for a total of 50 weeks in a year block. Interestingly, of the 106 respondents, 45 of them were not aware of the interest rates charged by the MFIs. This shows the lack of awareness of the borrowers about the interest rates charged by various MFIs. They had borrowed loan amount from these institutions without even knowing the minimum interest rates. Taking advantage of this scenario, MFIs charged them heavily, which became one of the main reasons for the collapse of the private microfinance industry in Andhra Pradesh. Access to adequate credit with affordable price is very important for the poor to start any small-scale business firm and further to make repayments in time. With the private microfinance institutions, however, the problem of high interest rates and forced recovery practices proved counterproductive, which further resulted in weakening the socio-economic conditions of the poor borrowers. The below Table 5.25 illustrates the purpose of borrowing loan from the MFIs.

The functioning of a financial institution that lends to the poor may be assessed by how the loan amount has been utilised by the borrowers. As far as MFIs are concerned, scholars argue that majority of the loans received by the MFI borrowers use for non-productive or consumption purpose and proportionately a nominal percentage of the borrowers use it for small-scale business ventures (Basu and Srivastava, 2005; Sylendra, 2010; Khan, 2012; and SERP report, 2013). From Table 5.25, of the 106 respondents, 33 used the loan for consumption/ daily needs purpose, 15 used the loan for buying agricultural equipments, four used for livestock rearing and 27 used the loan for small-scale business. Of the remaining 27 respondents, 25 used the loan for meeting emergencies and performing social ceremonies, and two of them used the loan for other purpose such as construction of house and repaying the old debts. In other words, of the 106 respondents, 45 per cent used the loan for productive purposes and the

Table 5.23: Purpose of borrowing from MFIs

S.No	*Name of the training programme*	*Name of the Village and District*			
		Chinabonala (Karimnagar)	*Diwancheruvu (East Godavari)*	*Taduku (Chittoor)*	*Total*
1.	Consumption/daily needs	14 (34)	11 (30)	8 (28)	33 (31)
2.	To buy agricultural equipment	4 (10)	5 (13)	6 (21)	15 (14)
3.	Livestock rearing	—	4 (11)	—	4 (4)
4.	Working capital for business	11 (27)	9 (24)	7 (25)	27 (25)
5.	Emergencies/Ceremonies	12 (29)	8 (22)	5 (19)	25 (23.5)
6.	Others	—	—	2 (7)	2 (1.5)
	Total Respondents	**41 (100)**	**37 (35)**	**28 (100)**	**106 (100)**

rest of them for non-productive purposes. As far as village-wise is concerned, a maximum of 41 respondents who have approached MFIs were from Chinabonala village of Karimnagar district followed by Diwancheruvu village of East Godavari district (37 respondents) and Taduku village of Chittoor district (28 respondents). Whereas in SHG-Bank Linkage Programme (SBLP) model, of the 150 respondents, 96 (64 per cent) availed bank loan and utilised it for productive purposes, the remaining 54 respondents (36 per cent) used it for non-productive purposes. In other words, the respondents who utilised the loan for productive purpose is 64 per cent in SBLP model, whereas it is 45 per cent in MFI model. In a similar vein, the respondents who used the loan for non-productive purposes is 36 per cent in SBLP model, whereas it is 55 per cent in MFI model. These figures indicate that those availing loan from SBLP model is apparently investing it in productive purpose as compared to the MFI wherein non-productive usage is high.

Table 5.24: Business Advice and Entrepreneurial Training for MFIs borrowers

Have you received any business advice and entrepreneurial training from your lending institution?	Yes	No	Total Respondents
	27 (24.5)	79 (74.5)	106 (100)

Source: Primary data.

Note: Figures in parentheses represent the number of respondents in percentage.

Providing business advice and entrepreneurial training for their clients is one of the main strategies of MFIs as it attracts the borrowers to receive loan from the MFIs and start small-scale business activities. In fact, the necessary business advice and entrepreneurial training significantly help the borrowers to use their loan amount for productive purpose. The field observations show that only 27 respondents have received some kind of business advice such as what kind of business activity is appropriate according to the nature of the place and competence of the person, skill development programmes for tailoring and embroidery. The remaining 79 respondents could not receive any kind of business advice and entrepreneurial training, as they highlighted that the staff of the MFIs have not spoken about this.

Table 5.25: Have you ever faced any harassment by the MFI staff

S.No.	*Have you faced any harassment by the MFI staff as for repayment is concerned*	*Respondents from the three villages*
1.	Yes	44 (41.5)
2.	No	25 (23.5)
3.	No idea	37 (35)
	Total Respondents	**106 (100)**

Note: Figures in parentheses represent the number of respondents in percentage.

As mentioned, in the aftermath of microfinance crisis in Andhra Pradesh (AP), the MFIs were questioned for illicit and unethical recovery methods practiced by their agents. The field survey findings show that the SHG women as Joint Liability Group (JLG) members had faced pressure from the MFI field agents in case of loan default. From Table 5.27 it is evident that of the 106 respondents, 44 of them faced harassment by the MFI agents in various types. In a focus group discussion with the SHG respondents in Taduku village of Chittoor district say that they (MFI borrowers) have faced harassment by the staff such as using abusive language, confiscating movable assets, and threatened to file a complaint in the police station in case of loan default, among others. The forced recovery practices employed by the MFI agents have shown an adverse effect on the poor borrowers, and in some places, these repercussions led to distress deaths by the MFI borrowers in AP. According to a fact-finding report by the Gender Unit of Society for Elimination of Rural Poverty (SERP) (2012), since 2008 onwards 54 people have committed suicides due to the high interest rates and coercive recovery methods practiced by the MFIs in AP.

Microfinance Crisis in Andhra Pradesh: Governance Issues and State Intervention

The success of any policy or programme depends on the legal and regulatory frameworks and the government's intervention in various phases (Priya Basu, 2005:1753). In the context of microfinance models, the SBLP is being run under state control. However, the government has not adequately controlled the institutions like MFIs and this has caused a tremendous setback in achieving the goals and objectives of the programme. The growth of these institutions at a frantic pace led to a phenomenal crisis even in March 2006 in Andhra Pradesh. The district authorities in the state had closed down about 50 branches of two major MFIs in Krishna district. There are three major allegations against the MFIs that came up during the crisis: (i) MFIs are collecting exorbitant interest rates. Further, MFIs lack transparency regarding their interest rate practices, which helps them to transfer various costs on the borrowers; (ii) MFIs are resorting to unethical ways of recovering loans by confiscating title deeds, using intimidation and abusive language; and (iii) MFIs are aggressively poaching from government and banks to capture their borrowers. Despite this incident, there was no proper action taken against the illicit practices of MFIs. Further, it is also said that some of these institutions are not familiar with the concept of MFIs, which made the rural poor borrow credit from multiple sources (Shylendra, 2008:1959).

In an interview with a key respondent, the SBI bank manager of Siricilla branch, some important observations were made regarding the functioning of MFIs in Siricilla Mandal of Karimnagar district. He says that there were three MFIs worked in Siricilla Mandal. Those are (i) Sharemula, (ii) Swayam Krushi Sangam (SKS) and (iii) Spandana. Due to exorbitant interest rates and coercive recovery practices, five MFI borrowers committed suicide in September 28, 2010. This incident forced the government to ban all the MFIs for six months. Since then there were no transactions of MFIs in Siricilla Mandal. Moreover, with the orders of AP MFIs (Regulation of Money Lending Act) 2010, all the MFIs have shut down. While talking about the operations of MFIs, he adds that the MFI agents used to take the sign of the MFI borrowers on insurance papers during the time of credit delivery, therefore, if they die or commit suicide, the amount, which the victim has borrowed, will be repaid by the bank. This is one of the reasons for the staff of the MFI harassing the borrowers for 100 per cent repayment. The suicide incident led the government to issue a special package of Rs 600 crore to the MFI borrowers and 14 SHGs who have borrowed from MFIs in Siricilla Mandal. Under the special package called as "Total Financial Assistance" scheme, all the MFI borrowers of this mandal have got some monitory compensation, which is disbursed by the government officials. With this financial assistance, the indebted

MFI borrowers repaid the debt loan. Since then, most of these people, including weavers and women have opened bank accounts and started taking loans from the Bank in the name of different schemes.

As a part of state intervention, in order to reduce the interest burden on the rural poor and to improve the profitability of SHGs, the Government of Andhra Pradesh has launched 'Sthreenidhi' scheme, with a corpus fund of Rs 1,000 crore on 15th September, 2012. This scheme has been claimed as an alternative to MFIs offering loans to SHGs at nominal interest rates. The main objectives of the Sthreenidhi scheme are to supplement credit to SHG members to meet financial exigencies and short-term loans for business purposes and to ensure timely credit availability of loans, preferably within 48 hours from the date of request for loan. Once the SHG member makes a loan request, the SHG scrutinises the member's request with reference to income-generating activity proposed, existing income and expenditure, and estimated income from proposed activity. If the SHG is satisfied with the member's eligibility, proposed income-generating activity, repaying capacity; then the SHG submits the loan application to VO for sanctioning the loan. The rate of interest charged under Sthreenidhi scheme is 14 per cent per annum (SERP report, 2013).

Andhra Pradesh Microfinance Institutions (Regulation of Money Lending) Act, 2010

The Andhra Pradesh Microfinance Institutions (Regulation of Money Lending) Act, 2010 primarily aims at protecting the very concept of SHG and the interest of the SHG members who are being trapped in a vicious debt cycle due to multiple lending by various MFIs. The ordinance became an Act with the approval of both the Houses of Andhra Pradesh Legislative Assembly in 2010. The Act provides stringent regulations for the operation of financial activities and stipulates a model code of financial ethics to the MFIs. According to this Act (2010), every MFI operating in the State is required to register at the registration authority in rural and urban areas and the MFIs operating in more than one district need to file separate applications for registration in each district. The Act aims at regulating and monitoring the functioning of MFIs in the state by imposing a ceiling on interest rates. It also emphasises that no MFI shall levy any charge or impose any cost on the borrowers except the interest rate. Further, to contain unethical financial practices, this Act bounds the registering authorities to serve a legal notice to MFIs in the event of any complaint of excess recovery of the loan and or the charging of interest rate exceeding the principal amount. The Act has banned due collections and prohibits the MFI agents visiting the borrowers home and collecting the repayments. Instead, it opens a provision for the agents to collect their dues from local gram panchayat offices. [Andhra Pradesh Micro Finance Institutions (Regulation of Money Lending) Act, 2010].

Malegam Committee Report by Reserve Bank of India (2011)

In the aftermath of microfinance crisis in Andhra Pradesh, a Sub-Committee of the Central Board of Directors of Reserve Bank of India was constituted in 2010 under the Chairmanship of Y.H. Malegam to look into the alleged abusive practices adopted by the MFIs involving in high interest rates, coercive recovery methods and multiple lending. In addition, the Committee was assigned to explore the scope for regulating the microfinance sector by the RBI and to suggest a regulatory framework. The Committee submitted its report in 2011, titled, 'Report of the Sub-Committee of the Central Board of Directors of Reserve Bank of India to Study Issues and Concerns in the MFI Sector', with a few important recommendations to revitalise the microfinance industry.

The key recommendations include[8] the following: First, restrict MFIs to lend those who possess a minimum of Rs 50000 annual income. In other words, the borrowers' whose annual income is up to Rs 50000 and above are only eligible for availing credit from the MFIs. However, Sa-Dhan (2012), a network body of India's Microfinance Institutions, argues that the household income limit of Rs 50000 is not acceptable, as it has not considered the rural-urban divide, occupational pattern and seasonal cash flow. The recommendation would exclude the poor in urban areas and also limit the scope for repeat loans for borrowers graduating from poverty. Sa-Dhan also raises concern that would be difficult for the MFIs to predict the household income of the borrowers, as the income levels of the poor communities are unstable and changes over a one-year period. The second recommendation of the Committee is related to reducing the debt burden and interest rate on the poor. It is recommended that the MFIs should not lend any loan above Rs 25000 to a low-income household. The Committee is of the view that if the size of the loan is less than Rs 25000, it would become easy for the poor borrower to repay the loan amount in-time and with low per cent of interest rate. Sa-Dhan (2012) argues that the maximum loan size of Rs 25000 is not sufficient to start an entrepreneurial activity, other sustained individual income generating activities and even for housing loan. In order to get supplementary capital to start such activities, poor people would look out for exploitative moneylenders.

The third recommendation of the Committee is related to fixing a cap on interest rates. The Committee, after taking critical note on the interest rates currently charged by the MFIs which sometimes exceeds 24 per cent, recommends to lay a ceiling on the maximum not to exceed beyond 24 per cent. The fourth recommendation aimed to avoid multiple lending and coercive recovery practices. The report observes that peer pressure among the Joint Liability Group (JLG) members formed by the MFIs can drive an individual to extreme humiliation and sometimes resulted in suicides. As far as financial security of the borrower is concerned, the fifth recommendation makes it mandatory that each MFI should register under the RBI guidelines and must maintain minimum capital of Rs 15 crores. This recommendation restricts the small range of MFIs from entering into the markets to just exploit the poor and to enhance their own financial sustainability. The Committee report considered financial sustainability as an important dimension and, therefore, recommended for a standard minimum capital to establish a MFI.

The sixth recommendation is that, besides the RBI, public sector banks should play key role in monitoring compliance of regulatory norms and transactions of the MFIs. However, the NBFC-MFIs are to be exempted from the provision of money lending, and from the Andhra Pradesh Microfinance (Regulation of Money Lending) Act, 2010. However, the Society for the Elimination of Rural Poverty report (2013), by the Government of Andhra Pradesh, argues that the exemption of NBFC-MFIs from the Andhra Pradesh Microfinance (Regulation of Money Lending) Act, 2010 undermines the provisions of the Act that solely aim to protect SHG members from the MFIs. The report is of the view that the microfinance crisis in Andhra Pradesh has had severe repercussions for the rural poor borrowers, particularly, on the lives of SHG women. With an objective to ensure that the loan is properly used for enhancing livelihood options, the seventh recommendation of the Committee report directs the MFIs to ensure 75 per cent of their loan must be utilised for income-generation activities. The last recommendation aimed at improving the repayment rates and reducing the weekly installment stress on the borrowers. In this regard, the committee recommends that the minimum tenure for loans up to Rs 15000 should be at least one year, and larger loans upto Rs 25000 can be relaxed for two years.

Summary of the Field Survey

The study analysed the impact of SHG-Bank Linkage Programme (SBLP) model in alleviating poverty of rural women and outlined its drawbacks. To assess its impact on some aspects such as the respondent's period of association with the group, purpose for availing loans, the correlation between respondent's caste and purpose of availing loan, improved income levels of the respondents before and after joining SHGs, and also their financial contribution to family expenditure were taken into consideration. The study inferred that availing microcredit through SBLP model with subsidized interest rates, that is, at three per cent per annum has a significant impact on the creation of various livelihood opportunities vis-á-vis alleviating poverty of the rural women. It is also emphasised that the active participation of SHG women in group functioning, collective participation in some of the training programmes and interaction with bank officials enhanced their participation in various developmental activities. Further, it has shown that utilising their loans in various prôductive activities like buying agricultural equipments, livestock rearing and creation of various self-employment activities has made considerable progress in improving their income levels. The contribution of their income for family expenditure like purchasing food items and electronic goods, children's education, health-care purpose, house construction and repaying old debts has significant impact in reducing their vulnerability to poverty.

Despite its potential contributions, the SBLP model suffers from certain limitations. The manifest challenges on the functioning of SBLP model operate from both ends bank officials as well as SHG members. To mention just a few, there is little evidence of mutual understanding within the group members, and the behaviour of the SHG president and handling of bank loan by the male member of her family, poor participation levels in the group meetings by members belonging to poor sections and mismanagement in book-keeping by some of the bookkeepers are serious irritants. In regard to loan disbursement, problems like partiality of the bank officials on some of the SHGs in sanctioning loan amount, deliberate delay in loan sanctioning for some SHGs, and repeated complaints by the respondents regarding distribution of loan amount among the group members are noticed. As far as the utilisation of loan is concerned, 36 per cent of the respondents used their loan for non-productive purpose like for daily consumption, performing social ceremonies and emergency (medical) purpose.

The study also dealt with an important aspect, that is, SBLP vis-á-vis rural entrepreneurship development. In recent times, the SBLP model has been appreciated due to its pro-active role in promoting entrepreneurial activities among SHG women. The study examines the possibilities of running various group-based small-scale business ventures by the SHG women. Along with agricultural activities and livestock rearing, some of the respondents have initiated income-generating activities like running photocopying centres, grocery shops, tailoring shops, handloom weaving, bangle stores, *chat bandar,* vegetable/fruit shop, basket, mat and broom making, and beedi-rolling. Though these women have been engaged in various individual self-employment activities, they have to go a long way in initiating group-based entrepreneurial activities, where women not only find employment for themselves but create employment opportunities for others as well. The study has shown that no group employment activity emerged in the selected three villages. It argues that, apart from small and untimely loans, lack of entrepreneurial and management skills to initiate and sustain various business ventures, has become a serious limitation. It also emphasises that mere provision of subsidized credit delivery is not sufficient and accordingly the desired results are not achieved. It is, therefore, vital to ensure access to adequate and timely credit and promoting entrepreneurial skills and business management for successful functioning of the model. The study also drew some observations regarding the functioning of microfinance institutions (MFIs) model and found certain constraints in its implementation through the feedback of the respondents. It outlined three main factors responsible for the microfinance crisis and the subsequent repercussions for the borrowers. Exorbitant interest rates and weekly repayment collection practices made the borrowers depend upon other private financial institutions or conventional moneylenders to repay the old debts. The third factor was the coercive and highhanded behaviour of MFI staff in recovering the loans. For instance, using abusive language, confiscating movable assets, threatening to file a complaint in the police station by the MFI's staff had a negative impact on the hapless borrowers, which in turn led to distress deaths.

References

1. One of the field surveyed districts, named Karimnagar now falls under the newly formed state of Telangana.
2. The Pavala Vaddi scheme is intended to provide interest subsidy on the bank loan availed by the SHGs in Andhra Pradesh. The scheme is applicable to all loans extended by banks on or after 01.07.2004. See, www.ap.gov.in/ initiatives
3. Sthree Nidhi Credit Cooperative Federation Ltd is considered as an important initiative in the realm of credit disbursement to the SHGs. It is promoted by the Government of Andhra Pradesh to provide affordable and timely credit to the poor SHG members. In order to stop the borrowing from MFIs at high interest rates, the government attempted to facilitate access to hassle-free credit from the Sthree Nidhi. Through this scheme, the SHG members who are in an urgent need of credit can avail loan from Sthree Nidhi within 48 hours of their loan application. See, https:// www.sthreenidhi.ap.gov.in.
4. Source: http://www.eastgodavari.ap.gov.in .
5. http://www.chittoor.ap.gov.in
6. Gram Panchayat Office, Taduku, Puttur Mandal, Chittoor District.
7. The analysis on group experience and self-employment activities of SHG women would be discussed in detail in the later pages of this chapter.
8. Report of the Sub-Committee of the Central Board of Directors of Reserve Bank of India to Study Issues and Concerns in the MFI Sector. Reserve Bank of India (2011).

Chapter VI

Microfinance Models and Initiatives on Financial Inclusion of the Poor: Findings from Andhra Pradesh and Telangana

The previous chapter assessed the impact of SHG-Bank Linkage Programme (SBLP) model on poverty alleviation of women in three districts of Andhra Pradesh and Telangana. It examined the functional aspects of Microfinance Institution (MFI) model in providing microfinance to the rural poor and identified the reasons that led to recent suicides by the MFI credit holders in both the states and the state government's response in mitigating the microfinance crisis. The present chapter attempts to testify another important aspect of the study: financial inclusion of the poor. In this regard, the chapter attempts to examine the impact of SBLP and Business Correspondent (BC) models on promoting financial inclusion of the poor in the selected three villages.

Introduction

In recent times, the phenomenon of financial inclusion, as mentioned in the literature review (Chapter II), has gained wider currency in the development discourse across the globe. Given the magnitude of poverty in the Third World economies, wherein a large segment of the population does not have access to basic financial services, the idea of financial inclusion commonly understood as banking to all acquires significance. Recent estimates show that, globally, over three billion people lack access to basic financial services, of which about 90 per cent are from Africa, Asia, Latin America and the Middle East. This has led to a considerable demand from the developing countries for a more inclusive financial system that would cater to the demands of the poor in these regions (John, Julius and Worapot, 2009 and Consultative Group to Assist the Poor (CGAP), 2012).

With reference to India, while emphasising the importance of access to adequate and affordable financial services, the recent Nachiket Committee Report on Financial Inclusion Government of India (2013) states that the basic financial services help the customers to maximise benefit from human and other resources that they possess while minimising the impact of adverse conditions on their lives. The Report (2013:6), however, estimates that in India nearly 70 per cent of the population lives in villages, a significant segment of about 6,50,000 villages do not have a coverage of any nationalised banks to access formal banking services. It further argues that about 90 per cent of small businesses do not have any formal links with banks and about 60 per cent of the rural and urban population does not have access to any banking related services. Thus, the lack of access to banking services pushed the large part of the population, rural communities in particular, to depend on informal financial sources such as chit fund companies and moneylenders for meeting their credit and other financial requirements. This scenario emphasises the need for two fundamental changes in the financial services offered to the poor: the necessity of providing various basic financial services and products to the low-income households, and need for initiating various banking models in order to reach out to the unbanked population. In this context, it is pertinent to examine and assess the impact of various microfinance models and initiatives being promoted by the Reserve Bank of India (RBI) and National Bank for Agricultural and Rural Development (NABARD) in ensuring the process of financial inclusion in rural areas.

The chapter primarily attempts to examine the impact of two microfinance models: (i) Self Help Group-Bank Linkage Programme (SBLP) model and (ii) Business Correspondent (BC) model on promoting financial inclusion of the poor in the selected three field sites surveyed in Andhra Pradesh and Telangana. The chapter is organised into two sections. Section I examines the contributions of SBLP model in promoting financial inclusion among the SHG women on the one hand, and on the other, identifies the challenges faced in its execution. For this purpose, data from follow up interviews with the same 150 respondents as stipulated in the earlier chapter is tabulated and analysed. Section II assess the impact of BC model in promoting the process of financial inclusion. The sample population for this study is picked up separately, both male and female, who are being enrolled under the BC model from the three selected villages. A total of 150 respondents has been selected by using stratified random sampling method. The chapter attempts to offer a comprehensive understanding of the formation and functioning of BC model vis-à-vis inclusion of the hitherto financially excluded sections into the banking fold. It also brings out the structural constraints involved in the BC model in achieving the said objective.

PART I

The Impact of SBLP Model on Financial Inclusion of Women: Field Survey Analysis

As discussed in the first chapter, Self-Help Group-Bank Linkage Programme (SBLP) is recognised as the largest and successful models of its kind in the world (Rajeev and Mahija, 2013). Accordingly, the Society for Elimination of Rural Poverty (SERP) report states that the SBLP model has been largely instrumental in mainstreaming more than 90 per cent of women, who have been by-passed by the formal banking system in Andhra Pradesh. In terms of loan recovery by the SHG women, the report is of the view that on-time recovery of the loan installments is one of the distinctive features of the Bank Linkage programme. The SERP report estimates that the recovery rates were as high as 90 per cent in commercial banks, 87 per cent in Regional Rural Banks (RRBs), and 86 per cent in cooperative banks (SERP Report, 2013). Considering the promising tie-ups between SHGs and bank under the SBLP model, SHGs in India acknowledged as potential intermediaries between the poor women and banks. Therefore, in order to understand the correlation between SHGs and financial inclusion of women, it is pertinent to examine the implementation of SBLP model in the three villages of Andhra Pradesh and Telangana. Accordingly, the following section aims to study whether this model fostered the process of financial inclusion and the role played by the SHG women become instrumental in realising the said objective.

No-frills Accounts (NFA)

In the process of making financial inclusion a reality, the RBI has come up with the policy of opening 'no-frills accounts' for low-income and unbanked sections. The present study deals with the SHG women, who apart from having their joint bank accounts under SBLP model, also have individual bank accounts under 'no-frills account' category. For the analysis, the study seeks to measure financial inclusion, that is, availability and usage of banking services by the surveyed respondents under their individual bank (no-frills) accounts (Sarma, 2008). According to this idea, if at least one member in the family has an individual bank account, availing basic financial services and continuing their financial transaction under the same, the family is referred to as financially included. Otherwise, it is considered to be financially excluded from the formal banking system. Based on the above idea of assessing financial inclusion the following tables aim at identifying the surveyed SHG women who claimed to have no-frills accounts. The data of the tables below further reports the number of no-frills accounts opened by the respondents, availing various financial services under the same accounts, awareness on Know Your Customer (KYC) norms, and so on. In recent times, no-frills accounts have played an important role in promoting the process of financial inclusion. In other words, promoting 'no-frills accounts' by opening zero or minimum balance bank accounts and delivering basic financial services become an important variable in measuring the extent of financial inclusion. The Table 6.1 identifies the no-frills accounts opened by the SHG members.

Table 6.1: Do you have No-frills Account

Responses	*Name of the Village and District*			
	Chinabonala (Karimnagar)	*Diwancheruvu (East Godavari)*	*Taduku (Chittoor)*	*Total Respondents*
Yes	21 (42)	38 (76)	33 (66)	92 (61)
No	18 (36)	7 (14)	11 (22)	36 (24)
No idea	11 (22)	5 (10)	6 (12)	22 (15)
Total Respondents	**50**	**50**	**50**	**150 (100)**

From the above Table 6.1, it is evident that, of the 150 respondents, 92 (61 per cent) have opened no-frills accounts in various public sector banks, 36 (24 per cent) of them have not opened no-frills accounts and the remaining 22 (15 per cent) respondents have no idea about no-frills accounts and its benefits. Ramji (2009), Majumdar and Gupta (2013) emphasise that no-frills accounts aim at inculcating the habit of savings behaviour among the poor and disadvantaged segments and ensuring basic banking facilities to them in a uniform manner. As far as the village-wise data is concerned, SHG women from Diwancheruvu have opened the highest number of no-frills accounts (38 respondents) followed by Taduku village (33 respondents) of Chittoor district and Chinabonala village (21 respondents) of Karimnagar district.

The interaction with bank managers has revealed that most of the no-frills accounts have been opened by farmers and SHG members. Apart from SHG accounts, a few farmers' joint liability group (JLG) accounts have been found. It is also observed that the provision of lending upto Rs 3 lakh to the farmers groups, under JLG account, considerably affects their cultivating patterns. Bankers are of the view that providing bank accounts with minimum or zero balance and accordingly lending various kinds of loans to the rural communities ensure financial inclusion of the hitherto excluded sections, if the bank accounts are in active mode. However, of the 150 respondents, 36 respondents (24 per cent) have not opened no-frills accounts. In response to the question 'why did you not open no-frills account', the respondents replied that insufficient income for savings and lack of financial awareness as to how to open a bank account are the major factors that obstructed them from opening an individual bank account, except as a member of SHG and stakeholder of SHG joint account.

Table 6.2: How did you know about No-frills Account?

S.No	*Source of Information*	*Name of the Village and District*			
		Chinabonala (Karimnagar)	*Diwancheruvu (East Godavari)*	*Taduku (Chittoor)*	*Total Respondents*
1.	Through SHG members	18 (46)	22 (49)	28 (64)	68 (54)
2.	Through Village Panchayat Officials	6 (16)	3 (7)	5 (11)	14 (10)
3.	Through Bank Officials	11 (28)	14(31)	9 (20)	34 (27)
4.	Through neighbors	4 (10)	6 (13)	2(5)	12 (9)
	Total Respondents	**39 (30)**	**45 (35.5)**	**44 (34.5)**	**128 (100)**

As mentioned in the Table 6.1, of the 150 respondents, 128 are familiar with no-frills accounts, and of the 128 respondents, 92 have opened no-frills accounts. A question was asked to all the 128 respondents regarding how they learnt about no-frills accounts. Of the 128 respondents, 68 (54 per cent) replied that they learnt about such accounts through SHG members, 14 (10 per cent) knew through village panchayat officials, 34 (27 per cent) aware of this accounts through bank officials and 12 (9 per cent) through neighbours. The above figures highlight the aspect of financial awareness among the SHG women. No-frills accounts are considered as the first step in the process of financial inclusion strategy. Through these accounts, the financially excluded sections become the clients of banks and they are educated about various financial services and government benefits that are being channelised through bank accounts such as MGNREGA wages, old-age pensions, gas subsidy through cash transfer and so on. It is therefore, inferred that opening no-frills accounts provides not only a permanent bank account but also promotes financial awareness among the clients. Table 6.3 analyses how the SHG women, apart from their SHG joint account under SBLP model, use their individual bank accounts that are opened under no-frills category.

As stated earlier, the mere opening of a bank account does not kick-start the process of financial inclusion. The bank account has to be in active mode with basic financial transactions being carried out by the account holder. It is, therefore, apparent that the use of no-frills accounts for various purpose is imperative for meaningful financial inclusion. The following Table 6.3 highlights how the account holder has been using these accounts. It further highlights one of the dimensions of measuring financial inclusion, that is, usage of financial services as proposed by Sarma (2008).

Table 6.3 reports that, of the 92 respondents, who opened bank account under no-frills category, 47 (51 per cent) use it for availing gas subsidy through direct cash transfer scheme, 21 (23 per cent) use it for availing Indiramma housing loan and 13 (14 per cent) of them use it for savings. The remaining 11 (12 per cent) respondents use it for availing any other loan facility through the accounts. The Government of Andhra Pradesh made it mandatory to open bank account to avail gas subsidy provided by the government in form of direct cash transfer to the beneficiary. However, it is evident that of

Table 6.3: Usage of no-frills account

S.No	*Responses*	*Name of the Village and District*			
		Chinabonala (Karimnagar)	*Diwancheruvu (East Godavari)*	*Taduku (Chittoor)*	*Total Respondents*
1.	To save money	02	06	05	13 (14)
2.	To avail Gas subsidy	12	21	14	47 (51)
3.	To avail Indiramma housing loan	04	10	07	21 (23)
4.	To avail any other loan facility	–	08	03	11 (12)
	Total Respondents	**18 (19.5)**	**45 (49)**	**29 (31.5)**	**92 (100)**

Source: Primary data.

Note: Figures in parentheses represent the percentages for usage.

the 150 respondents (SHG women), only 92 opened bank account under the no-frills accounts category; and of these 92 respondents, only 47 are able to access gas subsidy. It shows that of the 150 sample frame, 103 respondents are not utilising gas subsidy primarily for two reasons. They are either not having gas connections or not aware of this subsidy scheme through cash transfer. Availing Indiramma housing loan comes under second highest in utilising no-frills accounts by the SHG women. Of the 92 respondents, 21 (per cent) use the account for availing Indiramma housing loan. As it mentioned, under this scheme, the Government of Andhra Pradesh provides loan to construct houses for the poor households.

Know Your Customer (KYC) norms

In order to open any kind of bank account, a customer needs to meet the Know Your Customer (KYC) norms. In fact, KYC norms play a pivotal role in ensuring financial inclusion as the RBI has relaxed the KYC norms and made the banking procedures simple to open a bank account. The following Table 6.4 explicates the idea of KYC norms and its relation to financial inclusion.

Know Your Customer (KYC) norms facilitate opening a bank account. The literature on this subject argues that various cumbersome procedures in opening a bank account become a serious constraint in the process of inclusive banking system, that is, financial inclusion (Ramji, 2007 and Bhatia and Chatterjee, 2010). Raghuram Rajan, the Governor of RBI, recently expressed that "one roadblock to access, even to something as simple as a universal basic savings accounts, is stringent KYC requirements" followed by some public and private sector banks. He further adds that the stringent KYC norms keep a large number of sections out of the banking system, and lead to inconvenience for others.[1] The statement highlights the difficulty involved in meeting the KYC norms by the poor and illiterate sections of the society and emphasises for simplifying the requirements.

Table 6.4: Awareness about Know Your Customer (KYC) norms

S.No	*Response*	*Name of the Village and District*			
		Chinabonala (Karimnagar)	*Diwancheruvu (East Godavari)*	*Respondent's Taduku (Chittoor)*	*Total Respondents*
1.	Yes	14(28)	23 (46)	17(34)	54 (36)
2.	No	36 (72)	27 (54)	33(66)	96 (64)
	Total Respondents	**50**	**50**	**50**	**150 (100)**

As part of financial inclusion drive, the Government of Andhra Pradesh with the help of Reserve Bank of India (RBI) organises various training programmes for the SHG women. Table 6.5 represents some of the important programmes/awareness camps being conducted for the SHG respondents. During the field survey, it was observed that the SHG women are actively participating in some of the important training programmes. Data was collected on the top four training programmes being organised in the state and the respondent's participation levels on the same have been documented. Of the 150 respondents, 43 (29 per cent) attended an awareness camp on availing Sreenidhi Scheme, 29 (19.5 per cent) respondents have attended awareness camps on promoting financial inclusion (including financial literacy campaign), 17 (11.5 per cent) attended training programmes on formation and functioning of JLGs, and eight respondents (five per cent) attended an awareness camp on MFI Act (2010) and its usage. The remaining 53 respondents (35 per cent) have not attended. From all the above training programmes, most of the respondents (43 respondents) attended awareness camps on how to avail 'Sreenidhi scheme'. Since it is a new programme, which aims at providing interest free loans to the SHG members, the respondents showed interest in attending this programme. Of the 150 respondents, 29 have attended the awareness camp on promoting financial inclusion. This camp primarily intended to promote awareness on financial literacy of the SHG women. However, it is also pertinent to highlight that 53 (35 per cent) respondents did not participate in any of the awareness camps/training programmes. This significantly undermines the very objective of SHG, that is, 'collective participation'.

Table 6.5: What are the training programmes you have attended recently

S. No	*Name of the training programme*	*Name of the Village and District*			
		Chinabonala (Karimnagar)	*Diwanche-ruvu (East Godavari)*	*Respondent's Taduku (Chittoor)*	*Total Respondents*
1.	Awareness camp on promoting Financial Inclusion (including financial literacy)	11(22)	8 (16)	10 (20)	29 (19.5)
2.	Awareness camp on availing Sreenidhi Scheme	12 (24)	14 (28)	17 (34)	43 (29)
3.	Training Programme on formation and functioning of JLGs	3 (6)	9 (18)	5 (10)	17 (11.5)
4.	Awareness camp on MFI Act (2010) and it's usage	3 (6)	5 (10)	—(—)	8 (5)
5.	Not Attended	21 (42)	14 (28)	18 (36)	53 (35)
	Total Respondents	**50 (100)**	**50 (100)**	**50 (100)**	**150 (100)**

As far as the village-wise data is concerned, SHG respondents from Deevancheruvu village of East Godavari district were appeared to be active in attending various training programmes and awareness camps followed by the SHG respondents belong to Taduku village of Chittoor district. However, the participation of SHG members belong to Chinabonala village of Karimnagar district was less as compared with the above two villages. It is worth mentioning that, unlike Diwancheruvu and Taduku villages, Chinabonala village does not have a bank branch. Having a bank branch within the village may influence the participation level in various training programmes/awareness camps being conducted by the concerned bank branch.

The bankers' perspective emphasise the government and public sector banks initiatives in promoting financial awareness among the SHG women. However, it is inferred that despite these considerable efforts, a major section of the people, in particular women and farmers, still lack financial literacy regarding the formal financial system. This constraint gives scope for the private financial institutions to dominate the lending system in rural areas.

PART II

Business Correspondent (BC) Model

Business Correspondent model, also known as agent-client model, is an important banking model. It is envisaged in spreading the banking system even to the remotest regions of India. In particular, in order to provide an alternative banking structure to branch-based banking services, the RBI in January, 2006 adopted the technology-based agent bank model through business facilitators (BFs)/business correspondents (BCs) model.[2] This model enables public sector banks to use the services of Non-Governmental Organisations/Self-Help Groups (NGOs/SHGs), Microfinance Institutions (MFIs) and other Civil Society Organisations (CSOs) as intermediaries in providing financial and banking services (RBI, 2006). The model primarily intends to reach out to the geographically diverse population, particularly to those who are financially excluded from the mainstream banking services. The significant feature of this model is to ensure doorstep delivery of financial products and services (Khan, 2012). According to the RBI guidelines, the business correspondents (BCs) are permitted to carry out financial transactions on behalf of bank, as agents, which is also called branchless banking. This model is increasingly aided by technology such as Point of Service handheld devices (POS devices), mobile phones and a biometric scanner (Karmakar, 2009).

BC is an agent authorised to undertake transactions on behalf of a specified bank of a particular region. The BCs or bank agents have the advantage over bank branches as they can deliver banking services at the doorstep across the geographical landscape. The functions and responsibilities of BC include collecting small value deposits, disbursing and recovering small value loans; receiving and sending small value remittances; cross-selling third party products such as micro insurance, mutual funds and pension products, and engaging in bill payments for services (Frost and Sullivan, 2009). In addition, this model helps the target population to overcome regional barriers of language and culture, and inadequate infrastructure in rural areas. The role of BC is to bridge the gap between the service providers (the banks) and the service seekers (clients) who are under-served and unbanked. This model should enable up for the lack of required manpower to reach different sections of people in the current banking system Khan (2012). Considering the importance and necessity of the BC model in relation to spreading the banking system to the remotest regions, the following section examines the impact of BC model in promoting financial inclusion in three regions of rural Andhra Pradesh and Telangana.

Financial Services Available under Business Correspondent (BC) Model: Business Correspondent's Perception

Before analysing the field observations of the BC model, it is pertinent to understand the basic services available under this model. Theoretically, the literature on the subject lists out various financial services available under the BC model. Under the BC model, banks offer basic financial services such as holding bank accounts, savings, fixed deposits, money transfer etc. on a small-scale basis. However, a maximum limit is imposed on every financial service (Bhargava, 2009). During the key-informant interviews with the business correspondents, it is found that there are selected financial services available to the clients under BC model. Business Correspondents are of the view that opening a bank account under BC model facilitates some of the important financial services, which are available under public sector banks.

It is evident from the responses of business correspondents that savings, fixed deposit, cash transfers, cash withdrawals, availing various loans, availing scholarship facility by the students, availing gas subsidy in the form of cash transfer and pensions, and alike are some of the important financial services available to the clients of BC model. It is observed that the list of services mentioned by the BC not only matches with the services referred to in the literature but also includes additional services such as availing scholarships by students and gas subsidies through direct cash transfer. As bank agents, business correspondents explain their activities to be discharged under BC model. In the first phase, they identify the people who are in urgent need of banking services, collect the necessary information from the applicant and submit their application to the banks on their behalf. In the second stage, the application become an account holder of their bank branch, the BC mediate in lending credit and other financial services to the clients from the concerned bank branch, monitor the post-sanction activities and follow up the recovery procedure. Apart from delivering various financial services, the business correspondents state that they mobilise people and inculcate the savings habit and encourage them to save in fixed deposits.

Table 6.6: Gender distribution of the Respondents

S. No.	*Variable*	*Name of the Village and District*			
		Chinabonala (Karimnagar)	*Diwancheruvu (East Godavari)*	*Taduku (Chittoor)*	*Total Respondents*
1.	Male	24 (48)	23 (46)	26 (52)	73 (49)
2.	Female	26 (52)	27 (54)	24 (48)	77 (51)
	Total	**50 (100)**	**50 (100)**	**50 (100)**	**150 (100)**

Note: Figures in parentheses represent the number of respondents in percentage.

Table 6.6 shows the percentage of male and female members who are enrolled under Business Correspondent (BC) model. Of the 150 respondents, 73 (49 per cent) are male and the remaining 77 (51 per cent) are female members opened bank accounts under the BC model. It is interesting to note that in the total sample frame, female percentage is higher than the male percentage. One of the important reasons is that many of the subsidy schemes are being targeted at women such as gas subsidy, housing loan, loans for dairy farming and so on. Therefore, the female member of the family is given first priority to open a bank account either directly from the bank branch or through BC model. As far as the village-wise data is concerned, Diwancheruvu village has the highest number of bank accounts opened by women (27 respondents) under BC model, followed by Chinabonala (26 respondents) and Taduku (24 respondents) respectively.

Table 6.7: Age-wise distribution of the respondents

S.No	Age	*Name of the Village and District*			
		Chinabonala (Karimnagar)	*Diwancheruvu (East Godavari)*	*Taduku (Chittoor)*	*Total Respondents*
1.	20-30	19 (38)	20 (40)	22 (44)	61 (41)
2.	31-40	17 (34)	16(32)	12(24)	45 (30)
3.	41-50	8 (16)	9 (18)	11 (22)	28 (18.5)
4.	51 above	6 (12)	5 (10)	5 (10)	16 (10.5)
	Total	**50 (100)**	**50 (100)**	**50 (100)**	**150 (100)**

Source: Primary data.
Note: Figures in parentheses represent the number of respondents in percentage.

Age is one of the important variables in socio-economic analysis of a qualitative study. In this study, it provides an understanding on the customers of BC model from different age groups who are enrolled under BC model. Table 6.7 demonstrates that a majority of the respondents (41 per cent) fall under the age group of 20-30, whereas 45 (30 per cent) are from the age group of 31-40, and 28 respondents (18.5 per cent) are in the age group between 41-50. The remaining 16 respondents (10.5 per cent) are in the age group of 51 and above. From the Table 6.7, it is evident that the respondents fall under the age group of 20-30, who are opened a bank account under the BC model are high in number followed by the age group of 31-40. In other words, the younger people are showing greater interest in opening a bank account under the BC model rather than in opening a normal account in the bank branch. It appears that respondents in these age groups are aware of the services available under this model. Of the 150 respondents, only 16 (10.5 per cent) are above the age of 50 years.

Table 6.8: Caste-wise distribution of the Respondents

S.No.	Variable (Caste)	*Name of the Village and District*			
		Chinabonala (Karimnagar)	*Diwancheruvu (East Godavari)*	*Taduku (Chittoor)*	*Total Respondents*
1.	ST	6 (12)	5 (10)	3(6)	14 (10)
2.	SC	12 (24)	15 (30)	14 (28)	41 (27)
3.	BC	21 (42)	22 (44)	19 (38)	62 (41)
4.	Forward Caste	11 (22)	8 (16)	14 (28)	33 (22)
	Total	**50**	**50**	**50**	**150 (100)**

Source: Primary data.
Note: Figures in parentheses represent the number of respondents in percentage.

Table 6.8 demonstrates the number of respondents who are enrolled under the Business Correspondent model from various social groups such as Scheduled Castes (SCs), Scheduled Tribes (STs), Backward Castes (BCs) and Forward Castes (FCs). It shows that the respondents who are enrolled under Business Correspondent model are high among the BC (62 respondents) and SC (41 respondents) category, which is followed by Forward Caste (33 respondents). However, it is also observed that the enrollment of ST community in the Business Correspondent model is low (only 14 respondents). It reveals the lack of awareness about the Business Correspondent model and about how to avail various basic financial services. As far as the village-wise data is concerned, only three respondents from ST category are enrolled under BC model from Taduku village of Chittoor.

Education Levels of the Respondents

The educational background of the respondents is examined mainly to ascertain whether, if at all, the literacy levels of the respondents have an impact in utilising various financial services provided by the BC model. It was found that education levels of the respondents have, indeed encouraged their participation in financial awareness camps on how to open a bank account and the benefits available under BC model. It is also observed that the respondents who studied above Xth standard are active in knowing about the various loans available for the rural community such as educational loan, housing loan, farm loan, and alike. The following Tables 6.9 (a) and (b) report the educational levels, gender profile of the respondents and their participation in various financial activities.

Table 6.9 (a): Educational levels of the Respondents

S.No	*Variable (Education)*	*Name of the Village and District*			
		Chinabonala (Karimnagar)	*Diwancheruvu (East Godavari)*	*Taduku (Chittoor)*	*Total Respondent*
1.	No formal Education	11 (22)	7 (14)	14 (28)	32 (22)
2.	1st to 5th standard	18 (16)	13(26)	15 (30)	46 (30)
3.	6th to 10th Standard	12 (24)	11 (22)	13 (26)	36 (24)
4.	Intermediate to Degree	9 (18)	17 (34)	7 (14)	33 (22)
5.	Above Degree	–	2 (4)	1 (2)	3 (2)
	Total	**50 (100)**	**50 (100)**	**50 (100)**	**150 (100)**

The literacy levels of the respondents are categorised into five groups. These are: (i) no formal education, (ii) 1st to 5th standard, (iii) 6th to 10th Standard (iv) Intermediate to Degree and (v) above Degree. The Table 6.9 (a) shows that, of the 150 respondents, 32 (21 per cent) have not received any kind of formal education; 46 (31 per cent) have completed their primary education, that is, upto Vth standard; 36 (24 per cent) have studied up to Xth standard and 33 (22 per cent) have studied above Xth standard to Degree. The remaining three respondents (two per cent) have studied above Degree, that is, two of them studied M.B.A. and one passed B.Ed. These findings show that, of the 150 respondents, 118 (79 per cent) are found to be literate and received education starting from primary level to above graduation irrespective of their region. As far as the gender-wise data is concerned, from the Table 6.9 (b), it is evident that, of the 150 sample frame, 73 (49 per cent) are male and the remaining 77 (51 per cent) are female respondents. Of the 77 female respondents, a maximum of 22 (15 per cent) had not received any kind of formal education and 32 (21 per cent) received education upto Vth standard. The remaining 23 (15.5 per cent) received education upto Xth standard and above, and none of the respondents studied above graduation.

The above data reveals that though the education levels of the females are lower than males, the percentage of enrolling with the BC model is high in female category (51 per cent, whereas it is 49 per cent for male category). It is generally assumed that there is a positive correlation between educational levels and availing the benefits of various government schemes and services. However, from the above particular table, it can be inferred that there is no positive correlation between education levels and holding a bank account under BC model by the female respondents. The reason is that whether they are literate or not, women have opened bank accounts primarily to avail gas subsidy provided by the Government of Andhra Pradesh. It is not because of basic services as prescribed in BC model. It means the domestic necessity of homemaker encouraged them to open bank account in order to avail the subsidy. Apart from availing gas subsidy, only a nominal proportion of women are availing the same account for other financial services. During the focus group discussion with these women respondents, it was observed that they do not have much awareness about other financial services, which are available under this model.

In fact, other than availing gas subsidy, most of the women are not showing interest in operating/utilising the same account for various other financial services. In this context, attending various financial literacy camps and participating in various financial awareness programmes assume critical importance to know and understand the best utilisation of the BC model.

Respondent's Occupation

Through applying respondent's occupation as a variable in the analysis, some important observations could be drawn on whether respondent's occupations have any effect on accessing various financial services under Business Correspondent (BC) model. The selected respondents are broadly classified under five categories, viz. homemakers, daily-wage labourers, livestock rearing, farming and self-employed persons. Agriculture constitutes the major occupation in rural Andhra Pradesh, while livestock rearing is considered as one of the basic alternative sources of livelihood. Those who do not have landholdings are largely involved in agricultural and allied labour services. The following Table 6.10 (a) demonstrates the occupational representation of the respondents while Table 6.10 (b) represents the gender profile and occupational structure of the respondents.

Table 6.10: Respondents' occupation

S.No	*Respondents' Occupation*	*Name of the Village and District*			
		Chinabonala (Karimnagar)	*Diwancheruvu (East Godavari)*	*Taduku (Chittoor)*	*Total Respondents*
1.	Homemakers	9 (18)	7 (14)	4 (8)	20 (13)
2.	Daily Wage labour	17 (34)	21 (42)	19(38)	57 (38)
3.	Livestock rearing	8 (16)	5 (10)	14 (28)	27 (18)
	Farming	13 (26)	9 (18)	11 (22)	33 (22)
4.	Self employed	3 (6)	8 (16)	2 (4)	13 (9)
	Total	**50 (100)**	**50 (100)**	**50 (100)**	**150 (100)**

Source: Primary data.

Note: Figures in parentheses represent the number of respondents in percentage.

From Table 6.10 (a), it is observed that of the 150 surveyed respondents, 57 (38 per cent) work as daily-wage labourers, 33 (22 per cent) occupied in farming in their own land, 27 (18 per cent) engaged in livestock rearing and 20 (13 per cent) are homemakers,

The remaining 13 (9 per cent) are involved in various self-employment business ventures such as general store, bookstore and stationary, mobile repairing, footwear shop and so on. As far as the village-wise data is concerned, homemakers and respondents engaged in farming are high in Chinabonala village (9 and 13 respondents respectively), daily wage labourers are high in Diwancheruvu village (21 respondents) and respondents who engaged in livestock rearing are high in Taduku village (14 respondents). Respondents who involved in self-employment activities are high in Diwancheruvu village of East Godavari district.

Table 6.11: Knowing about the BC model

S. No.	*Source of information*	*Name of the Village and District*			
		Chinabonala (Karimnagar)	*Diwancheruvu (East Godavari)*	*Taduku (Chittoor)*	*Total Respondents*
1.	Friends	5 (10)	4 (8)	2 (4)	11 (8)
2.	Relatives	2 (4)	0	3 (6)	5 (3)
3.	Other members of BC model	18 (36)	12 (24)	14 (28)	44 (29)
4.	Through Business Correspondent	16 (32)	21 (42)	19 (38)	56 (37)
5.	Bank officials	9 (18)	13 (26)	12 (24)	34 (23)
	Total	**50 (100)**	**50 (100)**	**50 (100)**	**150 (100)**

From Table 6.12, it is reported that, of the 150 respondents 11 (8 per cent) knew this model through friends, five (three per cent) came to know through relatives, and 44 (29 per cent) from other active customers of the BC model. A maximum of 56 (37 per cent) knew this model through business correspondents, who run/supervise the model, and the remaining 34 (23 per cent) respondents got an idea about the BC model through the bankers from the nearby bank branch. From the above data, it is understood that business correspondents and bank officials play a proactive role in publicising the idea of BC model in rural areas. In other words, a total of 90 respondents, of the 150 sample, came to know about the BC model through the bankers and business correspondents. Interestingly, the members/clients of the BC model are also in the forefront in disseminating the information regarding the model. As the Table 6.12 shows that, of the 150 respondents, 44 (29 per cent) knew this model through the BC clients.

Table 6.12: Reasons for choosing to open Savings Bank Account under the BC model

S.No		*Name of the Village and District*			
		Chinabonala (Karimnagar)	***Diwancheruvu (East Godavari)***	***Taduku (Chittoor)***	***Total Respondents***
1.	To save money	7 (14)	11 (22)	6 (12)	24 (16)
2.	To avail bank loan	12 (24)	14 (28)	15 (30)	41 (27)
3.	To avail subsidy on Gas	21 (42)	17 (34)	22 (44)	60 (40)
4.	To avail ATM-Debit card facilities	10 (20)	8 (16)	7 (14)	25 (17)
	Total	**50**	**50**	**50**	**150**

Source: Primary data

Note: Figures in parentheses represent the number of respondents in percentage.

Table 6.13 is important for a number of reasons as it provides a detailed analysis on why people are choosing savings bank account under 'no-frills account' category. From the banker's and business correspondent's perspective, it analyses how this strategy relates to financial inclusion. During the interview with the respondents, there are several reasons identified on why people are interested in opening a bank account, particularly no-frills accounts. Four main reasons are taken into consideration for this analysis. From the Table 6.13, it is evident that, of the 150 respondents, a maximum of 60 (40 per cent) primarily to avail gas subsidy in the form of cash transfers. Interestingly, all the 60 respondents are from female category. In other words, of the 77 total female sample frame, 60 respondents are using their bank account essentially for availing gas subsidy. Thirty-three (22 respondents) opened for availing various loans and 25 respondents (17 per cent) are opened bank account to get the ATM-debit card facility. The remaining 24 (16 per cent) opened individual bank account for savings purpose. As far as the BC model is concerned saving, fixed deposits and availing various kinds of loans are the core objectives of the model. However, it is observed that availing loan facility and saving have received least priority by the beneficiaries. It shows that though the model is reached to the poor households, the very purpose of the same model has taken a back seat.

It is inferred that for women, in order to avail gas subsidy, it is necessary to open a bank account with Aadhaar Card as an identity proof. During the focus group discussion with the female respondents, however, it was found that opening a bank with Aadhaar Card as an identity proof became a major hindrance for most of the women, as many of them were yet to get their Aadhaar Cards. On the other hand, during an interview with one of the bankers in Taduku village of Chittoor district, it is revealed that the idea of providing gas subsidy in the form of cash transfer to the people is to promote banking habit among the rural population, particularly among the rural women. Thus, though the idea of inculcating banking habit among the rural women is laudable, it is equally important to ensure that the rural population has the Aadhaar Card in order to open an individual bank account. Otherwise, those who do not have Aadhaar Cards, but already have gas connections before the initiation of cash transfer scheme, may lose their gas connections or may not be able to reap the benefits of cash transfer. However, it is worth mentioning that the Supreme Court on March 24, 2014 directed the Central government to withdraw all notifications making Aadhaar cards mandatory for availing benefits under social security schemes.[3]

Table 6.13: Availability of Business Correspondent in a day

S.No.		*Name of the Village and District*			
		Chinabonala (Karimnagar)	*Diwancheruvu (East Godavari)*	*Taduku (Chittoor)*	*Total Respondents*
1.	2-5 hours	19	16	22	57 (38)
2.	5-8 hours	12	18	13	43 (29)
3.	8-10 hours	5	7	4	16 (10)
4.	No idea	14	9	11	34 (23)
	Total	**50 (100)**	**50 (100)**	**50 (100)**	**150 (100)**

Source: Primary data.

Note: 1. Figures in parentheses represent the number of respondents in percentage.

2. Although the banking timings are from 9 am to 5 pm, i.e. 8 hours in a day, the business correspondents on and average works 10 hours as he belongs to the same village. Following this, the study has taken 9-10 hours as one of the sub-groups in the above table.

Table 6.14 reports the availability of business correspondent to serve the financial needs of the clients in a day within their own village. In fact, daily availability of the business correspondent determines the successful functioning of the BC model. Of the 150 respondents, 57 (38 per cent) reported that the business correspondent is available for 2-5 hours in a day, 43 (29 per cent) opine 5-8 hours in a day and 34 (23 per cent) respondents do not have any idea of the availability of the business correspondent. The remaining 16 (10 per cent) are of the view that the agent is available 8-10 hours in a day. The presence of the business correspondent (BC) during the office hours in the village significantly helps the bank customers in various financial matters. The BC can facilitate required information regarding banking system not only to the bank customers of business correspondent model but also to the people who are willing to open an account under business correspondent model. According to the RBI guidelines, the business correspondent must available from 9 am to 5 pm. If the business correspondents do not give adequate time to serve the client's needs and problems, then the very purpose of the BC model, that is, delivering banking services at the doorstep becomes diluted. Ananth and Sabri (2014) in their recent study on business correspondent model in Andhra Pradesh believe that the help of business correspondent is essential to the inhabitants in villages where transportation is difficult. It is found that on an average the availability of business correspondents are 5-8 hours in a day. The availability of the business correspondent during the office hours in his outlet within the village, and addressing financial needs of the BC customers certainly builds the credibility of the business correspondents that in turn leads to the development of the BC model in the longer run.

Drawbacks of Business Correspondent Model

Although the Business Correspondent (BC) model holds the potential to cater to the financial needs of the rural unbanked populace, the field observations show some mixed results. From the interviews with the BC customers, business correspondents and bank managers, some observations made as part of field survey regarding the functioning and operational problems of the BC model are detailed below.

Customers' perspective

(i) Dissatisfaction over the loan facility

One of the problematic facets of this model is that banks are not taking seriously the loan applications, which come under BC model, into consideration to provide various types of loans. During the focus group discussion with the BC account holders in Chinabonala village of Karimnagar district, three respondents state:

> We opened a bank account under BC model primarily to avail various types of loans from the public sector banks. Though we have opened bank accounts without any difficulty, we are facing serious problems in availing loan facility. The bank officials are reluctant to consider our application for granting loans. We have applied for short-term loans three months ago, however still the loan applications are in pending mode. The bank manager says that first, they scrutinise the loan applications received by their normal branch account holders and then they look at the applications opened under BC model. We are disappointed with the discrimination against the customers of the BC model.

It is also said that, of the 50 respondents from Chinabonala village, 17 members have applied for short-term farm loan in which six of them received loans. The remaining 11 members are yet to receive loan facility from the bank. This is despite the fact that one of the main objectives of the BC model is to bring the under banked and unbanked sections into the banking fold through branchless banking system and serve them with basic financial services. However, when they are not receiving one of the basic financial services, that is, 'loan' facility, then the purpose of mere opening a bank account cannot fulfill the objective of financial inclusion.

(ii) Majority of the no-frills accounts are not in maximum utilisation

During the field study, it was found that though the BC model succeeded in opening many no-frills accounts with low or minimum balance, majority of these accounts were not being utilised multi-purpose. A nominal percentage of respondents were using these accounts for stable savings. As already mentioned, some of the respondents from Diwancheruvu village of East Godavari district complain that banks are not showing their willingness in providing loan facilities to the BC clients. In order to make these accounts active and profitable, banks need to offer equal treatment to all its accounts holders including the BC account holders which enables the BC account holder to avail in time.

(iii) Lack of financial awareness about this model

Lack of proper financial education of the bank customer is a barrier to the effective utilisation of various financial services available under this model. A respondent from Chinabonala village of Karimnagar district argues that "though we have opened a bank account, we are not provided with any kind of training on availing various financial services that are available under this model. There is no proper follow up mechanism by the bank officials on the performance of the BCs". In a focus group discussion with some of the BC clients, it is found that some of them expressed their dissatisfaction with its operational structure. They are not given any prior financial and technical education by the BCs regarding operational structure. They are of the view that the procedures to do financial transactions under the BC model are too technical, as it is predominantly assisted by technology and through online transactions. Due to these technical issues, we have to fully depend upon the business correspondent.

(iv) Credibility of the Business Correspondent

During the interview, respondents were asked about the reasons for not utilising the maximum services through bank accounts (for savings, fixed deposit etc) under the BC model. Of the 150 respondents, 72 (48 per cent) stated that they were yet to rely completely on the business correspondents. They are of the view that:

> As we are aware that the business correspondent is directly recruited by the SBI on contract basis. We cannot afford to trust him when it comes to savings as he neither a government employee nor a resident of our village. It is, therefore, whenever we need to save our money, to get various loans and withdrawals, we directly go to the correspondent bank branch and ask the bank staff for necessary help in this regard.

Apart from the above apprehensions noticed by the customers of the BC model, some other respondents, who are part of BC model, state that the business correspondent is not regular in operating financial transactions. He seldom visits the village and meets the clients of BC model.[4] They also add that if they need any urgency in operating their bank account, they have to visit the parent bank, in the absence of business correspondent, for any kind of technical/financial help. From theses observation, it is assumed that if the client has to visit the bank branch, which is away from their own village, then the actual purpose of opening the bank account under the BC model is of no use. Corroborating the field observations, Iyer (2015) in her recent study, believes that trust plays a dominant role in banking sector participation by households. As far the BC model is concerned, lack of trust among the households on business correspondents defeats the very purpose of making financial services more accessible and affordable for the poor.

(v) Smart cards and passbooks are not given to all the BC clients

Respondents express dissatisfaction with regard to issuing of smart cards and passbooks. Of the 150 respondents from the three field surveyed villages, 82 (54 per cent) are not satisfied due to the negligence and poor maintenance in issuing smart cards, passbooks and ATM-debit cards to the account holders. Some of them have said that their account is not yet activated, despite opening the account a month ago. A respondent from Chinabonala village of Karimnagar states that it took 45 days to activate his account after opening an account. In that case, if there is a delay in activating their account and providing various basic financial services, then the account holder lose his/her interest and credibility over the business correspondent, and accordingly the account become inactive.[5]

Business Correspondents' perspective

The study also attempts to highlight some of the practical problems faced by the business correspondents during their financial transactions under the BC model. Three business correspondents from the three villages have been interviewed for this purpose. Some of the drawbacks as presented by them are as follows:

(i) Inadequate financial resources to mobilise savings

Inadequate financial resources become one of the practical hindrances for most of the business correspondents in order to mobilise people to open a bank account under the BC model and inculcate savings habit among them. Apart from the financial resources for promoting the BC model, it is observed from the field survey that the business correspondents are not even getting sufficient wages to sustain as a business correspondent on longer run. Business correspondents from

Delwancheruvu and Chinabonala villages state that "we work under the supervision of nearby State Bank branch and draw salaries from the bank branch itself. However, we are not getting salaries in-time. Sometimes, we get a salary once in two months. This made us depend on the commission charged from the customers of the BC model as a service charge". This makes it clear that the drawback of not providing salaries in-time to the BCs became a burden on the bank customers.

(ii) Lack of Professional Orientation

During the interviews with the business correspondents, it is observed that they are not getting adequate professional training on how to operate POS devises online financial transaction from the correspondent bank branch and various strategies in mobilising the people to open bank accounts under the BC model. In order to run the BC model without any practical problems and to make the model as a successful banking model, adequate professional training for the business correspondents is indispensible. Beside professional orientation, moral support from the bankers to the business correspondents is crucial in making the model feasible. Otherwise, lack of professionalism and support by the bankers certainly affects the performance of the business correspondent and that in turn, impedes the functioning of the BC model. In fact, pertaining to the performance of the BC model, FICCI's report (2012) highlights the lacunae regarding the recruitment of BCs and functioning of BC model. Although RBI permitted a variety of individuals to work as BCs, very few have been engaged by banks. Regarding the performance of BC staff, the report identifies that the BC staff are mostly irregular in the maintenance of records and delay the processing of loans, which subsequently generates a low volume of business for banks.

(iii) Lack of technical infrastructure

Business correspondents from the three field villages surveyed expressed their dissatisfaction over the technological assistance provided by the concerned bank branch. They are of the view that "though the bankers have encouraged us to work as a business correspondent, due to lack of sufficient technological infrastructure, it became difficult to run the BC model". Apart from the operational problems, both from the client's and business correspondent's perspective, some shortcomings are observed from the banker's side as well. During the key-informant interviews with the bank managers, it is observed that the bank managers, who appointed business correspondents to discharge their responsibilities, are not showing enough care and enthusiasm in developing and promoting the BC model. Bankers replied "we do not have complete authority to manage the business correspondents and the BC model. We are running a small bank branch here and we do not have sufficient funds to manage the model. We have to depend upon the district level authorities".

SHG Women and BC Model: A Potential to Foster Financial Inclusion

The field study observations offer a possible link between SHG women and the BC model. These observations generate a possibility that if the banks use SHG women as business correspondents, it may improve the functioning of BC model in mobilising people to be a part of BC model and to avail various financial services. In fact, the RBI in a circular released on 25 January 2006, recognised the potentialities of the SHGs in delivering various financial services to the poor in general and women in particular. The RBI states that with the objective of ensuring financial inclusion and increasing the outreach of the banking sector, it has been decided in public interest to enable banks to use the services of SHGs as one of the potential intermediaries in providing financial services using business correspondent model (RBI, 2006).

Similarly, in a recent study on the BC model in Andhra Pradesh, Ananth and Sabri (2014) found some of the SHG women working as business correspondents in Kurnool and Chittoor districts of the state. They believe that encouraging village organisations (VOs) or the district level SHG federations (Zilla Samakhyas) to become business correspondents can be considered for the forward integration of the SHG movement into the BC model. They argue that the SHG women, who are successfully running various self-employment activities, have the potential to save money, however these sections have been so far ignored in opening individual bank accounts. Corroborating the above statement, P. Chidambaram, the then Finance Minister of Union Government, at the inauguration of the first Bharatiya Mahila Bank

(BMB) in Mumbai on November 19, 2013 estimated that only 26 per cent of women in India have bank accounts and per capita credit for women is currently 80 per cent lower than that for men. He further argues, "there is deep-seated bias, at institutional and individual levels against women. Since fewer women have bank accounts, fewer women get bank loans."[6] These arguments emphasise the urgent need of improving the banking habit among women. Considering the magnitude of the problem of exclusion of women from the banking system, it is essential to include them in every activity that promotes and promises financial inclusion. The idea of appointing SHG women as business correspondents, therefore, could be seen as an effective strategy for including the hitherto financially excluded sections in the banking ambit.

Recognising the importance of financial inclusion of women and appointing SHG women as business correspondents to promote the BC model, this study has attempted to identify and examine the possible linkages between SHG women as a business correspondent and the development of the BC model in all the three field areas surveyed. However, the study found that no woman is appointed as a business correspondent yet and, in particular, nobody from the SHG. The literature proved that the SHG women can maintain a strong communicative network within the village. As a group, they can have easy access from the village president to households of poor women (Ananth and Sabri, 2014). If an active SHG member is appointed as a business correspondent, then the possibility of opening a bank account by the SHG women will increase. If female members come forward to open a bank account within the family, it may not only ensure financial inclusion but also increase women's participation in the financial domain. Moreover, with regard to the functioning of the BC model, having a SHG woman as business correspondent, the problem of irregularity and unavailability of the business correspondent will be relatively reduced. There is a possibility of the female business correspondents, as SHG members, making themselves more accessible and frequently available to the other SHG members of the village. It is therefore, high time to look at the possibilities of appointing active SHG members as a business correspondent in order to develop the BC model.

Summary of the Field Survey

The present chapter examined the impact of SHG-Bank Linkage Programme (SBLP) model and Business Correspondent (BC) model in the process of promoting financial inclusion of the rural poor. As far as the former model is concerned, the study inferred that the public sector banks, apart from providing SHG-Bank Linkage loan to the SHG women, are encouraging SHG members to open individual bank accounts under 'no-frills account' category. The study reported that, of the 150 SHG women respondents, 92 (61 per cent) had opened no-frills accounts in various public sector banks. It is also observed that these banks are encouraging these customers to utilise various basic financial services such as savings, fixed deposits, availing gas subsidy through cash transfer, availing Indiramma housing loan, availing any other loan facility and so on. On the other hand, the bankers are also encouraging rural communities, particularly SHG women to open individual bank account by simplifying the Know Your Customer (KYC) norms. Apart from these initiatives, the Government of Andhra Pradesh, with the help of Reserve Bank of India (RBI), has been promoting various training programmes for the SHG women such as awareness camp on promoting financial inclusion, awareness camp on availing Sreenidhi scheme, training programme on formation and functioning of JLGs and so on. From these findings, it is clear that SBLP model in Andhra Pradesh has become instrumental in not only providing loans to the women as a group, but also attributing significant impact in bringing rural women to formal financial fold through various initiatives.

However, of the 92 respondents, who opened bank account under no-frills category, 47 (51 per cent) use it for availing gas subsidy through cash transfer scheme. With reference to Business Correspondent model, of the 150 respondents, a maximum of 60 (40 per cent) opened bank account primarily to avail gas subsidy and interestingly, all the 60 respondents are from female category. From both the SBLP and BC model, the majority of the female respondents who opened bank accounts under the BC model are using the account only for availing gas subsidy; and availing loan facility and savings have received least priority. This observation could be seen as a limitation of promoting no-frills accounts as well as implementation of the BC model. In fact, in a recent study, Iyer (2015) argues that if there is no financial capacity to save and use of other financial services by the people through BC model, then it is difficult to envisage its contributions in promoting financial inclusion. The study found that insufficient income for savings and lack of financial awareness on how to open a bank account are the major drawbacks in operating the individual bank accounts. Of the 150-sample frame, 96 (64 per cent) respondents are not aware of KYC norms. As far as women's participation in training programmes is concerned, the study found that 53 (35 per cent) respondents have not participated in any awareness camps/training programmes that undermine the very objective of SHG, that is, 'group participation'. The study, therefore, highlights the importance of financial literacy and emphasises the need to put more efforts to give wider publicity to bridge the gap between the beneficiaries and the SBLP model. It also emphasises the need for promoting various kinds of loans to the rural communities for on-farm and off-farm activities, which may increase their income levels and further improve their savings capacity.

With regard to Business Correspondent (BC) model, the study inferred that the model can be seen as 'an alternative formal banking structure' to the traditional banking process. It aims at improving banking facilities to the remote regions. It can be understood that this model has the potential to bridge the gap between the service providers (the banks) and the service seekers (clients) who are under-served and unbanked. The field observations, however, show some mixed results. The operation/utilisation of the bank account under the BC model by the respondents is not satisfactory. They are yet to utilise the discernible benefits of an active bank account and various financial services being provided under the BC model. The study found several operational problems of the BC model and brought out few important shortcomings both from the customer's and business correspondent's perspective. While highlighting the importance of financial inclusion of the poor in general and women in particular, the study concludes that the linkages between SHG women as a business correspondent may enhance the development of the BC model.

References

1. Keynote address delivered by Dr. Raghuram Rajan, Governor, Reserve Bank of India, on 'Financial Inclusion: Technology, Institutions and Policies' at

the NASSCOM India Leadership Forum in Mumbai on Febrauray12, 2014. For more details, see www.rbi.org.in.speeches

2. On the basis of recommendations made by an Internal Group of Reserve Bank of India (RBI) on 'Rural Credit and Microfinance'. For more details, see Khan Committee 2006.
3. Matthan, Rahul (2014) 'Identity Crisis: The Supreme Court order on Aadhaar averted a looming disaster', *The Indian Express*, 3 April, p.8.
4. During the field study, it is observed that due to lack of sufficient staff, one business correspondent supervising more than six villages in the East Godavari district. It certainly, diminishes the quality of work, and accountability in financial transactions of the business correspondent.
5. Micro Save India (2011), one of its research paper argues that there are now 25 million 'no-frills' accounts in India, of which less than 3 million (11 per cent) are active.
6. "Mahila bank to offer universal banking services", *The Hindu,* November, 20, 2013.

Chapter VII

Conclusion

This chapter primarily synthesises various arguments put forth in the preceding theoretical chapters and summarises the main findings of the empirical chapters. In doing so, the chapter highlights and analyses the potential of SHG-Bank Linkage Programme (SBLP) and Business Correspondent (BC) models in terms of the two main claims: poverty alleviation and financial inclusion of the poor. Further, it offers a few suggestions for the successful functioning of SBLP and BC models with a special emphasis on Microfinance Institutions (MFIs). The chapter draws three inferences: First, the provision of delivering subsidized credit through SBLP has a positive impact on creation of various livelihood opportunities for the rural poor. However, it is argued that merely providing subsidized credit and individual bank accounts may not address the multidimensional nature of poverty. Second, financial inclusion is an ongoing and a progressive process. Its success depends upon access to adequate, affordable and timely credit along with the availability of basic financial services and its optimum usage by the people. Third, as far as the BC model is concerned, it is primarily an agent driven model and its success depends upon the efficiency and motivation of the business correspondents in connecting with the customers and creating awareness among them.

With the ascendancy of the concept of microcredit in development literature, access to credit is widely debated. It is believed that lending small loans to the rural unbanked population would create small-scale self-employment opportunities to improve their income levels and uplift them from the clutches of poverty. An argument has been put forward that besides various welfare and developmental policies, it is imperative for women to become financially aware and economically independent. Accordingly, an alternative strategy to poverty alleviation has been advanced to not only uplift the poor, particularly women, but also to enhance their resilience. It did not take much time for the policy-makers to understand that offering tiny loans and promotion of self-employment opportunities alone may not be a substitute for the holistic development of rural people. In the larger developmental discourse, it has been argued that the need of the hour is to bring the hitherto unbanked poor and women into the ambit of institutional finance by providing basic financial services. On this assumption, academicians and policymakers have searched for various microfinance and banking models and initiatives to promote financial inclusion. In this discourse, the achievement of poverty alleviation and financial inclusion is all about integrating the potentialities of various microfinance and banking models which are aimed at providing adequate credit and other financial services at an affordable cost.

Given this backdrop, the study made an attempt to conceptualise the multidimensional nature of poverty and understand the concept of microfinance in relation to poverty alleviation. The study assumed that the notion of poverty is a multifaceted phenomenon in its content and definition, and its scope has been widened over time. The study further argues that poverty is not only related to lack of income, education, health, housing, social security and so on but also about lack of access to adequate and affordable institutional credit. With this assumption, first, the study attempted to find out the potential linkage between microfinance intervention and livelihood promotion of rural women. This line of thought has brought the concepts of Self-Help Groups (SHGs) and microfinance intervention through SHG-Bank Linkage Programme (SBLP) model to the forefront. Second, having realised the need for financial inclusion of the rural poor, the Government of India, with the help of Reserve Bank of India, has come up with a new model in the realm of banking sector called the Business Correspondent (BC) model. This model, it is claimed, is an important banking model that intends to provide various financial services to the geographically diverse population, particularly in rural areas, and those who remained financially excluded from the banking system (Karmakar, 2009). Thus, the study made an attempt to assess the impact of the BC model on respondents' access to various financial services. Third, in the light of the recent microfinance institutions (MFIs) crisis in the undivided state of Andhra Pradesh, the study also attempted to examine the reasons for the recent microfinance crisis, and the state government's response to mitigate this crisis. Before examining these issues, the study briefly provides theoretical insights of microfinance and financial inclusion.

The study highlights that in the late 1970s and early 1980s, the idea of microfinance was invoked as a small-scale philanthropic movement, intended to provide small loans for unbanked poor households, particularly women. Later on, this practice matured into a financial approach which aimed to break gender barriers in accessing credit services. The study approaches microfinance from two perspectives. The first is an attempt to understand the ideological circumstances in which microfinance emerged. It situates the microfinance intervention in neoliberal policies in the early 1990s, whereby the governments in different countries have encouraged private (non-state) financial institutions to provide credit facilities to poor. It is evident that before the advent of neo-liberalism, the state had been the major player in steering the economy and providing credit and subsidies to rural community. The initiation of neo-liberal policies altered the role of the state by shrinking its space, which has now come to be dominated by the market and private institutions. A significant change brought by this shift has been in the area of credit availability.

The second perspective is more practically oriented. This is the recognition of a new alternative mechanism for poverty alleviation by Professor Muhammad Yunus through the establishment of Grameen Bank in 1984. Having influenced by the success and popularity of Grameen Bank model, the concept of microcredit has been recognised as an important strategy to alleviate poverty in many developing countries. In addition, the concept gained broad acceptance due to the World Bank's attempts to authorise microcredit as a poverty alleviation project. During the 1990s, the World Bank and other international agencies have officially adopted and promoted microcredit schemes for poverty reduction in developing countries. Such promotion took place either through active government intervention whereby state sponsored banks took the lead or through private organisations such as MFIs. It is understood that though the concept of microfinance was initially encouraged by the private players, later on, owing to its popularity, potential market and credit need of the poor, this intervention has also been encouraged and promoted by public sector banks in many developing countries through various models.

The study also deals with financial inclusion which is a global phenomenon in the banking system. The idea of financial inclusion has assumed greater importance in many developing countries as a large segment of the population does not have access to basic financial services. The study reviewed various concepts related to financial inclusion and its significance, besides identifying the problems in the process of achieving it. In India, a variety of microfinance and banking models have been introduced in order to achieve financial inclusion. Holding a bank account, delivery of products and services through a variety of banking models, promoting financial literacy, facilitating technological assistance in accessing various financial services and active participation and optimum utilisation of financial services by the end users are the important stages in the process achieving financial inclusion (Frost and Sullivan, 2009). In this regard, the SBLP model and Business Correspondent (BC) model have emerged as the favoured delivery channels to promote financial inclusion. The former model aims at providing credit and other financial services to women through SHGs. The latter model intends to reach out to the geographically diverse population, particularly those who are financially excluded from the mainstream banking services; and to ensure doorstep delivery of financial products and services.

Having recognised the potential synergy between microfinance, poverty and financial inclusion, the study has adopted a broader objective, assessing the impact of SBLP model, MFI Model and BC model on poverty alleviation and financial inclusion of the poor in Andhra Pradesh and Telangana. The study tested the following hypotheses:

H1: SHG-Bank Linkage Programme (SBLP) and Business Correspondent (BC) model may have a positive impact on alleviating poverty and promoting the process of financial inclusion of the poor.

H2: The easy accessibility of microcredit may lead to over dependency on the MFIs that lead to serious repercussions for the rural poor.

Key observations on the Impact of SBLP model on Poverty Alleviation

- From the field survey, it is observed that the respondents who are in the age group of 31-40 years actively take part in the SBLP model. Of the 150 respondents, 58 fall under this category. It was found that a total of 32 women with more than five years of experience as a group member undertook self-employment activities in all the three villages. This observation could be seen as a positive sign as respondents' experience as a group member for more than five years has a significant impact in improving their livelihood opportunities.
- The study found a positive correlation between education levels of the respondents and the functioning of the SHGs. It was observed that education levels of some SHG members enabled them to operate their accounts, and negotiate with group leaders and bank staff to access better facilities. It also enhanced their participation in various training programmes, financial literacy workshops and livelihood promotion programmes undertaken at the block and district level.
- As far as the utilisation of loans is concerned, availing microcredit with subsidized interest rates has had a significant impact on the creation of various livelihood opportunities in the study area. Among the total 150 respondents, 96 have availed a bank loan and utilised it for various income-generating activities such as livestock rearing, tailoring, bangle store, fruit selling, vegetable shop, chat bandar etc. Most of the respondents saved money from the income they earned and repaid their monthly loan installments. In contrast, the remaining 54 respondents did not use the loan amount productively. They used it for daily consumption, social ceremonies and emergencies. This feature is predominant among the SHG members belonging to SC and BC communities. It is to be noted that larger proportion of them are landless and daily-wage labourers. Thus, it is seen that women from socially advanced castes gain from the practices of SHGs whereas respondents from deprived backgrounds fail to benefit.
- It is also observed that the respondents who utilised their loan for various self-employment activities showed improvement

in their income levels. It has a considerable impact on their living standards and their contribution to family income. The 96 respondents who utilised the loan for income-generation were able to purchase food items and electronic goods, invest in children's education, healthcare, house construction and repaid old debts. In other words, it is understood that utilisation of loan for productive purposes can improve the purchasing capacity of the people.

- As far as the participation of women in socio-economic and political activities are concerned, it was found that of the 150 women respondents, 77 have participated in various developmental activities organised at the village level. The participation of women, even at the mandal level is one of the encouraging trends.
- About half of the total respondents have shown interest in renovating their houses from the surpluses they made from small businesses. It is a good sign that they are investing the profits that they have made from businesses rather than the amount they have borrowed.
- The study also observed a few limitations in the operations of SBLP model. Some of the respondents expressed their dissatisfaction over the functioning of SHGs. They cited the following reasons: lack of mutual understanding within the group; disappointment over the behaviour of their group president; unaccountability in distribution of the loan; and lack of participation by some of the group members in monthly meetings. These problems not only reflect the poor governance of the SHGs, but also talk about lack of effective leadership that evidently have a negative impact on the functioning and sustenance of a group.
- The study examined the possibility of running various group-based small-scale income generating activities by the SHG women. Though the respondents have been engaged in various individual self-employment activities, the study found that no group employment activity emerged in the selected three villages. Lack of entrepreneurial and management skills to initiate and sustain medium scale entrepreneurial ventures have

become a considerable limitation. The study concludes that mere provision of subsidized credit delivery alone is not sufficient to achieve poverty alleviation.

Key Observations on the Impact of SBLP Model on Financial Inclusion

- Of the 150 women respondents, 92 have opened no-frills accounts in various public sector banks. However, majority of the no-frills accounts are not in active mode as the respondents operate them once in two months for banking purposes. Those who have not opened no-frills accounts replied that insufficient income to save, and lack of financial awareness are the major factors that obstructed them in opening an individual bank account.
- Most of the respondents are not aware of Know Your Customer (KYC) norms. For instance, of the 150 respondents, only 54 knew about the KYC norms and the remaining 96 were not aware of these norms. It can be concluded that financial awareness and financial literacy are important vis-à-vis promotion of financial inclusion. As far as the saving pattern is concerned, 42 per cent of the respondents in Chinabonala village stated that they do not have sufficient income to save money or keep the bank account in an active mode. The observations emphasise the need of promoting financial literacy and various awareness programmes among the rural unbanked people.
- The study found that majority of the respondents had not participated in any awareness camps/training programmes. Hence, it undermines the very objective of SHG, that is, 'group participation'.
- It is observed that banks which have their branches in villages may encourage people to open bank accounts and also influence the participation levels in various training programmes/awareness camps being conducted by the concerned bank's branch. For instance, it is observed that both Diwancheruvu and Taduku villages have branches of State Bank of India (SBI). This one of the reasons for the higher number of customers and active participation of people in various training programmes in both the villages as

compared to Chinabonala village of Karimnagar district. It indicates the necessity of establishing rural bank branches in every gram panchayat.

Key Observations of Microfinance Institution (MFI) Model

The study also attempted to draw some important observations regarding the functioning of MFI model in the wake of recent microfinance crisis in undivided Andhra Pradesh. Significant inputs were received from the respondents related to issues such as the MFIs operational structure, rate of interest, purpose of lending, reasons for suicides, and other necessary information. This first-hand information helped the researcher to draw some important observations on the functioning of MFIs. A total of 106 respondents (out of 150) of this study (71 per cent) have previously borrowed from MFIs. Therefore, the analysis related to MFI functioning is restricted to the inputs received from 106 members of the total sampling.

- Majority of the respondents who borrowed from MFIs were belonging to BC and SC communities. For instance, of the 106 respondents, 18 belong to Forward caste, 34 belong to SC community, 11 belong to ST community and 43 belong to BC community.
- The average loan amount provided by any MFI was between Rs 20000-50000 and occasionally it has reached the upper limit. As stated, MFI borrowings are in addition to the borrowings from SHGs. Multiple borrowing shows the high aspirations for credit and reflect the financial need of the poor rural households.
- What emerged quite strange is the fact that the majority of those who had borrowed from MFIs were unaware of the exact interest rate charged by the MFIs. When inquired, there were discrepancies in the response from the respondents as different respondents cited various interest rates being charged by MFIs. This shows the lack of awareness among the borrowers about the interest rates charged by various MFIs.
- Less than 45 per cent of the respondents used the loan for income-generation activities and the rest of them used it for consumption purposes. On the other hand, in the SBLP model, of the 150 respondents, 96 (64 per cent) availed bank

loan and utilised it for income-generation, the remaining 54 respondents (36 per cent) used it for consumption purposes. It can be concluded that those availing loan from the SBLP model are investing in productive purposes as compared to beneficiaries of the MFI whose consumption usage is high. It is found that there was no encouragement by the MFIs in relation to the creation of income-generating activities.

- An important observation related to training and skill development is that a total of 79 respondents expressed that they could not receive any kind of business advice or entrepreneurial training. They further went on to say that the staff of the MFIs have not spoken anything about the business advice or skill development.
- From the study, three main factors have been observed to be responsible for the current microfinance crisis: (i) exorbitant interest rates, (ii) weekly repayment collection practices and (iii) coercive and highhanded behaviour of MFI staff in recovering the loans.

Key Observations of the Business Correspondent (BC) Model

With regard to the BC model, the study concluded that the model can be seen as an alternative to the formal banking structure and the traditional banking process.

- From the responses of the business correspondents, it is found that savings, fixed deposit, cash transfers, cash withdrawals, availing various loans, availing scholarship facility by the students, and availing gas subsidy in the form of cash transfer and pensions are some of the important financial services available to the customers of the BC model.
- It is interesting to note that in the total sample frame of 150 respondents, female respondents (77) are higher than the male respondents (73). It is mainly because many subsidy schemes are being targeted at women such as gas subsidy, housing loan, loans for dairy farming and so on.
- The respondents who are enrolled under the BC model are high among the BCs followed by SCs. It is lowest among the ST category. It reveals that the BC model has not received

proper attention among the rural poor, particularly disadvantaged sections like SCs and STs. This defeats the very purpose of creating the BC model in rural areas.

- There is no correlation between education levels and holding a bank account under the BC model by the female respondents. For instance, women have opened bank accounts primarily to avail gas subsidy in the form of cash transfer. It is not because of basic services as prescribed in the BC model. It means that the domestic necessity of cooking and availing gas subsidy have encouraged them to open bank accounts. It is, however, observed that a few respondents also use the same account to avail additional financial services. To conclude, it is found to be more of an account opening exercise rather than on focused on the real task of ensuring financial inclusion.
- It is also found that the occupational pattern of a few respondents has significant impact on opening a bank account and utilising it for availing loan services. For instance, a recent initiative by the public sector banks in providing Rs 5 lakh to start dairy farming in rural areas has influenced some of the respondents of the BC and forward castes to open an individual bank account.
- According to the RBI guidelines, business correspondents need to be well educated and should come from the same village. However, the business correspondent from Diwancheruvu village of East Godavari district is acting as a business correspondent for six villages. This shows the banker's lackadaisical approach towards developing the BC model.
- As far the inadequate infrastructure is concerned, it is observed that the Point of Service handheld devices (POS devices) have not been given to the business correspondents. It is found that banks are tardy in issuing smart cards to all the account holders who have opened savings bank accounts under the BC model. It needs to be highlighted that without POS device, smart cards and other infrastructure, it is very difficult to run the BC model.
- Due to poor internet connectivity in the villages, the business correspondents are facing technical problems in opening a

bank account and to carry out other transactions online. The basic purpose of the BC model is to ensure hassle free banking services to the poor at their doorstep without any time loss. However, due to poor infrastructure, the implementation of the BC model has not yielded positive results.

Recommendations

- As far as the SBLP model is concerned, apart from providing subsidized credit to rural women to start small-scale business ventures, the government with the help of banks should promote various skill-based training programmes. Further, the government should come forward to create market linkages and required infrastructure to promote the indigenous goods produced by rural communities. In fact, respondents opine that they are not excited to open a new business activity as they may fail to cope-up with the market trends.
- The RBI should also take necessary measures in promoting skill-based training programmes for SHG women. In Andhra Pradesh and Telangana, the Society for the Elimination of Rural Poverty (SERP) must come up with various necessary training programmes and encourage women self-employers. The public sector banks may also partner with SERP in organising such training programmes.
- Rural banks must encourage SHG women to take up innovative income-generating activities against the conventional work they carry out such as beedi-rolling, basket-making, mat-weaving and so on.
- Development of the 'Sthreenidhi' scheme in both the states of Andhra Pradesh and Telangana is immediate need of the hour as it has the potential to reduce rural women's dependency on MFIs and local money-lenders.
- With reference to MFI model, the idea of providing small loans to the poor people through MFIs requires structural changes. In particular, the changes are required in its functioning, charging of interest rates and the behaviour of the MFI staff in approaching the poor borrowers.
- As far as the recovery method is concerned, MFIs should increase the grace period and reduce the frequency of

repayment from 50 equitable weekly repayments to monthly repayments as practiced in the SBLP model. In other words, MFIs should come up with long-term loans that would give enough time to the borrowers to earn and save money out of their business ventures.

- Lending procedures should be modified and business schemes and training programmes should be restructured to address the customised need of the business venture. As advocated by Huff (2011) and Flores (2014) MFIs should try to synchronise both the institutionist and welfarist approach. In other words, both the 'organisational sustainability' of the institutionist approach and the 'depth of outreach' of the welfarist stance should go hand-in-hand.
- As far as the governance issues are concerned, MFIs must ensure transparency in its management and act as responsible financial institutions. In particular, with regard to interest rates, these institutions need to show accountability. After all, success of any lending institutions depends upon improving the well-being of its borrowers through their services. Importantly, the microfinance institutions must follow the recommendations of 'Andhra Pradesh Microfinance Institutions (Regulation of Money Lending) Act, 2010 and the Malegam Committee report (2011).'
- Proper training for the MFI field staff/agents in recovering loans from the borrowers is necessary. It is also important to make them free from target pressure of their officers.
- There is also a need to create a follow up mechanism by the banks. For instance, the RBI must allow rural bank branches to monitor the operations of MFIs in rural areas to ensure transparency and adherence to best practices.
- As far as the BC model is concerned, the salaries of the Business Correspondents (BCs) need to be increased as they are not satisfied with the salary of Rs 5000 provided to them. It is found that insufficient salary has a negative effect on their performance and it encourages them to collect unauthorised service charges from the customers in the form of commissions.

- The study suggests that recruiting active SHG women as business correspondents may solve the demand side problems. If an active SHG member is appointed as a business correspondent, then the possibility of opening a bank account by the other SHG women will increase. They may undertake the banking formalities on behalf of the illiterate or semi-literate women and other people. In addition, they can also financially educate many illiterate women and make them aware of various financial services and schemes.
- The successful functioning of the BC model depends on the effective performance of the BCs. In this regard, the parent bank branch in the concerned area must provide required technological assistance and skill development training sessions regularly to the BCs. In particular, POS devices should be given to BCs in order to ensure proper functioning and quick services of the BC model.
- Smart cards should be given to the BC model customer as soon as they open the bank account under the BC model so that they can use the account and make transactions easily. In fact, issuing smart cards could be seen as one of the strategies to promote the BC model by the bankers.

On the whole, it is observed that the goal of poverty alleviation through promoting financial inclusion of women in rural areas, through different microfinance and banking models is a laudable attempt. In particular, encouraging women to start self-employment activities, encouraging them to be economically independent and further promoting them to be a part of formal banking system through SBLP and BC models could be seen as a forward linkage from poverty alleviation to financial inclusion. From the field-survey observations, it can be inferred that the provision of delivering tiny loans, particularly through SBLP model has a positive impact on creation of various livelihood opportunities in relation to alleviating rural poverty. However, merely providing subsidized credit for self-employment through SBLP model and providing individual bank account alone through the BC model may not address the multidimensional nature of poverty. It is also pertinent to understand that without addressing multidimensional nature of poverty, an effort to achieve full-cycle of financial inclusion is not possible.

Financial inclusion is an ongoing and a progressive process in the banking system. Its success depends upon various factors including access to adequate, affordable and timely credit along with availability of basic financial services and its optimum usage by the people. In other words, achieving financial inclusion is a concerted effort of government, bankers and the end users or beneficiaries. As far as the BC model is concerned, it is primarily an agent driven model and its success depends upon the efficiency and motivation of the business correspondent in connecting with the customers and creating awareness among them. The government's thrust on financial inclusion largely hinges on the role played by the business correspondents. The BC model, however, has important limitations. The usage of the accounts opened under the BC model is low and most of the accounts lie dormant. This underscores the need to pay greater attention to provide customer centric products and services that would motivate the customers to utilise the bank accounts and avail the appropriate services. Moreover, the business correspondents are facing serious problems in maintaining wide network and quality service due to lack of infrastructure and technical inadequacy. It is evident from the field survey that both the demand and supply side factors are equally responsible for the poor performance of the BC model.

Amid promoting the strategies to achieve financial inclusion, it is worth mentioning that the Government of India recently came up with an initiative, named, the Pradhan Mantri Jan-Dhan Yojana (PMJDY) on 28 August, 2014. It is primarily intended to financially empower people by opening bank accounts for two adults in every household and providing various basic banking services. It is reported that as of February 6, 2015 there are a total of 12.65 crore bank accounts opened under PMJDY, however, 8.5 crore of such accounts lie dormant. While these figures emphasise the government's efforts in providing bank accounts to the hitherto financial excluded households, on the one hand, the inactivity of bank accounts on the other highlights the lackadaisical approach of the bankers in propelling the scheme. This suggests that the public sector banks must ensure an optimum utilisation of these services by the needy sections. The banks, therefore, ought to play an instrumental role in building an effective credit information system, creating awareness of how to utilise various financial services, promoting financial education and counseling on management of credit, savings, debt repayment and so on. From the community side, the beneficiaries, especially women and low-income groups must be empowered to utilise all the available financial services and reap the perceptible benefits, which are essentially designed and aimed at their economic upliftment and to achieve the larger goal of financial inclusion.

Bibliography

Books

Abdullah-Al-Mamum and Ridhwan, F. (2008), 'Micro-Finance: An Overview'. In: Daniel, Lazar and Palanichamy, P. eds. *Micro-Finance and Poverty Eradication: Indian and Global Experience*. New Delhi: New Century Publications. pp. 43-55.

Ahmad, Rais (2008), 'Role of Micro-Finance in Empowering Women'. In: Sinha, Ajit Kumar eds. *New Dimensions of Women Empowerment*. New Delhi: Deep and Deep Publications. pp. 150-162

Bateman, Milford (2010), *Why Does not Microfinance Work? The Destructive Rise of Local Neoliberalism*. London: Zed Books.

Besley, T. (1995), 'Saving, Credit and Insurance'. In: Behrman, J. and Srinivasan, T.N. eds. *Handbook of Development Economics*, Vol. IIIa, Amsterdam: North Holland.

Bhat, G.M. and Hussain Altaf Kira (2009), 'Changing Dynamics of Microcredit in India: Transition from NGO to Non-Banking Financial Company'. In: Thakur, Anil Kumar and Praveen Sharma eds. *Microcredit and Rural Development*. New Delhi: Deep and Deep Publications. pp. 134-163.

Bhattacharya, B.B. (1988), *Financial Reforms and Financial Development in India*. New Delhi: Shri Jainendra Press.

Das, Sabyasachi (2005), 'Self-Help Groups and Micro-Credit Synergic Integration'. In: Verma, S.B and Pawar, Y.T. eds. *Rural Empowerment through SHGs, NGOs and PRIs*. New Delhi: Deep & Deep Publications, Pvt. Ltd., pp. 27-35.

De Aghion, A.B. and Jonathan, Morduch (2004), 'Microfinance: Where do we Stand?'. In: Goodhart, C.A.E. eds. Financial Development and Economic Growth. United Kingdom: Palgrave MacMillan. pp. 135-148.

De Aghion, A.B. and Jonathan, Morduch (2005), *The Economics of Microfinance*. London: The MIT Press Cambridge.

De Haan, Arjan and Naila, Kabeer (2008), *Social Exclusion: Two Essays*. New Delhi: Critical Quest.

Dichter, Thomas and Harper, Malcolm (2007), *What's Wrong with Microfinance?*. New Delhi: Practical Action Publishing.

Elango, K. (2010), 'Performance of Micro Finance on Women Entrepreneurs of SHGs in Aranthangai Taluk of Pudukkotai District'. In: Lazer, Danial, Natarajan. P. and Malabika Deo eds. *Macro dynamics of Microfinance*. New Delhi: Excel Books. pp. 303-323.

Ghate, Prabhu (2007), *Indian Microfinance: The Challenges of Rapid Growth*. New Delhi: Sage Publications.

Ghosh, B. K. and Patel, K. V. (1991), 'Institutional Credit for Farm Sector in India with Particular Reference to Small and Marginal Farmers'. In: Shah. S. eds. *Rural Credit Issues for Nineties*. New Delhi: IBA Publishing Company.

Giles, Mohan (2009), 'Structural Adjustment'. In: Kitchin, R. and Thrift, N. eds. *International Encyclopedia of Human Geography* (1-9). Oxford University Press: United Kingdom.

Goodhart Charles, A. E. (Ed.). (2004), *Financial Development and Economic Growth: Explaining the Links*. New Delhi: Palgrave Macmillan.

Hans-Dieter, Roth (2007), *Indian Money Lenders at Work: Case Studies of the Traditional Rural Credit in Dhanbad District, Bihar*. New Delhi: Manohar Publishers & Distributors.

Harper, Malcolm (2003), *Microfinance: Evolution, Achievements and Challenges*. New Delhi: Samskriti Publications.

Higinbothan, S.H. (1995), *Managing to Empower: The Grameen Bank's Experience of Poverty Alleviation*. Dhaka: University Press Ltd.

Hulme, David (2007), 'Is Micro debt good for poor people? A not of the dark side of microfinance'. In: Dichter, Thomas and Malcolm, Harper eds. *What's Wrong with Microfinance?*. New Delhi: Practical Action Publishing. pp. 53-69.

Hulme, David and Arun, T. (2009), 'The Future of Microfinance'. In: Hulme, David and Arun, T. eds. *Microfinance: A Reader.* New York: Routledge Publications.

Iddi Makombe, Eulalia, Tembo and Aggrey Kihombo (2005) 'Micro-Credit and Women's Empowerment: Evidence from the Credit Scheme for Productive Activities of Women in Tanzania'. In Menon Vineetha, Nair, Gopinath and Nair, K.N. eds. *Alleviating Poverty: Case studies of Local-level Linkages and Process in the Developing World.* Noida: Rainbow Publishers. pp. 233-251.

Ismi, Asad (2004), *Impoverishing a Continent: The World Bank and the IMF in Africa.* Canada: Canadian Centre for Policy Alternatives.

Jain, B.M. (2009) 'Microfinance for Inclusive Growth and Inclusive Finance: Issues and Policy Options'. In: Thakur, Anil Kumar and Praveen Sharma eds. *Microcredit and Rural Development.* New Delhi: Deep and Deep Publications Pvt.Ltd. pp. 416-429.

Jodka, Surinder. S. (2014), *Caste in Contemporary India.* Delhi: Routledge Publishers.

Joshi, Deepali Pant (2011), *The Financial Inclusion Imperative and Sustainable Approaches.* Delhi: Foundation Books.

Kamdar, Sangita (Ed.). (2007), *Microfinance, Self-Employment and Poverty Alleviation.* New Delhi: Himalaya Publishing House.

Karmakar, K.G. (2011), *Towards Financial Inclusion in India.* New Delhi: Sage Publications.

Katuri, Nageswara R. (Ed.). (2002), *Bank Credit: Emerging Trends.* The ICFAI University Press.

Kochhar, Sameer (2014), *Defeating Poverty: Jan-Dhan and Beyond.* New Delhi: Skoch Media Pvt. Ltd.

Kumar Karthick, Fazil, M. and Anbarasu (2010), 'Risk Based Pricing in Microfinance'. In: Lazer Danial, Natarajan. P. and Malabika Deo eds. *Macro Dynamics of Microfinance.* New Delhi: Excel Books. pp. 152-162.

Kumar, Abhishek and Alpana Sharma (2009), 'Microfinance: Some Important Variables of Microfinance Programme in India'. In: Thakur, Anil Kumar and Praveen Sharma eds. *Microcredit and Rural Development*. New Delhi: Deep and Deep Publications. pp. 246-267.

Kurien, C.T. (1987), *Analysing Redistribution Policy.* New York: Cambridge University Press.

Lakshmi Narasaiah, M. (2008), *Microcredit and Women*. New Delhi: Discovery Publishing House Pvt. Ltd.

Lalitha, N. (2004), 'Women in Panchayat Raj System: Empowerment through Self-Help Groups'. In: Palanithurai (Ed.). *Dynamics of New Panchayati Raj System in India*. Vol. IV, *Empowering Women.* New Delhi: Concept Company.

Lazar, Daniel and Palanichamy. P. (Ed.) (2008), *Microfinance and Poverty Eradication.* New Delhi: Century Publications.

Lazar, Daniel, Matarajan P. and Malabika Deo (Ed.). (2010), *Macro Dynamics of Micro Finance*. New Delhi: Excel Books.

Lazar, Daniel, Matarajan P. and Malabika Deo (Ed.). (2010), *Microfinance: Enabling Empowerment*. Chennai: Vijay Nicole Imprints (P) Ltd.

Madeline, Hirschland (2005), *Savings Services for the Poor: An Operational Guide.* New Delhi: Kumarian Press, Inc.

Mahadeva, M. (2008), 'Financial Inclusion in India'. In: Lazer, Daniel and Palanichamy, P. eds. *Microfinance and Poverty Eradication*. New Delhi: New Century Publications. pp. 179-182.

Marguerites, S. and Robinson (1997), *Microfinance in Indonesia.* The Unesco Courier, Pro Quest Research Library.

Menon, Vineetha, Nair Gopinath, P.R. and Nair, K.N. (Ed.). (2005), *Alleviating Poverty: Case Studies of Local-Level Linkages and Process in the Developing World.* Uttar Pradesh: Rainbow Publishers.

Milgram, L. (2006), 'Banking on Bananas, Crediting Crafts: Financing Women's Work in the Philippine Cordillera'. In: Fernando, J.L. eds. *Microfinance Perils and Prospects*. Routledge Publications: London and New York. pp. 12-186.

Misra, B. S. and Rau, P.K. (2008), 'Regional Rural Banks in India: Past, Present and Future'. In: Sharma, Maboranjan eds. *Dynamics of Indian Banking: Views and Vistas*. New Delhi: Atlantic Publishers & Distributors (p) Ltd. pp. 274-293.

Mohan, Rakesh (2008), 'Economic Growth, Financial Deepening and Financial Inclusion'. In: Sharma Maboranjan eds. *Dynamics of Indian Banking: Views and Vistas*. New Delhi: Atlantic Publishers & Distributors (p) Ltd. pp.142-157.

Mujumdar, N.M. (2002), *Financial Sector Reforms: Indian's Economic Development.* New Delhi: Academic Foundation.

Murthy, R.K. and Sankaran, L. (2001), *Denial and Distress: Gender, Poverty and Human Rights in Asia.* Bangalore: Books for Change.

Navin Anand and Monika, Khanna (Ed.). (2010), *Ready Reckoner on Microfinance.* New Delhi: UNDP.

Neera, B., Joy Deshmukh-Ranadive and Ranjani K. M. (2005), *Micro-Credit, Poverty and Empowerment: Linking the Triad.* New Delhi: Sage Publications.

Niranjana, B. R. (2010), 'Socio-Economic Impact of Microfinance: An Empirical Study with Special Reference to Mysore Dist., Karnataka'. In: Lazer, Danial, Natarajan. P, and Malabika Deo eds. *Macro Dynamics of Microfinance*. New Delhi: Excel Books. pp. 261-265.

Nussbaum, Martha C. (2000), *Women and Human Development: The capacities Approach*. New Delhi: Kali for Women.

————(Ed.). (2003), *Essays on Gender and Governance.* New Delhi: UNDP, Human Development Resource Centre.

Omari, C.K. (1991), *The Social Dimension of Women in the Informal Sector*, Professorial Inaugural Lecture, University of dar es Salaam.

Panigrahi, Anupam and Shobit (2008), 'Micro-Finance for Poverty Reduction in India'. In: Daniel, Lazar and Palanichamy, P. eds. *Micro-Finance and Poverty Eradication: Indian and Global Experience*. New Delhi: New Century Publications. pp. 34-42.

Panikar, P.G.K. (1980), *Rural Savings in India.* Bombay: Somaiya Publications Pvt Ltd.

Paramashivaiah, P. (2010), 'Micro Insurance in India: Protecting the Poor'. In: Lazer Danial, Natarajan. P. and Malabika Deo eds.

Macro Dynamics of Microfinance. New Delhi: Excel Books. pp. 442-450.

Parr, Sakiko and Fukuda (Ed.). (2003), *Readings in Human Development.* New Delhi: Oxford University Press.

Pathak, D.C. and Pant, S.K. (2009), 'Microfinance: A Magic Wand for Poverty Alleviation: A Case Study of SGSY'. In: Thakur, Anil Kumar and Praveen Sharma eds. *Microcredit and Rural Development.* New Delhi: Deep and Deep Publications Pvt. Ltd. pp.111-133.

Pawar and Thiruvengala (2010), 'Impact of Microfinance on Tribal Development in Andhra Pradesh'. In: Lazer, Danial, Natarajan. P. and Malabika Deo eds. *Macro Dynamics of Microfinance.* New Delhi: Excel Books. pp. 35-46.

Peter, Westman (Ed.). (2010), *Knowledge Products of Microfinance: A Synthesis of Consolidated Replies.* New Delhi: UNDP.

Rajesh, Chakrabarti (2006), *The Financial Sector in India: Emerging Issues.* New Delhi: Oxford University Press.

Ramachandran, Lalitha, Victor. A. D. and Williams Albert (2010), 'Microfinance to Decimate Child Labour in Bhutan'. In: Lazer, Danial, Natarajan. P. and Malabika Deo eds. *Macro Dynamics of Microfinance.* New Delhi: Excel Books. pp. 412-423.

Rangarajan, C. (2009) *India: Monetary Policy, Financial Stability and Other Essays.* New Delhi: Academic Foundation.

Rengarajan, V. (2010), 'Microfinance: Is it a Panacea for Alleviation of Poverty or Aggravation of Poverty?'. In: Lazer, Danial, Natarajan. P. and Malabika Deo eds. *Macro Dynamics of Microfinance.* New Delhi: Excel Books. pp. 390-406.

Rhyne, E. (2001), *Mainstreaming Microfinance: How Lending to the Poor Began, Grew, and Came of Age in Bolivia.* Bloomfield, CT: Kumarian Press.

Robinson, M. S. (1998), 'Microfinance: The Paradigm Shift from Credit Delivery to Sustainable Financial Intermediation'. In: Kimenyi, M.S., Robert C. W. and J D Von Pischke eds. *Strategic Issues in Microfinance.* England: Ashgate Publishings. pp. 35-49.

Robinson, M.S. (2001), *The Microfinance Revolution. Volume 1: Sustainable Finance for the Poor.* Washington, DC: World Bank.

Roodman, D. and Qureshi, U. (2006), *Microfinance as Business*. Washington, DC: Center for Global Development.

Roy, Debesh (2008), 'Microfinance and Rural Non-Farm Sector: Thinking out of the Box'. In: Sharma, Manoranjan eds. *Dynamics of Indian Banking: Views and Vista*. New Delhi: Atlantic Publishers. pp. 359-386.

Sandhu, B.S. (1996), *Banking and Rural Development: Promises and Performance*. New Delhi: Deep & Deep Publications.

Selvam, S. (2005), *Empowerment and Social Development: Issues in Community Participation*. New Delhi: Kanishka Publishers & Distributors.

Sen, Amartya (2000), *Development as Freedom*. New Delhi: Oxford University Press.

________(2007), *Social Exclusion: Concept, Application and Scrutiny*. New Delhi: Critical Quest.

Sharan, Vyuptakesh (2009), *India's Financial Sector: An Era of Reforms*. New Delhi: Sage Publications.

Sharma, Manoranjan (Ed.). (2008), *Dynamics of Indian Banking: Views and Vistas*. New Delhi: Atlantic Publishers (P) Ltd.

Shubhashis, Gangopadhyay and Wilima Wadhwa (Ed.). (2000), *Economic Reforms for the Poor*. New Delhi: Konark Publishers Pvt Ltd.

Singh, C. P. (1989), *Poverty Alleviation Programmes under the Plans*. New Delhi: Indus Publishing.

Singh, Katar (2010), *Rural Development: Principles, Polices and Management*. New Delhi: Sage Publications.

Singh, S.R. and Srivastava, M. P. (2009), 'Microfinance: Scope and Linkages with Faster and Inclusive Growth'. In: Thakur Anil Kumar and Praveen Sharma eds. *Microcredit and Rural Development*. New Delhi: Deep and Deep Publications Pvt.Ltd. pp. 309-324.

Sinha Frances, Tankha, Ajay and Raja R. K. (2009), *Microfinance and Self-Help Groups in India: Living up to Their Promise?*. Warwickshire: Practical Action Publishing.

Srinivasan, N. (2008), *Microfinance India-State of the Sector Report-2008*. New Delhi: Sage Publications India Pvt. Ltd.

Stephanie, Charitonenko and Rahman, S.M. (2002), *Commercialisation of Microfinance: Bangladesh*, Manila: Asian Development Bank.

Stephanie, Charitonenko, Anita Campion and Nirmal A. F. (2004), *Commercialisation of Microfinance: Perspectives from South and South-East Asia.* Manila: Asia Development Bank.

Susan, H.H. (1995), *Managing to Empower: The Grameen Bank's Experience of Poverty Alleviation.* Dhaka: University Press Ltd.

Thakur, B.K. (2009), *Microfinance and its Relevance after Reforms: A Special Focus on Rural Credit in India.* In Anil Kumar Thakur & Praveen Sharma eds. *Microcredit and Rural Development.* New Delhi: Deep and Deep Publications Pvt.Ltd. pp. 441-455.

Thakur, Anil Kumar and Sharma Praveen (Ed.). (2009), *Micro-Credit and Rural Development*, New Delhi: Deep and Deep Publications.

Thakur, Sharma and Jain, S.P. (2010), 'Microfinance: A Tool for Poverty Control (with Special Reference to Gwalior and Chambal Division of Madhya Pradesh)'. In: Lazer Danial, Natarajan. P. and Malabika Deo eds. *Macro Dynamics of Microfinance.* New Delhi: Excel Books. pp. 61-72.

Tisdell, Clem (2008), *Poverty, Poverty Alleviation and Social Disadvantage: Analysis, Case Studies and Policies.* New Delhi: Serials Publications.

Uppal, R.K. (Ed.) (2008), *Financial Sector of India: Emerging Challenges.* New Delhi: New Century Publications.

Uppal, R.K. and Rimpi Jatana (Ed.). (2007), *E-banking in India: Challenges and Opportunities.* New Delhi: New Century Publications.

Vaidyanathan, A. (2014), *India's Evolving Economy: Puzzles and Perspectives.* New Delhi: Academic Foundation.

Vaish, Arun and Sharad, Agarwal (2010), 'Indian Microfinance Industry: Resilience during Economic Downturn'. In: Lazer Danial, Natarajan. P. and Malabika Deo eds. *Macro Dynamics of Microfinance.* New Delhi: Excel Books. pp. 412-423.

Weber, H. (2006), 'The Global Political Economy of Microfinance and Poverty Reductions: Locating Local Livelihoods in Political Analysis'. In: Fernando, J.L. eds. *Microfinance Perils and Prospects.* Routledge: London: New York. pp. 43-64.

Yunus, Mohammad and Jolis, A. (1998), *Banker to the poor: The autobiography of Muhammad Yunus, founder of the Grameen Bank*. Dhaka: The University Press.

Yunus, Muhammad (2008), *What Is Microcredit?* Dhaka: Grameen Bank.

Zeller, M. and Meyer, R. L. (Ed.). (2002), *The Triangle of Microfinance: Financial Sustainability, Outreach and Impact,* Baltimore: Johns Hopkins for the International Food Policy Research Institute.

Articles

Ahmed, F., Brad, Brown and Perry, Williams (2013), 'Is it time to regulate microfinance?', *Progress in Development Studies,* 13 (3), pp. 209-220.

Alain de Crombrugghe, Michel T. and Julie, Sureda (2008), 'Performance analysis for a sample of microfinance institutions in India', *Annals of Public and Cooperative Economics,* 79 (2), pp. 269-299.

Aloysius, P. F. (2007), 'A Microfinance Institution with a Difference', *Economic and Political Weekly*, pp. 1185-1189.

Ambec, S. and Treich, M. (2007), 'Roscas as Financial Agreements to Cope with Self-control Problems', *Journal of Development Economics*, 82, pp. 120-137.

Arora, Sangeeta and Meenu (2010), 'Microfinance Intervention- An insight into related literature with special reference to India', *American Journal of Social and Management Sciences,* 1 (1), pp. 44-54.

Bandyopadhyay, D. (2001), 'Andhra Pradesh: Looking beyond Vision 2020', *Economic and Political Weekly,* 36 (11), pp. 900-903.

Banerjee, Tanmoyee (2009), 'Economic Impact of Self-Help Groups- A Case Study', *Journal of Rural Development*, 28 (4), pp. 451-427.

Basu, Priya (2005), 'A Financial System for India's Poor', *Economic and Political Weekly*, pp. 4008-12.

Basu, Priya and Srivastava, P. (2005), 'Exploring Possibilities: Microfinance and Rural Credit Access for the Poor in India', *Economic and Political Weekly*, 40 (17), pp. 1747-1756. Stable URL: http://www.jstor.org/stable/4416534

Beck, Kunt and Patrick (2009), 'Access to Financial Services: Measurement, Impact and Policies', *The World Bank Research Observer*, 24 (1), pp. 122-33.

Calomiris, C. and Rajaraman, I. (2009), 'The role of Roscas: lumpy durables or event insurance?', *Journal of Development Economics*, 56 (1), pp. 207-216.

Campbell, Gregor (2010), 'Micro financing in the Developing World: How Small Loans Empower Local Economies and Catalyse Neoliberalism's End Game', *Third World Quarterly*, 31(7), pp. 1081-1090.

Chavan, Pallavi (2007), 'Access to Bank Credit: Implication for Dalit Rural Households', *Economic and Political Weekly*, pp. 3219-24.

Chiu, Tzu-Kuan (2014), 'Putting Responsible Finance to Work for Citi Microfinance', *Journal of Business Ethics*, 119, pp. 219-234.

Chowdhury, P. R. and Ray, Jaideep (2009), 'Public-private partnership in micro-finance: Should NGO involvement be restricted?'. *Journal of Development Economics,* 90 (2), pp. 200-208.

Dandekar, V. M. and Nilkantha, Rath (1971), 'Poverty in India', *Indian School of Political Economy,* pp. 145-156.

Dasgupta, Rajaram (2001), 'Working and Impact of Rural Self-Help Groups and Other Forms of Micro financing: An Informal Journey through Self- Help Groups', *Indian Journal of Agricultural Economics,* 56 (3).

Datt, G, V. K. and Ravallion. M. (2003) 'A Model Based Assessment of India's Progress in Reducing Poverty in the 1990s', *Economic and Political Weekly*, pp. 355-61.

Dev, Mahendra S. and Ravi, C. (2007), 'Poverty and Inequality for All-India and Major States, 1983 to 2004-05', *Economic and Political Weekly.*

Dev, Mahendra. S. (2006), 'Financial Inclusion: Issues and Challenges', *Economic and Political Weekly,* pp. 4310-4313.

Divya, K. (2014), 'A Study on Impact of Financial Inclusion with Reference to Daily Wage Earners', *Journal of Business Management & Social Sciences Research*, 2 (6), pp. 85-92.

Dorado, Silvia (2013), 'Small Groups as Context for Institutional Entrepreneurship: An Exploration of the Emergence of Commercial

Microfinance in Bolivia', *Organisation Studies*, 34 (4), pp. 533-557.

Dulal, Bansha, Chris, D. and Stough (2008), 'Do Microfinance Programmes Really Serve the Poor? Evidence from Rural Southeast Nepal', *Journal of South Asian Development,* 3(2), pp. 253-268.

Flores, Raquel (2014), 'The Microfinance Sector in Vietnam: An overview of its Present State and Future Prospects', *Local Economy*, 29 (3), pp. 213-227.

Floro, Maria and Gary, Dymski (2000), 'Financial Crisis, Gender and Power: An Analytical Framework', *World Development.* 28 (7), pp. 1269-83.

Gaiha, R. (1989), 'Are the Chronically Poor also the Poorest in Rural India?', *Development and Change*, 20, pp. 295-322.

Gangopadhyay, Kausik and Singh, Kamal (2013), 'Extent of Poverty in India: A Different Dimension', *Economic and Political Weekly,* xlviii (6), pp. 75-83.

Garmaise, M. J. and Gabriel Natividad (2010), 'Information, the Cost of Credit, and Operational Efficiency: An Empirical Study of Microfinance', *The Review of Financial Studies*, 23 (6), pp. 2560-90.

Ghosh, Jayati (2013), 'Microfinance and the Challenge of Financial Inclusion for Development', *Cambridge Journal of Economics*, 37, pp. 1203-1219.

Golait, Ramesh (2007) 'Current Issues in Agriculture Credit in India: An Assessment', *Reserve Bank of Indian Occasional Papers*, 28 (1), 1-22.

Guha and Gupta (2005), 'Microcredit for Income Federation: The Role of Rosca', *Economic and Political Weekly,* pp. 1470-73.

Hashemi, S. M., Sidney Ruth Schuler and Ann Riley, P. (1996), 'Rural Credit Programmes and Women's Empowerment in Bangladesh', *World Development,* 24 (4), pp. 635-53.

Hazare, Anupam (2011), 'Ensuring Better Access to Credit in Rural India', *Kurukshetra*, 59 (8), pp. 7-9.

Hermes, Niels and Robert, Lensink (2007), 'Impact of Microfinance: A Critical Survey', *Economic and Political Weekly*, pp. 462-465.

Hisako, Kai (2009), 'Competition and wide outreach of Microfinance Institutions', *Economics Bulletin*, 29 (4), pp. 2628-2639.

Hudon, Marek (2009), 'Should Access to Credit be a Right?', *Journal of Business Ethics*, 84, pp. 17-28.

Huff, G. (2011), 'Finance and Long-term Development issues in Southeast Asia', *Asian-Pacific Economic Literature*, 25(1), pp. 56-78.

Hulme, David (2000), 'Is Micro Debt Good for Poor People? A Note on the Dark Side of Microfinance', *Small Enterprise Development,* 11(1), pp. 26-28.

Hulme, David and Mathilde Maitrot (2014), 'Has Microfinance Lost Its Moral Compass?', *Economic and Political Weekly*, Vol. xlix, (48), pp. 77-85.

Hulme, David and Thankom, Arun (2011), 'What's Wrong and Right with Microfinance', *Economic and Political Weekly*, XLVI (48), pp. 23-26.

Imran, Sharif, Chaudhry and Farhana N. (2009), 'The Determinants of Women's Empowerment in South Punjab (Pakistan): An Empirical Analysis', *European Journal of Social Sciences,* pp. 216-224.

Jayaraman, R. and Peter Lanjouw (1999), 'The Evolution of Poverty and Inequality in Indian Villages', *The World Bank Research Observer*, 14 (1), pp. 1-30.

Jodhka, Surinder S. (2014), 'Changing Face of Rural India', *Economic Political Weekly*, Vol. XLIX, (14), pp. 28-31.

John, Weiss and Heather, Montgomery (2005), 'Great Expectations: Microfinance and Poverty Reduction in Asia and Latin America', *Oxford Development Studies*, 33 (3&4), pp. 391-415.

Johnson, Margaret A. (1998), 'An Overview of Basic Issues Facing Micro-enterprise Practices in the United States', *Journal of Developmental Entrepreneurship*, 3 (1), pp. 5-23.

Johnson, Susan (1998), 'Programme Impact Assessment in Microfinance: The Need for Analysis of Real Markets', *IDS Bulletin*, 29 (4), pp. 21-30.

Johnston, Don and Morduch Jonathan (2008), 'The Unbanked: Evidence from Indonesia', *The World Bank Economic Review*, 22 (3), pp. 517-537.

Jung, D. H. (2008), 'Microfinance in India: SHG-Bank Linkage Program', *International Area Review*, 11 (2), pp. 127-52.

Kabeer, Naila (1999), 'Resources, agency, achievements: Reflections on the measurement of women's empowerment'. *Development and Change.* 30(3), pp. 435-64.

————(2001), 'Conflicts over Credit: Re-evaluating the Empowerment Potential of Loans to Women in Rural Bangladesh', *World Development*, 29 (1), pp. 63-84.

Kakwani, N. and Subbarao, K. (1990), 'Rural Poverty and Its Alleviation in India', *Economic and Political Weekly*, 25 (13), pp. 2-16.

Kaladhar, K. (1997), 'Microfinance in India: Design, Structure and Governance', *Economic and Political Weekly*, 18, pp. 2687-2706.

Kalpana, K. (2011), 'An Anthropological Critique of Microfinance in Bangladesh', *Economic and Political Weekly*, XLVI, 35, pp. 33-35.

Kamath, Rajalaxmi (2007), 'Financial Inclusion vis-á-vis Social Banking', *Economic and Political Weekly*, 14, pp. 1334-35.

Kamath, Rajalaxmi, Mukherji, Arnab and Maria, Sandstrom (2010) 'Accessing Institutional Finance: A Demand Side Story for Rural India', *Economic & Political Weekly*, XLV (37), pp. 56-62.

Kameswari, P. (2011), 'Credit Facilities in Rural India', *Kurukshetra*, 59 (8), pp. 3-6.

Karmakar, K.G. and Mohapatra, N.P. (2009), 'Emerging Issues in Rural Credit', *The Microfinance Review*, 1 (1), pp. 1-17.

Katsushi, S. I., Thankom, Arun and Samuel, K.A. (2010), 'Microfinance and Household Poverty Reduction: New Evidence from India', *World Development,* 38 (12), pp. 1760-1774.

Kaur, Prabhjit and Soma Dey (2013), 'Andhra Pradesh Microfinance Crisis and its Repercussions on Microfinancing Activities in India', *Global Journal of Management and Business Studies*, 3 (7), pp. 695-702.

Khan, R. H. (2012), 'Issues and Challenges in Financial Inclusion: Policies, Partnerships, Processes and Products', *RBI Monthly Bulletin*, pp. 1447-57.

Khandelwal, Anil K. (2007), 'Microfinance Development Strategy for India', *Economic and Political Weekly*, XLII.13, pp. 1121-26.

Khandker, S. R. (2000) 'Savings, Informal Borrowings and Microfinance', *Bangladesh Development Studies*, 26 (2-3).

———(2005), 'Microfinance and Poverty: Evidence Using Panel Data from Bangladesh', *The World Bank Economic Review*, 19 (2), pp. 263-286.

Kirkpatrick, C. (2000), 'Financial Development, Economic Growth, and Poverty Reduction', *The Pakistan Development Review*, 39 (4), pp. 63-88.

Klonner, S. (2003), 'Rotating Savings and Credit Associations when participants are risk averse', *International Economic Review*, 44 (3), pp. 979-1005.

Knight, Tonya, Farhad Hossain and Christopher J. R. (2009), 'Microfinance and the Commercial Banking System: Perspectives from Barbados', *Progress in Development Studies,* 9 (2), pp. 115-25.

Kochar, Anjini (1997), 'Does Lack of Access to Formal Credit Constrain Agricultural Production? Evidence from the Land Tenancy Market in Rural India', *American Journal of Agricultural Economics,* Oxford University Press. 79 (3), pp. 754-763. Stable URL: http://www.jstor.org/stable/1244417.

Kumaran, K. P. (2001), 'Self-Help Groups of the Rural Poor in India: An Analysis', *National Bank News Review*, pp. 31-37.

Lutfun Osmani, N.K. (1998), 'Impact of credit on the relative Well-being of Women: Evidence from the Grameen Bank', *IDS Bulletin,* 29(4), pp. 31-38.

Mark, J. G. and Gabriel Natividad (2010), 'Information, The Cost of Credit, and Operational Efficiency: An Empirical Study of Microfinance', *The Review of Financial Studies*, 23(6), pp. 2560-2590.

Maulick, Barna (2012), 'Financial Inclusion in Bihar-A Step Towards Development', *Kurukshetra*, 60 (5), pp. 35-40.

Mayoux, L. (2001), 'Microfinance Impacts in Enterprise', *Impact News*, 1 (3), pp. 2-4.

Misra, B.S. (2006) 'The Performance of Regional Rural Banks in India: Has Past Anything to Suggest for Future?', *RBI Occasional Papers*, Vol. 27 (1-2).

Mohanty, Bidyut (2013), 'Microfinance in India: Whither Microfinance?', *Social Change,* 43 (3), pp. 495-505.

Morduch, Jonathan (1999), 'The Microfinance Promise', *Journal of Economic Literature*, 37 (4), pp. 1569-1614.

Morduch, Jonathan (2000), 'The Microfinance Schism', *World Development,* 28 (4), pp. 617-29.

Mosley, P. (2001), 'Microfinance and Poverty in Bolivia', *Journal of Development Studies,* 37, pp. 101-32.

Muhammad, Abdul Latif (2001), 'Micro-Credit and Savings of Rural Households in Bangladesh', *Bangladesh Development Studies*, 27.

Muhammad, Anu (2009), 'Grameen and Microcredit: A Tale of Corporate Success', *Economic and Political Weekly*, Vol. xliv (35), pp. 35-42.

Mujumdar, N. A. (1999), 'Reviving Rural Credit', *Economic and Political Weekly*, 19 (25), pp. 1577-1586.

Mukhopadhyay, Bappaditya and Rath Sambit (2011), 'Role of MFIs in Financial Inclusion', *Review of Market Integration*, 3 (3), pp. 243-286.

Nagayya. D. and Koteswara Rao, D. (2009) 'Micro Finance and Support Organisations in the Southern States of India', *Journal of Rural Development*, 28 (3), pp. 285-301.

Nair, Tara, S. (2000), 'Rural Financial Intermediation and Commercial Banks: Review of Recent Trends', *Economic and Political Weekly*, 29.

————(2011), 'Microfinance: Lessons from a Crisis', *Economic and Political Weekly*, Vol. xlvi (6), pp. 23-26.

Namboodri, N. V. and Shiyani, R. L. (2001), 'Working and Impact of Rural Self-Help Groups in Rural Financial Deepening', *Indian Journal of Agricultural Economics*, 56 (3).

Nanayakkara, Gemunu (2012), 'Measuring the Performance of Micro financing Institutions: A New Approach', *South Asia Economic Journal*, 13 (1), pp. 85-104.

Nayyar, Gaurav (2005) 'Growth and Poverty in Rural India: An Analysis of Inter-State Differences', *Economic and Political Weekly*, 40 (16), pp. 1631-1639. Stable URL: http://www.jstor.org/stable/4416505.

Otero, M. (1999), 'Bringing Development back into Micro-Finance', *Journal of Micro-Finance,* 1 (1), pp. 8-14.

Parthasarathy, G. (1995), 'Public Intervention and Rural Poverty: Case of Non-Sustainable Reduction in Andhra Pradesh', *Economic and Political Weekly,* 30 (41/42), pp. 2573-2586. Stable URL: http://www.jstor.org/stable/4403333

Rahman, Aminur (1999), 'Micro-Credit Initiatives for Equitable and Sustainable Development: Who Pays?', *World Development* 27 (1), pp. 67-82.

Rajasekhar, D. (2000), 'Microfinance Programmes and Women's Empowerment: A Study of Two NGOs, from Kerala', *Journal of Social and Economic Development*, 3 (1), pp. 76-94.

Ramalakshmi, C. S. (2003), 'Women Empowerment through Self-Help Groups'. *Economic and Political Weekly,* 36 (12).

Rautela, Reeta, Gaurav Pant, Swati Anand and Deepika Sharma (2010), 'Micro Finance: A New Mantra for Rural Development', *International Journal of Science, Technology & Management,* pp. 1-11.

Rena, Ravinder (2009), 'Rural Entrepreneurship and Development – An Eritean Perspective', *Journal of Rural Development*, 28 (1), pp. 1-9.

Rosengard, Jay. K, Richard H. Patten, Don E. Johnston and Widjojo Koesoemo (2007), 'The Promise and The Peril of Microfinance Institutions in Indonesia', *Bulletin of Indonesian Economic Studies*, 43(1), pp. 87-112.

Sadegh, Bakhtiari, (2006), 'Microfinance and Poverty Reduction: Some International Evidence', *Journal International Business & Economics Research*.

Sarma, E. A. S. (2004), 'Is Rural Economy Breaking Down? Farmers' Suicides in Andhra Pradesh', *Economic and Political Weekly*, 39 (28), pp. 3087-3089. Stable URL: http://www.jstor.org/stable/4415247

Satish, P. (2005) 'Mainstreaming of Indian Microfinance', *Economic and Political Weekly,* 23, pp. 1731-39.

Savita, Shankar and Mukul, Asher, G. (2010), 'Regulating Microfinance: A Suggested Framework', *Economic and Political Weekly*, Vol. XLV, (1), 15-18.

Schicks, Jessica (2007), 'Developmental Impact and Coexistence of Sustainable and Charitable Microfinance Institutions: Analysing BancoSol and Grameen Bank', *The European Journal of Development Research*, 19 (4), pp. 551-568.

Sengupta, Arjun (2007), 'A Right-Based Approach to Removing Poverty: Eradicating Poverty as Realizing Human Rights', *Indian Journal of Human Development*, 1 (6), pp. 55-68.

Sengupta, Niranjana (2013), 'Poor Women's Empowerment: The Discursive Space of Microfinance', *Indian Journal of Gender Studies*, 20 (2), pp. 279-304.

Sengupta, R. and Aubuchon, C.P. (2008), 'The Microfinance Revolution: An Overview', *Federal Reserve Bank of St. Louis Review,* 90(1), pp. 9-30.

Shivamaggi, H.B. (2000), 'Reforms in Rural Banking: Need for Bolder Approach', *Economic and Political Weekly,* 35 (20), pp. 1714-1718.

Shylendra, H. S. (2003), 'South Africa: Some Impressions from a Recent Visit', *Network,* 9(4).

————(2006), Microfinance Institutions in Andhra Pradesh Crisis and Diagnosis, *Economic and Political Weekly*, pp. 1959-63.

Silva, Indunil De (2012), 'Evaluating the Impact of Microfinance on Savings and Income in Sri Lanka: Quasi-experimental Approach Using Propensity Score Matching', *Margin—The Journal of Applied Economic Research*, 6 (1), pp. 47-74.

Singh Tejmani, N. (2009), 'Micro Finance Practices in India: An Overview', *International Review of Business Research Papers,* 5(5), pp. 131-146.

Singh, Naresh (2004), 'Finance at the Grass Roots', *Economic and Political Weekly*, 39(17), pp. 1718-1720.

Singh, Swati (2014), 'The Effects of Microfinance Programs on Women Members in Traditional Societies', *Gender, Place & Culture: A Journal of Feminist Geography*. pp.1-17.

Sinha, Sanjay and Meenal, Patole (2003), 'Microfinance and the Poverty of Financial Services: A Perspective from Indian Experience', *South Asia Economic Journal*, 5 (2), pp. 301-319.

Sinha, Saurabh and Imran, Matin (1998), 'Informal Credit Transactions of Microcredit Borrowers in Bangladesh', *IDS Bulletin,* 29 (4), pp. 66-80.

Srikanth, R. (2013), 'A Study on - Financial Inclusion - Role of Indian Banks in Reaching Out to the Unbanked and Backward Areas', *International Journal of Applied Research and Studies*, 2 (9).

Sriram, M.S. (2005), 'Micro-Finance and the State: Exploring Areas and Structures of Collaboration', *Economic and Political Weekly*, pp. 1699-1703.

———(2010), 'Microfinance: A Fairy Tale Turns into a Nightmare', *Economic and Political Weekly*, Vol. XLV (43), pp. 10-13.

Subbiah, Nalini (2014), 'Role of Banks in Financial Inclusion', *Research Journal of Commerce and Behavioral Science*, 1 (4), pp. 83-91.

Thorat, Usha (2006), 'Financial Inclusion and Millennium Development Goals', *RBI Bulletin*.

———(2007), 'Financial Inclusion-The Indian Experience', *Reserve Bank of India Bulletin*, pp. 1165-71.

Toye, John (2007), 'Poverty Reduction', *Development in Practice*, 17 (4/5), pp. 505-510. Stable URL: http://www.jstor.org/stable/25548247

Upalankar, Ambaroo (2005), 'Empowerment of Women'. *Mainstream,* 11 (17), 19-23.

Varman, Mahendra, P. (2005), 'Impact of Self-Help Groups on Formal Banking Habits', *Economic and Political Weekly*, pp. 1705-1713.

Vatta, Kamal (2003), 'Microfinance and Poverty Alleviation', *Economic and Political Weekly,* 38(5), pp. 432-433.

Venugopal, Rajesh (2015), 'Neoliberalism as a Concept', *Economy and Society,* pp. 1-25. Stable ULR: http://dx.doi.org/10.1080/03085147.2015.1013356

Vetriveln, S.C. and Chandra Kumarmangalam, S. (2010), 'Role of Microfinance Institutions in Rural Development', *International*

Journal of Information Technology and Knowledge Management, 2 (2), pp. 435-441.

Visaria, Leela (2008), 'Violence against Women in India: Is the empowerment a Protective Factor?', *Economic and Political Weekly*. 6 (3), pp. 60-66.

Visaria, Leela (2011), 'India's 15th Population Census: Some Key Findings', *Yojana*, pp. 16-19.

Vonderlack, M. Rebecca and Mark, Schreiner (2002), 'Women, microfinance, and savings: lessons and proposals', *Development in Practice*, 12 (5), pp. 14-23.

Weber, Heloise (2004), 'The New Economy and Social Risk: Banking on the Poor?', *Review of International Political Economy*, 11 (2), pp. 356-386.

Weiss, J. and Montgomery, H. (2004), 'Great Expectations: Microfinance and Poverty Reduction in Asia and Latin America', *Oxford Development Studies*, 33(3-4), pp. 391-416.

Woller, Gary M., Dunford, Christopher and Warner Woodworth (1999), 'Where to Microfinance?', *International Journal of Economic Development*, 1(1), pp. 29-64.

Wong Ka Wai and Veronique (2014), 'Betting on Women in the Fight Against Poverty', *The Asia Foundation*.

Reports

Achola, P, Mennonite (2006), 'Economic Development Associates. Impact of HIV/AIDS on Microfinance: With a Case Study on HIV/AIDS Mitigation'. Washington, DC: Microcredit Summit/ Results Educational Fund.

Alkire, Sabina, Chatterjee, Conconi, Seth and Vaz (2014), 'Global Multidimensional Poverty Index'. Oxford Poverty & Human Development Initiative, Oxford Department of International Development. University of Oxford.

APDPIP Report (2000), 'Andhra Pradesh District Poverty Initiatives Project Appraisal Document (PAD)'. Report No. 20089. South Asia Regional Office.

Asia Development Bank (2000), 'Finance for the Poor: Microfinance Development Strategy'. Manila, pp.1-51.ULR: http:// www.adb.org/Documents/Slideshows/Finance_Poor/default.asp

———(2000), 'The Role of Central Banks in Microfinance in Asia and the Pacific'. Asian Development Bank.

Bryceson, D. and M. Kirimbai (Ed.). (1980), 'Subsistence or Beyond? Money Earning Activities of Women in Rural Tanzania'. BRALUP, Research Report No. 45. Dar-es-Salaam; University of Dar-es-Salam.

CGAP (2004a), 'Building Inclusive Financial Systems. Donor Guidelines on Good Practice in Microfinance'. Washington, DC: Consultative Group to Assist the Poorest.

———(2005), 'Funding Microfinance Technology', CGAP Donor Brief No. 23.

———(2009), 'Advancing Financial Access for the World's Poor'. Annual Report, World Bank, pp. 1-64.

Charitonenko, Stephanie and Rahman, S.M. (2000), 'Commercialisation of Microfinance'. Asian Development Bank, Manila, Philippines.

Economic Survey (2010-11), 'Micro foundations of Micro-economic Development'. Chapter II, Planning Commission, Government of India, New Delhi, pp. 23-41.

Financial Inclusion Strategy: 2010-2015 (2010), 'Australian Agency for International Development (AusAID)', Canberra. pp.1-13.

Frost and Sullivan (2009), 'Bringing Financial Services to the Masses: An NCR', White Paper on Financial Inclusion. NCR.

Government of India (1998), 'Report of Committee on Banking Sector Reforms'. Ministry of Finance, Government of India.

Government of India (2011), 'Report of the Sub-Committee of the Central Board of Directors of Reserve Bank of India to Study Issues and Concerns in the MFI Sector'. Ministry of Finance, Government of India.

Grameen Bank (2005), 'Grameen: Banking for the Poor'. Grameen Bank, Dhaka.

———(2010), 'Annual Report'. Grameen Bank, Dhaka.

International Fund for Agricultural Development (IFAD) (2009), 'The State World Rural Poverty- Am Inquiry into its Causes and Consequences'. New York University Press, New York.

Kaganda, C.P. (1991), 'Towards an Efficient System of Financing Small Cooperatives in Tanzania'. OSSREA. Ethiopia: Unpublished Research Report.

Malegam Committee Report (2011), 'Issues and Concerns in the MFI Sector'. Reserve Bank of India, Government of India, New Delhi. pp. 1-65.

MCDWAC (1992), 'Policy on Women in Development in Tanzania'. Dar es Salaam: MCDWAC.

NABARD (2002), 'Ten Years of SHG-bank Linkage: 1992-2002, NABARD and Microfinance'. *Mumbai.*

————(2005), 'Progress of SHG-Bank Linkage in India 2004-05'. *Mumbai.*

————(2008), *'Status of Micro Finance in India 2007-08'*. Mumbai, pp. 1-193.

————(2010-2011). Annual Report. NABARD, Mumbai. pp. 1-130.

Planning Commission (2009), 'Report on Financial Sector Reforms'. Ministry of Finance, Government of India.

Radcliffe, Dan (2012), 'A Digital Pathway to Financial Inclusion'. Bill & Melinda Gates Foundation.

Rangarajan, C. (2008), 'Report of the Committee on Financial Inclusion', Ministry of Finance, Government of India, New Delhi.

RBI (2005), 'Report on Rural Credit and micro finance'. IIMB-WP No. 474 31.

RBI (2014a), 'Report on comprehensive financial services for small businesses and low Income households'. Ministry of Finance, Government of India, New Delhi. (Chairman: Dr N. Mor).

RBI (2014b), Report of the Technical Committee on Mobile Banking. Ministry of Finance, Government of India, New Delhi. (Chairman: Mr. B Sambamurthy).

Report of the Steering Committee on Micro-finance and Poverty Alleviation: The Eleventh Five Year Plan (2007-08 - 2011-12) 'Development Policy Division', Planning Commission, Government of India, New Delhi. pp. 1-48.

UNCDF (2005) 'Microfinance and the Millennium Development Goals'. A Reader's Guide to the Millennium Project Reports and other UN documents.

Women's World Banking Annual Report (2010), 'Women's World Banking', New York. pp.1-21.

World Bank (1997), 'India: Achievements and Challenges in Reducing Poverty'. Washington D.C: Oxford University Press.

———(2008), 'Finance for All?: Policies and Pitfalls in Expanding Access', World Bank Policy Research Paper, Washington D.C. Oxford University Press.

———(2009), 'Banking the Poor: Measuring Banking Access in 54 Economies', World Bank Research Paper, Washington DC.

———(2011), 'Understanding Poverty in India', Washington D.C: Oxford University Press.

World Development (2000-01), 'Attacking Poverty, World Development Report'. Washington D.C: Oxford University Press.

Working Papers

Basu, Priya and Srivastava, Pradeep (2005), *Scaling-up Microfinance for India's Rural Poor*, Working Paper No. 3646. World Bank Policy Research.

David O' Brien, Joamma, W., De Haan, Arjan and Simon Maxwell (1997), *Poverty and Social Exclusion in North and South,* IDS Working Paper No. 55. Institute of Development Studies and Poverty Research Units, University of Sussex.

Ellis, Karen (2007), *Is Financial Liberalisation enough to promote Financial Inclusion?*, Working Paper No. 2475. Overseas Development Institute, pp. 82-83.

Frost and Sullivan (2009), *Bringing financial services to the Masses: An NCR White Paper on Financial Inclusion*, Working Paper No. 97. NCR Corporation.

Kelly Bird, Kelly Hattel, Eiichi Sasaki, and Luxmon Attapich (2011), *Poverty, Income Inequality and Microfinance in Thailand,* ADB Southeast Asia Working Paper Series. Manila: Asia Development Bank, pp. 1-18.

Mahmoud, Mohieldin, Iqbal Zamir, and Xiaochen Fu (2011), *The Role of Islamic Finance in Enhancing Financial Inclusion in*

Organisation of Islamic Cooperation (OIC) Countries, Policy Research Working Paper No. 5920. World Bank, pp. 1-59.

Misra, Alok (2010), *Micro Finance in India and Millennium Development Goals: Maximizing Impact on Poverty*, Discussion paper for Workshop on World Bank. Singapore, pp. 1-20.

Mitra, Subrata Kumar (2005), *Asking Price of Microfinance Loan to Poor Borrowers*, Working Paper No. 191. Anand: Institute of Rural Management Anand.

Nair, A. (2005), *Sustainability of Microfinance and Self-Help Groups in India: Would federating help?*, World Bank Policy Research Working Paper 3516.

Oommen, M.A. (2008), Micro-Finance and Poverty Alleviation: The Case of Kerala's Kudumbashree, Working Paper. No.17. Kerala: Centre for Socio-economic & Environment Studies (CSES), pp. 1-17.

Ramji, Minakshi (2009), *Financial Inclusion in Gulbarga: Finding Usage in Access*, Working paper series No. 26. Institute for Financial Management and Research, Centre for Microfinance, pp. 1-36.

Ratti (2012), *Indian Financial System & Indian Banking Sector: A Descriptive Research Study*, pp. 1-8.

Reddy, C.S. and Sandeep, Manak (2005), *Self-Help Groups: A Keystone of Microfinance in India-women empowerment & social security*. Hyderabad: Mahila Abhivruddhi Society, Andhra Pradesh (APMAS), pp. 1-19. Available at: www.empowerpoor.org/downloads/SHGs-keystone-paper.pdf.

Sarma, M. (2010), *Index of Financial Inclusion*. Discussion Papers in Economics, India: Centre for International Trade and Development, School of International Studies, Jawaharlal Nehru University, pp. 10-18.

World Bank (1997), *India: Achievements and Challenges in Reducing Poverty,* Washington D.C: Oxford University Press.

———(2008), *Finance for All?: Policies and Pitfalls in Expanding Access,* World Bank Policy Research Paper No. 2464. Washington DC: Oxford University Press.

———(2008), *Finance for All?: Policies and Pitfalls in Expanding Access,* World Bank Policy Research Paper No. 3142. Washington D.C: Oxford University Press.

———(2009), *Banking the Poor: Measuring Banking Access in 54 Economies*, World Bank Policy Research Paper. Washington DC: Oxford University Press.

———(2009), *Banking the Poor: Measuring Banking Access in 54 Economies*, World Bank Policy Research Paper No. 3275. Washington DC: Oxford University Press.

World Development (2000-01), *Attacking Poverty*, World Development Report. Washington D.C: Oxford University Press.

Zaman, Hassan (2000), *Assessing the Poverty and Vulnerability Impact of Microcredit in Bangladesh: A Case Study of BRAC*, Working Paper 2145.

Web sources

Andhra Pradesh State Portal: www.ap.gov.in

Asian Development Bank: www.adb.org

Department of Rural Development: Government of Andhra Pradesh. http://rd.ap.gov.in

Finance Commission, Government of India: http://fincominda.nic.in

Grameen Bank Website, http://www.grameenbank.org

Ministry of Finance, Government of India: http://finmin.nic.in

NABARD: http://www.nabard.org

National Institute of Rural Development (NIRD): www.nird.org.in

Planning Commission, Government of India: http://planningcomission.nic.in

Reserve Bank of India: https://rbi.org.in

Society for the Elimination of Rural Poverty: http://www.serp.ap.gov.in

Telangana State Portal: www.telangana.gov.in

The World Bank: www.worldbank.org

Index

S

T

U